The
New
Public
Personnel
Administration

The New Public Personnel Administration

FELIX A. NIGRO

University of Georgia

LLOYD G. NIGRO

Syracuse University

F. E. PEACOCK PUBLISHERS, INC.

Itasca, Illinois 60143

Library of Congress Catalog Card Number 75–17316
Printed in the United States of America

ISBN 0–87581–185–X

To E.H.N., C.L.N., and K.F.N.

Preface

Although there have been some extraordinary changes in public personnel administration in the past two decades, no book has been written which captures the most significant developments and adequately describes the field as it exists today. Our purpose has been to fill this gap with a concise treatment of the most important public policy issues and the major problems in formulating and implementing public personnel programs.

It is not possible to focus on these policy issues and operating problems without first developing a valid theoretical framework for understanding the role of the personnel function in modern organizations. Such a framework based on the systems resource model is presented in Chapter 2. Because the policy implications of public personnel administration have received little intensive analysis, a tendency has developed to view the field as narrowly vocational and, within government itself, as necessary but routine and removed from the center of agency policymaking. Recent developments make the policy role of public personnel very clear, yet its potential for improving the effectiveness of agency programs often has not been grasped.

We have not attempted to cover everything on the subject; basically, this is an analytical, problem-centered book, not an encyclopedic, descriptive account. Obviously, such matters as retirement, leaves, and records are important, but including them is essential neither to our purposes nor to users of this book in institutions of learning or government agencies. Bibliographical guides such as the U.S. Civil Service Commission's monthly index of *Personnel Literature* can be consulted to obtain information on all the detailed aspects of the personnel function.

Edna H. Nigro typed all drafts of the manuscript, read the proofs, and prepared the index, continuing her indispensable role for us in these matters. Ed Jackson of the Institute of Government of the University of Georgia prepared the various charts for the printer. To those who supplied us with materials and commented on portions of the manuscript, we give thanks, but we name no one because we want to make it entirely clear that we take full responsibility for the opinions expressed.

Athens, Georgia
January, 1976

FELIX A. NIGRO
LLOYD G. NIGRO

Contents

Historical Background and Present Challenges

 1

Public personnel administration in the United States is the product of a long evolution in which different concepts and emphases have played a part, and it therefore eludes precise definition. In this opening chapter, we will describe this evolution and indicate the challenges of the present period, a critical one for the determination of public personnel policy. Finally, we will suggest a definition of the field as it appears to us in the mid–1970s.

■ APPROACHES TO PUBLIC PERSONNEL ADMINISTRATION

Throughout world history there have been various approaches to public personnel administration. One method bases appointments, promotions, and other personnel decisions on ability to perform efficiently in the position assigned — this is the *merit principle*. Merit systems in the United States have ranked candidates for appointment and promotion in order of examination scores and then filled requests for eligibles with the names of those ranking highest on the employment registers, usually the top three names.

The British do not use rank-order employment lists, nor do they give appointing officers any fixed number of names to consider. Through written tests, interviews, and other selection devices they evaluate the candidates and then offer appointments to those judged the most suitable, according to the number of posts available.[1] Thus procedures may vary for determining ability to perform efficiently and for making appointments and other decisions. Personnel specialists disagree about which policies and procedures implement and preserve the merit principle, and, of course, practices followed in one country may not be suitable in another.

A very different approach is to consider the most deserving candidates for government jobs those who campaigned for or otherwise rendered valuable service to the party in power. In this view, the "spoils of office" justly belong to the victorious party. Politicians who make appointments to patronage jobs or otherwise control them often insist that they apply selection standards and name or propose qualified persons only. Since they confine their screening to political supporters, they in fact ignore a cardinal principle of merit systems — open competition.

A third approach is to provide government jobs to those who otherwise would be unemployed. This is sometimes called the welfare concept of public employment. The policy is commonly associated with the developing nations where mass unemployment makes it a matter of necessity for many political leaders. It is also far from unknown in the developed nations, where many advocate government as the employer of last resort. In the United States, Congress has recently enacted legislation providing for the creation of hundreds of thousands of jobs for the unemployed and the underemployed. In terms of permanent rather than temporary jobs, it is argued that "public service employment is a virtually unlimited area for achieving two major inseparable goals of American society, (1) full employment and (2) a

---

[1] Interview with K. M. Reader, Civil Service Commission, Great Britain, October 19, 1972.

decent, livable environment."[2] The reasoning here is that government should greatly increase its expenditures for pollution control, transportation, education, health services, recreation, and similar functions.

Another policy is to give preference in public employment for certain reasons, such as service in the armed forces (veterans' preference). Preference may also be granted to assure equitable representation of the different geographic areas, social classes, and ethnic groups of a country.

One approach may be used in filling certain kinds of jobs, another in filling other kinds. The approaches emphasized change with particular periods in a nation's history, and, of course, in the United States state and local government personnel policies are not uniform. All four of the approaches described above have influenced public personnel policy in the United States.

■ POLICIES OF THE FIRST SIX PRESIDENTS (1789 to 1829)

At the national level, the first application of the principle of basing appointments on ability came very early, indeed, with the first six Presidents.[3] From George Washington to John Quincy Adams the policy was to fill federal jobs with competent persons, although political factors were taken into account: Washington appointed persons friendly to the Federalist cause, and Jefferson openly made some political removals. Still, although by 1800 the spoils system had become entrenched in some state and local governments, it did not spread to the national government during this period. Indeed, most federal employees enjoyed permanent tenure, with few removals, and these generally for cause.[4]

Yet this first federal "merit system" was very exclusive. The top administrative posts were filled with persons "drawn

[2] Harold Shepard, "Job Design, New Careers and Public Service Employment—Their Potentials and Limits," Good Government, 87, No. 3 (Fall 1970), 2.

[3] See Paul P. Van Riper, History of the United States Civil Service (New York: Harper & Row, Publishers, 1958), pp. 18–27.

[4] Frederick C. Mosher, Democracy and the Public Service (New York: Oxford University Press, 1968), p. 59.

from the elite of the society in general"[5] — the upper crust in terms of family background and education. The rest of the work force came mostly from the middle and upper-middle classes, so the service as a whole was far from representative of the country's population. In making appointments, efforts were made to give fair representation to residents of all regions so as to strengthen the Union.

■ THE PERIOD FROM 1829 TO 1883

Andrew Jackson's views on public personnel policy differed in important respects from those of his predecessors. He wanted to democratize the service and open it to all segments of society; accordingly, to him rotation in office was the best policy. He believed that the duties of most federal jobs were simple, thus easily learned, so there was no need for permanence. However, in making appointments Jackson emphasized competence as much as his predecessors had. The supply of qualified persons was limited because of restricted educational opportunities, so he did not have much success in opening the service to the common man.[6]

Unfortunately, the long-term effect of Jackson's public service philosophy was to open the gates for the spoils politicians at the national level. His successors made many more removals, the objective being principally to strengthen the party machinery — a conception of political reality, rather than an egalitarian ideal. Concurrently, the spoils system spread to many other state and local governments, and prevailed at all levels of government until 1883.

Some scholars, such as the historian Carl Russell Fish, believe that for much of American history the President's patronage club over members of Congress strengthened his leadership in the system of separation of powers.[7] Yet Abraham Lincoln, looking at a crowd of job seekers in his

---

[5] Ibid., p. 58.

[6] Van Riper, *History of Civil Service*, pp. 30–41, Mosher, *Democracy and Public Service*, p. 62.

[7] See Carl Russell Fish, *The Civil Service and the Patronage* (Cambridge, Mass.: Harvard University Press, 1904).

outer office, remarked that "the spoils system might in course of time become far more dangerous to the Republic than the rebellion itself."[8]

The civil service reform movement

According to one interpretation, the civil service reform movement was basically negative in character because it aimed at "keeping out the rascals" rather than finding the most competent persons available. This is a perspective from a later period in American history; the objectives of the civil service reformers were very positive for their times. That the spoils system went hand in hand with graft was revealed by the scandals of the Grant Administration, and it was viewed as an evil which had to be extirpated from American society. The writings of the reformers abounded in emotional appeals and rhetoric.[9] Essentially they were moral crusaders, yet they clearly wanted the spoils system eliminated as a first step towards providing more efficient public service. Looking back, it was the responsibility of those who in later years administered civil service systems to adapt them to new needs. The really negative minded were those who continued to concentrate on "fighting the spoilsmen" in circumstances where the spoilsmen had ceased to be much of a threat.

Success came to the moral crusade in 1883 with the passage of the Pendleton Act. President Garfield's assassination by a disappointed office seeker demonstrated that "spoils equalled murder,"[10] but the immediate reason for approval of the legislation was the Republicans' fear that the next President would be a Democrat who would remove all Republican officeholders. The victory was not an overwhelming one; coverage of the new competitive system was limited to only about 10.5 percent of the positions in the executive branch. The administrative machinery established was a Civil Service Commission rather than an executive

---

[8] Van Riper, *History of Civil Service*, p. 44.
[9] See Dorman B. Eaton, *Civil Service in Great Britain* (New York: Harper & Bros., 1880).
[10] Van Riper, *History of Civil Service*, p. 89.

department or agency directly under the President. This was a crucial decision, for the Commission still exists and that form of organization was the model copied by state and local governments when they instituted civil service systems. The commission form was chosen to protect the system from partisan political control (as discussed in detail in Chapter 3). However, the President was given an important role because he appoints the three Civil Service commissioners, subject to Senate confirmation, and approves the civil service rules and regulations. He also is empowered both to place additional positions under the system and to remove positions from coverage.

■ CIVIL SERVICE FROM 1883 TO WORLD WAR II

The first civil service systems were poorly funded and struggled to survive. Besides being limited in coverage, they were narrow gauged; basically they gave examinations mostly of an unimaginative character, maintained records, and did little else. They were staffed largely with clerks, and clerks also took care of the personnel chores in the departments.

The first state to adopt civil service was New York, in 1883, followed by Massachusetts in 1884. That civil service was not a flood of reform is revealed by the fact that no new state civil service laws were approved in the next two decades. Albany, New York—now a stronghold of the old machine politics—was the first municipality to adopt civil service (1884). Cook County, Illinois, another example of boss control, was the first county to do so (1895). Often when civil service was adopted it was taken over by machine politicians and the commissions became "a front for spoils."[11]

Although the establishment of civil service systems increased during the first three decades of the 20th century, the activities conducted in these systems remained restricted. During this time the scientific management movement had some impact on government and the efficiency

---

[11] Albert H. Aronson, "Personnel Administration, the State and Local Picture," *Civil Service Journal*, 13, No. 3 (January–March 1973), 38.

concept was of increasing importance in American society, but civil service at all levels of government remained much the same.

Birth of modern personnel administration

In 1938 Franklin D. Roosevelt issued an executive order requiring the principal administrative agencies to establish bona fide, professionally staffed personnel offices. It may seem inconceivable that this should have occurred so late in American history, because today the personnel function, although much criticized, is generally accepted. Then, however, its necessity was questioned.

Roosevelt's order signaled the arrival of "modern" personnel administration, based on the efficiency approach. "Modern" meant expanded services, personnel offices staffed with specialists, recruitment and retention of efficient employees, improvement of basic techniques such as tests, and in general the use of the scientific method in selection and other personnel processes. This logically led to the employment of individuals with appropriate training, and college graduates began to replace the clerks. The modernization of the Civil Service Commission dates from this period, as it became much more efficiency conscious and positive in its outlook. The efficiency approach also began to have some effect in state and local governments.

Looking back on this period, the accomplishments and even some of the thinking may not seem impressive compared with improvements since then, but by the end of World War II personnel administration was establishing itself as a tool of executive management, joining other staff activities such as budget and finance. The old era of civil service as a routine activity with limited technical content and little relation to management needs began to recede into the past.

■ BETWEEN WORLD WAR II AND THE 1960s

The efficiency approach soon revealed weaknesses of its own. Basically, two criticisms of the new personnel offices were heard: they frequently hampered rather than helped line officials, and they concentrated on procedures and paper work, neglecting human considerations.

A familiar complaint was that the personnel workers carried a rule book they followed rigidly and were always saying no and refusing to cooperate. Whereas formerly line officials were held in suspicion for fear that they might violate the merit principle, now they seemed to be held in contempt as being unappreciative of the advantages of an efficiently functioning personnel office. This kind of criticism was inevitable; it is made of all staff specialists, since in their sphere of expertise they exercise control over line officials. Yet there was enough justification in the complaints for leaders in the personnel field to appeal to their colleagues to adopt a more flexible attitude. Many speeches were made and articles written in which the personnel technicians were reminded that, after all, their mission was to facilitate the work of the line agencies. Such admonitions are still being made, although more recently the phraseology is to "bring personnel into the mainstream of management," or some such statement. It is always difficult to mesh the personnel function with the line organization, and efforts to do so will probably continue for many years.

As to the second criticism, although the objective of personnel programs presumably was the obvious one of serving human needs, personnel workers did not seem at all "people minded." They spent most of their time on day-to-day personnel tasks, applying technical skills (as in classifying positions) but showing little interest in developing the potential of the employee as a valuable human resource. The human relations approach, stemming from the research of Elton Mayo and his Harvard University associates at the Hawthorne plant of the Western Electric Company in the late 1920s and early 1930s, was having some effect in the private sector but hardly any in the mechanistic world of public personnel administration.

This began to change after World War II as an "accent-on-people" emphasis—a term used by the executive director of the Public Personnel Association — gained adherents.[12] The human relations approach is, of course, immense in its implications, but it became clear in the 1950s that it could be applied to the personnel function in the following specific ways:

1. Stimulating employees to give forth their best efforts. It does not suffice simply to find qualified persons and place them in the right jobs; they must be properly motivated.
2. Developing the people-centered phases of the personnel program. An excellent example is in-service training, which had been given little attention. Analyzing employees' training needs and helping them develop their potential shows concern for them as human beings and also benefits the organization.
3. Recognizing that supervisors constitute the focal element in the personnel program because they have the closest contact with employees. Accordingly, they should be helped in all their personnel relations.
4. Undertaking personnel research because it is essential to understand the wellsprings of human motivation and effort. Very little such research was being conducted at the time. Hardly enough is today, but the need for it is far better appreciated.
5. Expecting personnel workers to have sufficiently broad backgrounds of training and experience to understand human behavior. The mark of their value should not be solely expertise in techniques such as classification or testing; they should be schooled as well in human relations theory and its application. The personnel profession could not be remade overnight (indeed, too many personnel workers are still narrow technicians) but the desirability of broader preparation and deeper insights became increasingly recognized.

Basically, the period was one in which, at the federal level and in a growing number of state and local jurisdictions,

---

[12] Kenneth O. Warner, "What's Ahead for Personnel?" *Personnel Administration*, 10, No. 2 (November 1947).

progress was made in making personnel systems more efficient, better related to management needs, and more concerned with the employee as a person. Just how much progress was made is a matter of opinion; in many state and local jurisdictions civil service remained negative and unimaginative in outlook. For the country as a whole, however, the conception of the personnel function had perceptibly broadened.

■ THE NEW PUBLIC PERSONNEL ADMINISTRATION

In the most recent period of American history — beginning with the 1960s — the changes have been so great that it can be said that a "new public personnel administration" has been created. The merit principle, redefined in important ways, still prevails, but the methods of making personnel policies, the policies themselves, and the procedures used in administering them are different in important respects. Public employee organizations now have a much more important role, and the equal employment opportunity concept has had considerable effect.

The spread of collective bargaining

Prior to 1960, only one state (Wisconsin in 1959) had passed legislation requiring the public employer (in this case municipal governments) to bargain collectively with public employees. In the federal government, the employee had the right to join a union, based on the Lloyd–La Follette Act of 1912, but there was no law or executive order providing an affirmative, governmentwide labor relations policy. Collective bargaining had taken place for years in the Tennessee Valley Authority and some parts of the Department of the Interior, but many federal agencies did not even have stated employee relations policies. The Post Office was strongly organized but union membership was small in most agencies, sometimes consisting of only a few employees.[13]

---

[13] See President's Task Force on Employee-Management Relations in the Federal Service, *A Policy for Employee-Management Cooperation in the Federal Service* (Washington, D.C.: Government Printing Office, 1961), pp. 2–3.

By the end of 1971, 35 states had "some positive labor relations legislation or procedure for dealing with their public employees."[14] In the remaining states, much bargaining takes place on a de facto basis, since increasingly the courts are ruling that, in the absence of state legislation prohibiting collective bargaining, the public employer may legally engage in such activity. In the federal government, where President Kennedy's Executive Order 10988 of January 17, 1962, introduced collective dealings with employee organizations, 57 percent of the employees outside the Postal Service are represented by an exclusive bargaining agent (union with majority support in a bargaining unit); the comparable figure for the Postal Service is 87 percent.[15] Nationwide, one of every three public employees belongs to an employee organization, exceeding the one in four union membership figure in the private sector.[16] (The term "employee organization" includes labor-affiliated and independent associations.)

There are many reasons for this rapid increase in collective bargaining in the public service, but they can all be summarized in one basic explanation: the public employee's new conception of his role.* He sees no reason why he should be expected to tolerate pay and working conditions inferior to those of comparable workers in the private sector. He wants to be treated with dignity, which means that he should have a voice in the determination of personnel policies. In the vast government machine, the union has proved an effective instrument for gaining such a voice. Besides, the public employee sees nothing unprofessional in joining unions, which in recent years have demonstrated

---

* Masculine forms of expression are used in this book in the indefinite sense; they should be taken to refer to both men and women.

[14] U.S. Department of Labor, *State Profiles: Current Status of Public Sector Labor Relations*, Labor Management Services Administration, Division of Public Employee Labor Relations (Washington, D.C., November, 1971), p. iii.

[15] *Federal Times*, March 12, 1975.

[16] *LMRS Newsletter*, 6, No. 3 (March 1975), 1. Published in Washington, D.C., by the Labor Management Relations Service of the National League of Cities, the United States Conference of Mayors, and the National Association of Counties.

an ability to improve his situation. Government workers in general cannot be said to have been captives of the outside labor movement, and collective bargaining is now strongly supported by many non-labor-affiliated public employee organizations. While the competition with the labor-affiliated unions has impelled the independents to become more militant, public employees and their leaders have been expressing themselves and have not been the pawns of "labor."[17]

The bilateral principle. Collective bargaining is innovative in the public service because it is based on *bilateralism,* whereas traditional personnel administration was built on paternalistic *unilateralism.* Under collective bargaining the employer and the union agree to bargain until they reach agreement on the matters subject to negotiation. The employer does not simply listen and then make its own decision which it imposes on the union. The parties sometimes do not come to an agreement and strikes or lockouts may result, but the employer knows that the bargaining represents a joint decision-making process, not simply a means whereby the union communicates with management.

Civil service was not conceived as a bilateral arrangement. The intention was to benefit the employee through enlightened personnel policies, but the employer—the legislature and the civil service commission—unilaterally decided these policies. The employees might be consulted and employee organizations could petition the legislature, but there was no thought of bargaining personnel policies with the employees. Nor were the employees at the time civil service was adopted demanding a bargaining relationship, for they were not thinking in those terms then. That many of them now are doing so has created inevitable conflict with public employers who find it difficult to understand why the workers cannot trust in their good intentions. In Britain, particularly since World War II, the official and staff sides

_____

[17] See Felix A. Nigro (ed.), "A Symposium, Collective Bargaining in the Public Service: A Reappraisal," *Public Administration Review,* 32, No. 2 (March–April 1972).

have been jointly deciding a wide range of personnel policies, but there has been no similar development in the United States.[18]

Union views of "merit." Attitudes of many public employers in the United States have also changed, so that they now accept collective bargaining. As to its compatibility with the merit principle, they believe that certain demands if accepted would compromise that principle, but bargaining carries with it no obligation to accept a given proposal. The unions claim that their input is injecting *true merit* into the personnel system. Historically, civil service administrators did not think of pay as part of the merit system, which they saw as consisting of appointment, promotion, and other personnel transactions. The unions insist that there can be no merit system if pay is poor by comparison with private employment. Interestingly, Columbia University's American Assembly in a recent report stated that "The Assembly . . . believes that comparability between public and private sector wages and fringe benefits is . . . more likely to be achieved through collective bargaining than through traditional civil service procedures."[19]

Unions press for negotiated grievance procedures which they regard as the sine qua non of justice for the worker and, therefore, of the merit principle. In traditional civil service the final decision on grievances and appeals is made by the department head or the civil service commission—by management, as the union sees it. In negotiated procedures a final step, binding arbitration, is frequently provided for, which means that a true neutral—the arbitrator—rules for or against the employee. At a minimum, grievance may be defined in the contract to mean any failure of the parties to correctly interpret or apply the terms of the agreement. It is sometimes defined to include complaints over *any* matter in

---

[18] Henry Parris, *Staff Relations in the Civil Service, Fifty Years of Whitleyism* (London: George Allen and Unwin, Ltd., 1973).
[19] The American Assembly, *Collective Bargaining in American Government,* Report of the Fortieth American Assembly, Columbia University, October 28–31, 1971, p. 8.

which the employer has discretion. Labor experts stress that most disputes between workers and management arise out of the application of personnel policies or, in other words, over grievances. The unions have no confidence in a system under which management decides whether or not it has lived up to the contract.

Earlier in this chapter mention was made of the role of the supervisor in personnel administration. Grievance arbitration makes that role a pivotal one in labor relations, since it is the supervisor's decisions, right or wrong, that lead to most grievances. Management knows that the success of the labor relations program largely depends on the competence of its supervisors, and supervisors' decisions are continuously monitored by union stewards ready to file grievances. Public personnel administration has been criticized for failure to study sufficiently and deal effectively with personnel problems at the supervisor-subordinate level. Grievance arbitration provides a built-in protection against such failure. A prominent feature of the new personnel administration is the union steward, who symbolizes the union role as a partner in the carrying out of personnel policies.

Some unions are obtaining contract provisions which expand the personnel program and thus make for better merit systems. In New York City, in agreements signed with District Council 37 of the American Federation of State, County, and Municipal Employees (AFSCME), the city pledged itself to make payments to a training fund to be "used to provide additional training and education opportunities beyond those presently provided by the Department of Personnel, designed to increase the effectiveness and efficiency of employees covered . . . and to prepare them for advancement and upgrading." The union participates in the planning of the programs and in the selection of the trainees.[20] In contracts for bargaining units represented by the Civil Service Employees Association (CSEA), New York state

---

[20] Contract between the City of New York and District Council 37, AFSCME, AFL–CIO, covering certain clerical-administrative employees of the City of New York for the period January 1, 1969, to June 30, 1971.

agreed to conduct certain training activities and to recommend to the legislature the appropriation of the necessary funds. Contract-established state–CSEA committees "assist the State by recommending priorities and criteria for development of courses and selection of participants, and by assisting in the resolution of problems in implementing specific programs."[21] The judgment of New York state training officials is that these contract provisions have produced a "significant supplement to the state's in-service training" and represent a departure from "traditional management training philosophy."[22]

Broad bargaining scope – The potential dangers. Since the dynamic of unionism is constantly to try to increase the scope of the bargaining, it holds potential dangers for the essential elements in a merit system. If, for example, unions obtain contract clauses providing for promotions strictly on the basis of seniority, the merit principle would be violated unless longer service could be demonstrated to reflect greater ability – which it often does not. Some unions do press for promotions principally by seniority, yet under civil service substantial weight has often been given to length of service. The past mistaken policies of civil service do not, however, justify acceptance of union requests which cannot be reconciled with the principle of distinguishing between individuals on the basis of ability.

Collective bargaining has been taking place now for some years in many jurisdictions which have had civil service for generations. In these jurisdictions, the civil service laws and regulations *together with the current labor contracts* constitute the personnel system. When agreements are negotiated, civil service administrators examine each union request carefully for possible conflict with core merit concepts. Increasingly, they are recognizing that some policies

---

[21] Herbert M. Engel and Ronald W. James, "Negotiating for Employee Training and Development Programs: The New York State Experience," *Public Personnel Management*, 2, No. 2 (March–April 1973), 103.
[22] Ibid., 107.

and procedures can be eliminated or changed without under-
mining the system. Recently the United States Civil Service
Commission completed a thorough review of the voluminous
Federal Personnel Manual to identify those matters that
could be opened up for negotiation because not prescribed
by law. As the result of this study, the Commission declared
negotiable certain aspects of merit promotions, performance
rating appeals, incentive awards, withdrawal of resignation
or retirement application, minimum charge for leave, and
distribution of health benefit brochures.[23]

In some state and local jurisdictions, contracts are negotiated with provisions which conflict with existing law, but
then the entire contract or the provisions in question are
adopted by the legislature. This has the advantage of quick
legislative change to eliminate rigidities and make other
improvements in the merit system—but it could also mean
discarding the basics of the merit system. While there is
much disagreement about the compatibility of some contract
clauses with the essentials of merit, the experience to date is
that collective bargaining has not destroyed civil service.
For that matter, the often-made prediction that civil service
commissions would be limited to recruitment, with most
other parts of the personnel program governed by union
agreements, has not been borne out. There are signs in this
direction, but generally while civil service commissions have
lost power in salary setting and in the settling of grievances
and appeals, they have not done so seriously in appointments, promotions, and other status changes.[24] The effects of
collective bargaining on different aspects of the personnel
program are discussed in other chapters of this book.

---

[23] See "Worth Noting," *Civil Service Journal,* 13, No. 4 (April–June 1973),
front and back covers, and Raymond Jacobson, "Are We Giving Away the
Store?" *Civil Service Journal,* 13, No. 2 (October–December 1972), 13–17.
[24] See Jerry Lelchook and Herbert J. Lahne, *Collective Bargaining in
Public Employment and the Merit System,* U.S. Department of Labor,
Labor-Management Services Administration (Washington, D.C.: Government Printing Office, 1972); David T. Stanley, *Managing Local Government under Union Pressure* (Washington, D.C.: Brookings Institution,
1972) and Sterling D. Spero and John M. Copozzola, *The Urban Community
and Its Unionized Bureaucracies, Pressure Politics in Local Government
Labor Relations* (New York: Dunellen, 1973), pp. 210–11.

Making the merit system inclusive

Under traditional civil service, the very low representation of minority groups in the public service was generally not viewed as a violation of the merit principle. So long as there was no overt discrimination, the failure of blacks, people with Spanish surnames, and other minorities to qualify for appointment in anywhere near the same numbers as the rest of society was viewed as unfortunate but no fault of the civil service system. Actually, there was overt discrimination, as documented by the findings of the U.S. Commission on Civil Rights in a 1969 report on state and local government personnel systems: "Administrators of merit systems have frequently violated the merit principle and practiced conscious, even institutionalized discrimination."[25] The Commission's basic finding, however, was that "static" civil service procedures were mostly responsible for excluding minority groups; it cited as examples the use of unvalidated written tests, rigid education requirements, and automatic disqualification for an arrest record. The report also stressed that most merit system agencies made no positive efforts to recruit minorities, as by visiting colleges with large enrollments of blacks or sending recruiters into the ghettos.[26]

At the time this report was issued, equal employment opportunity had made some progress in the nation, and some federal lower court decisions, based on the 14th Amendment to the Constitution and the Civil Rights Act of 1866 and 1871, had made clear that the judiciary would void discriminatory practices and insist on affirmative action programs if public employers did not do so.[27] In 1971, the U.S. Supreme Court made its now famous ruling in *Griggs* v. *Duke Power Company*, the only decision to date by the Court on job employment standards. We will discuss this case and

---

[25] U.S. Commission on Civil Rights, *For All the People . . . By All the People: A Report on Equal Opportunity in State and Local Government Employment* (Washington, D.C.: Government Printing Office, 1969), p. 64.
[26] Ibid., pp. 32–37, 65.
[27] 401, U.S. 424, 433 (March 8, 1971). See National Civil Service League, *Judicial Mandates for Affirmative Action* (Washington, D.C., 1973), pp. 22–32.

discrimination for reasons of race first and then take up sex discrimination.

In 1964, the Duke Power Company ended a policy of confining blacks to low-paying laborers' jobs but at the same time established the new requirement that to qualify for better jobs the employee, black or white, had to have a high school diploma and pass certain intelligence and aptitude tests. The black employees bringing the court action charged that in practice this continued the old discriminatory policies because the only jobs exempted from the new requirements and therefore the only ones for which they could qualify were menial ones in the company's labor department. The Court found that the new standards were not demonstrably related to successful job performance and that they served to disqualify blacks at a substantially higher rate than whites. As to the company's defense that its intentions had been good, the Court said that "good intent or absence of discriminatory intent does not redeem employment procedures or testing mechanisms that operate as 'built-in headwinds' for minority groups and are unrelated to measuring job capability."[28]

The Court emphasized that nothing in the Civil Rights Act of 1964 precluded the use of testing or measuring procedures and that Congress had not

> . . . commanded that the less qualified be preferred over the better qualified simply because of minority origins. . . . Far from disparaging job qualifications as such, Congress has made such qualifications the controlling factor, so that race, religion, nationality, and sex become irrelevant. What Congress has commanded is that any tests used must measure the person for the job and not the person in the abstract.[29]

The effect of this decision is that if employers, public employers included, use a selection requirement that has a disparate effect on the basis of race, sex, religion, or national origin, they must prove the requirement is job related. If

---

[28] Ibid., p. 17.
[29] Ibid., p. 18.

they cannot do so, the requirement constitutes unlawful discrimination.

Lower court decisions rendered both before and after *Griggs* reveal that in many cases the judiciary is prescribing the details of personnel policy and procedure. One such example is *Carter* v. *Gallagher*, in which the plaintiffs were black applicants who asked the district court to enjoin the city of Minneapolis from further use of its firefighters' test on grounds that it discriminated against blacks and lacked validity.[30]

The court, noting the gross disparity between the city's 6.4 percent nonwhite population and the 0.0 percent minority employment in the all-white, 535-member fire department, found the charges of discrimination substantiated. Not only did it enjoin the use of the test, it also ordered changes in many aspects of the personnel program. Specifically, it ordered arrest questions stricken from the application form because, although the form stated applicants would not necessarily be rejected for having been arrested, in the court's opinion asking about arrests discouraged persons with arrest records from making application. The court also found that the 20-year minimum age limit was not job related and hampered the recruitment of young blacks, and it was ordered lowered to 18. The high school education requirement was also voided as not being an essential qualification for firefighters.

Since the city's firefighters' examination had never been validated, the court ordered a new one constructed and validated under Equal Employment Opportunity Commission Guidelines on Employee Selection Procedures. The test in use consisted of questions on English vocabulary and firefighting equipment and techniques. Since no substantive job knowledge was required of recruits entering the firefighter training school, it was stipulated that the new examination should test for ability to be trained as a firefighter.

---

[30] Ibid., pp. 25–26. 452 F. 2d 315. 3 FEP Cases 121 (*8th* Cir. 1972).

To remedy the effects of past discrimination, the court ordered an affirmative action program, to include outreach recruitment and pretest tutoring sessions, and absolute preference in appointment for the first 20 qualified minority applicants for firefighter. Maintaining that such absolute preference denied qualified white applicants equal protection of the laws under the 14th Amendment, the city appealed in circuit court. This court, reviewing decisions of other courts on hiring quotas, found that while hiring ratios had been specified, absolute preference had not been decreed in any of these cases. Since the nonwhite population of Minneapolis was only 6.4 percent, substantially less than that in areas where courts had ordered one-to-one hiring ratios, the circuit court ordered a one-to-one ratio until 20 qualified minority persons had been hired. The Supreme Court denied the Minneapolis Civil Service Commission's request for appeal of this decision; to date, it has not ruled on the legality of remedial numerical ratios in cases of this type.

Since in 1972 Congress brought state and local governments under the antidiscrimination provisions of the Civil Rights Act of 1964, federal court decisions and regulations of the Equal Employment Opportunity Commission (EEOC) now also apply to all state and local governments. The 1972 legislation also provides a statutory basis for the nondiscrimination program in the federal government which is administered by the U.S. Civil Service Commission.[31]

Goals versus quotas

Affirmative action plans often include goals and timetables for the employment of minority-group persons. These stipulations have been attacked as essentially quota systems and thus a violation of the merit principle.

In March 1973, the U.S. Civil Service Commission, the Justice Department, the EEOC, and the Labor Department's Office of Federal Contract Compliance issued a joint state-

---

[31] Public Law 92–261, 92nd Cong., H.R. 1746, March 24, 1972.

ment[32] in which *quota systems* are described as imposing a fixed, mandatory number or percentage of persons to be hired or promoted, regardless of the number of potential applicants who meet the qualifications. If the employer fails to hire or promote the necessary number or percentage, he is subject to sanctions, no matter how unrealistic the quota and how hard he may have tried in good faith to recruit qualified persons.

In the same statement, *goal* is defined as a

> . . . numerical objective, fixed realistically in terms of the number of vacancies expected, and the number of qualified applicants available in the relevant job market. Thus, if through no fault of the employer, he has fewer vacancies than expected, he is not subject to sanction, because he is not expected to displace existing employees or to hire unneeded employees. . . . Similarly, if he has demonstrated every good faith effort to include persons from the group which was the object of discrimination into the group being considered for selection, but has been unable to do so in sufficient numbers to meet his goal, he is not subject to sanction.[33]

The joint statement further elaborates that goals do not obligate the employer to hire an unqualified person in preference to a qualified one, or a less qualified person in preference to a better qualified one.

How goals can be converted into quotas is seen in the following policy adopted by the Federal Aviation Administration and dropped at the insistence of the Commission: "If a minority group person cannot be appointed in each succeeding fifth vacant position, then neither that position nor any further position should be filled until a minority group person is appointed."[34] Those criticizing goals and timetables contend that in some cases minority group members are rated qualified or better qualified when they are not — thus leading to discrimination in reverse.

---

[32] Federal Policies on Remedies Concerning Equal Employment Opportunity in State and Local Government Personnel Systems, March 23, 1973.

[33] Ibid., p. 3.

[34] Don Mace, Jr., "FAA Modifies Minority Hiring Program," *Federal Times*, April 21, 1971.

Although they provide for the employment of *qualified* minority group members only, some federal lower court decisions prescribing numerical remedial ratios do require the employment of less qualified persons in preference to more qualified ones. If in every case a more qualified majority group member could not be passed over for a qualified minority person, the remedial ratios could not be observed. The courts requiring these ratios consider them temporary and therefore not quotas. As the court of appeals said in *Carter* v. *Gallagher,* once the trial court's order was fully implemented, all hirings would be on a nondiscriminatory basis "and it could well be that many more minority persons or less, as compared to the population at large, over a long period of time would apply and qualify for the positions."[35]

Most of the federal circuit courts of appeal have upheld these remedial ratios. In one such recent case, sustaining "a 25 percent black hiring quota to correct historic discrimination in the Alabama Department of Public Safety," the judges said it was a

> . . . temporary remedy that seeks to expend itself as promptly as it can by creating a climate in which objective, neutral employment criteria can successfully operate to select public employees solely on the basis of job-related merit. For, once an environment where merit can prevail exists, equality of access satisfies the demand of the Constitution.[36]

Sex discrimination

Like members of minority groups, women have been discriminated against in public employment, and their employment is heavily concentrated in the lower grades. As in the private sector, they have traditionally been considered for secretarial, clerical, typing, bookkeeping machine operator, switchboard operator, and similar jobs but not for executive and higher level posts. Although in time minority groups were rarely "blatantly excluded from em-

---

[35] See "The National Civil Service League's Policy Statement on Equal Employment Opportunity," in *Advance,* 1, No. 2 (Summer, 1973), p. 29 (Studies in Public Manpower Modernization from the National Civil Service League's National Program Center for Public Personnel Management).
[36] *The NCSL Exchange,* 4, No. 8 (October–November 1974), 3.

ployment by name," women were simply told they were not acceptable for nonroutine jobs.[37]

The Civil Rights Act of 1964 prohibited discrimination for reasons of sex, and this prohibition was extended to federal, state, and local government employers by the 1972 amendments to the act. Even before 1972 the federal government and some state and local governments had adopted policies to combat sex discrimination. With the amendments and recent Supreme Court decisions, women are being employed in many kinds of jobs from which they previously were excluded.

Although the federal courts regard classification based on race as inherently suspect, they have not so regarded classification by sex. Now, however, they are "closely examining" sex classifications and "increasingly have been finding them improper."[38] If their constitutionality is be upheld, such classifications must have a rational basis. As one example, in *Reed* v. *Reed* (1972) the Supreme Court declared invalid a statute giving men preference over women in administering estates because the classification was unrelated to any purpose sought by the statute. In *Frontiero* v. *Richardson* (1973), the Supreme Court invalidated a regulation which permitted men in the armed forces to declare their wives as dependents, whether or not the wives actually were dependents, but required servicewomen to prove that their husbands were dependents in order to receive the dependency allowance. Four of the justices concurred that sex classifications, like those based on race, are inherently suspect, but the fifth judge concurring in the majority decision based his decision on the "rational basis" doctrine.

Under the law, classification on the basis of religion, sex, or national origin is permissible only when it is a bona fide occupational qualification. The courts are interpreting "bona fide" narrowly, voiding laws and regulations that bar women

---

[37] William H. Brown, III, "Sex Discrimination—It Isn't Funny, It Is Illegal, and the Battle Has Just Begun," *Good Government*, 88, No. 4 (Winter 1971), 19.

[38] See "Legal Decisions," *Civil Service Journal*, 14, No. 2 (October–December 1973), 30–32.

from certain work for reasons which cannot be justified by business necessity. In declaring unconstitutional a state legislative provision barring a woman from tending bar unless she was the owner or wife of the owner of the bar, the Supreme Court said, "The pedestal upon which women have been placed has all too often, upon closer inspection, been revealed as a cage."[39]

■ OTHER ASPECTS OF THE CURRENT PICTURE

There are still some state and local governments where the old-style spoils systems is very strong. An article in the July 11, 1971, *New York Times* reported that the application form used by the Indiana State Highway Department asked, "How long have you been a member of the Republican party?" and "Would you be willing to contribute regularly to the Indiana Republican State Central Committee?" Spaces were provided for the applicants to obtain the "endorsement signatures" of the following: precinct vice committeeman, precinct committeeman, ward vice chairman, ward chairman, county vice chairman, county chairman, district vice chairman, state vice chairman, and state chairman. There were about 40,000 patronage employees in Indiana state, county, and local governments, virtually all of whom were required to kick back 2 percent of their salaries to the political party controlling their jobs.[40] Another article dated October 10, 1971, reported some unprecedented resistance in Jersey City to the 3 percent salary kickback that had been exacted from employees, whether or not under civil service, since the creation of the Hague political machine 50 years back. Hague's successor, John V. Kenny, was under indictment, charged with masterminding an extortion conspiracy involving public contracts.[41]

The number of patronage posts varies greatly; the gover-

---

[39] Ibid.

[40] John Kifner, "Kickbacks Still Thrive in Indiana," *New York Times*, July 11, 1971.

[41] Ronald Sullivan, "Employees of Jersey City Now Balk at Political Tithes," *New York Times*, October 10, 1971.

nors of New York and Illinois directly control thousands of such jobs, the governor of Oregon less than a dozen.[42] When President Richard Nixon took office in 1969, about 6,500 positions were being filled through political channels, including top political policymaking posts to which Presidents have often named highly qualified persons, including career civil servants. In early 1969, Nixon by executive order placed under merit procedures the jobs of some 70,000 postmasters and rural letter carriers, the last remaining large group of patronage employees in the federal service.

Later developments, especially revelations of the existence in a number of agencies of "patronage rings" instigated and directed by the White House, created what some observers believe to be the most serious threat to the merit system in its history. A manual prepared by the White House personnel office instructed these "special referral" offices in how to circumvent the civil service regulations and obtain the appointment or promotion of Nixon loyalists. In the spring of 1975, the House Committee on Post Office and Civil Service began hearings to investigate fully and determine whether new legislation was needed to protect the merit system from future such manipulation.[43] Employee leaders were demanding that the merit system be tightened, and one was recommending that "all but a small handful of Federal positions"[44] be brought under civil service. The merit system in the federal service had seemed secure for so many years that these revelations, corroborated by the Civil Service Commission, surprised and shocked many people; they also bore out the statements of personnel administrators that resurgence of the spoils systems in some guise is always a threat.

Since the 1950s there has been a steady increase in the number of states passing civil service laws; there are now

---

[42] Martin Tolchin and Susan Tolchin, *To the Victor . . . Political Patronage from the Clubhouse to the White House* (New York: Vintage Books, 1972), p. 96.

[43] See Arthur Levine, "I Got My Job Through CREEP," *Washington Monthly*, 6, No. 9 (November 1974), 35–46.

[44] *The Federal Employee*, 60, No. 2 (February 10, 1975), 11.

about two thirds of the states with comprehensive legislation of this type. About 75 percent of municipal workers (outside education) are under civil service, but in recent years there have been "no spectacular gains" in civil service coverage. In 1953, 254 cities over 25,000 population (49 percent of the number reporting) had civil service programs for all employees. By 1963, ten years later, there had been a gain of only four cities.[45] The view is often expressed that public support for merit systems has waned, but this is largely due to dissatisfaction with the way in which civil service has been administered.

Intergovernmental Personnel Act of 1970

A big boost for the merit principle came with passage of the Intergovernmental Personnel Act of 1970 (IPA).[46] Despite the great increase in services rendered by state and local governments, personnel practices in many of these governments were poor, "thereby resulting in the loading of agencies with incompetent, uninspiring, and often indifferent personnel."[47] Beginning with amendments to the Social Security Act in 1939, Congress over the years had imposed merit system requirements applicable to over 300 state agencies and affiliated local agencies. The Office of State Merit Systems in the Department of Health, Education, and Welfare (HEW) provided the technical expertise for overseeing these requirements.

The IPA provides federal financial and technical assistance to strengthen personnel administration in state and local governments in a manner consistent with the following merit principles:

1. Recruiting, selecting, and advancing employees on the basis of their relative ability, knowledge, and skills, in-

---

[45] Rosaline Levenson, "The Merit Principle in Municipalities — Strengthened or Eroded?" *Personnel Administration and Public Personnel Review,* 1, No. 1 (July–August 1972), 47.

[46] Public Law 91–648, 91st Cong., S. 11, January 5, 1971.

[47] Senate Subcommittee on Intergovernmental Relations, *Intergovernmental Personnel Act of 1967, Intergovernmental Manpower Act of 1967,* 90th Cong., First Sess. (Washington, D.C.: Government Printing Office, 1967), p. 2.

cluding open consideration of qualified applicants for initial appointment.

2. Providing equitable and adequate compensation.
3. Training employees, as needed, to assure high-quality performance.
4. Retaining employees on the basis of the adequacy of their performance, and separating employees whose inadequate performance cannot be corrected.
5. Assuring fair treatment of applicants and employees . . . without regard to political affiliation, race, color, national origin, sex, or religious creed and with proper regard for their privacy and constitutional rights as citizens.
6. Assuring that employees are protected against coercion for partisan political purposes and are prohibited from using their official authority for the purpose of interfering with or affecting the result of an election or a nomination for office.[48]

The IPA authorizes federal grants to state and local governments to establish merit personnel systems or improve existing ones. If a jurisdiction seeks to improve its personnel program without establishing a merit system or extending one it has, it may qualify for a grant at the discretion of the U.S. Civil Service Commission which administers the legislation. (The IPA transferred the programs and the staff of the HEW Office of State Merit Systems to the Commission.) We will refer to detailed provisions of the IPA in later chapters of this book; it is mentioned here because of its potential for greatly improving personnel administration at the state and local levels. The new public personnel administration is distinguished by a heavy intergovernmental emphasis.

■ DEFINITION OF PUBLIC PERSONNEL ADMINISTRATION

The six merit principles of the Intergovernmental Personnel Act constitute a definition of public personnel administration which incorporates the best of the latest thinking. Although in the opening paragraph of this chapter we noted the diffi-

---

[48] Public Law 91–648, Section 2.

culty of formulating a precise definition of the field, in concluding the chapter we can suggest the following short
definition:

> *Public personnel administration is the process of acquir-
> ing and developing skilled employees and of creating or-
> ganizational conditions which encourage them to put
> forth their best efforts.*

BIBLIOGRAPHY

Case, Harry L. *Personnel Policy in a Public Agency: The TVA Experience.* New York: Harper & Row, Publishers, 1955.

The Civil Service, Vol. 1, *Report of the Committee 1966–68.*
London: Her Majesty's Stationery Office, Cmnd. 3638, 1968.

Civil Service Journal, 13, No. 3 (January–March 1973) (articles reviewing current developments on 90th anniversary of the U.S.
Civil Service Commission).

Fish, Carl Russell. *The Civil Service and the Patronage.* Cambridge, Mass.: Harvard University Press, 1904.

Golembiewski, Robert T., and Michael Cohen (eds.). *People in
Public Service: A Reader in Public Personnel Administration.*
2nd ed. Itasca, Ill.: F. E. Peacock, Publishers, 1975.

Good Government, 91, No. 3 (Fall 1974) (text of National Civil
Service League's Model Public Personnel Administration Law
and progress report on its implementation).

Harvey, Donald R. *The Civil Service Commission.* New York:
Frederick A. Praeger, 1970.

Hoogenboom, Ari. *Outlawing the Spoils: A History of the Civil
Service Reform Movement, 1865–1883.* Urbana, Ill.: University
of Illinois Press, 1961.

House Subcommittee On Manpower and Civil Service, *Violations
and Abuses of Merit Principles in Federal Employment,* Pts. I
and II, 94th Cong., 1st Sess. (Washington, D.C.: Government
Printing Office, 1975).

Krislov, Samuel. *Representative Bureaucracy.* Englewood Cliffs,
N.J.: Prentice-Hall, 1974.

Levine, Charles, and Lloyd G. Nigro. "The Public Personnel Sys-
tem: Can Juridical Administration and Manpower Management
Coexist?" *Public Administration Review,* 35, No. 1 (January–
February 1975).

Macy, John W., Jr. *Public Service: The Human Side of Government.* New York: Harper & Row, Publishers, 1971.

Mosher, Frederick C. *Democracy and the Public Service*. New York: Oxford University Press, 1968.

Municipal Manpower Commission. *Governmental Manpower for Tomorrow's Cities*. New York: McGraw-Hill Book Co., 1962.

National Civil Service League. *Judicial Mandates for Affirmative Action*. Washington, D.C., 1973.

Nigro, Felix A. *Management-Employee Relations in the Public Service*. Chicago: International Personnel Management Association, 1969.

Nigro, Lloyd G. (ed.). "A Mini-Symposium, Affirmative Action in Public Employment." *Public Administration Review*, 34, No. 3 (May–June 1974).

Norris, James D., and Arthur H. Shaffer (eds.). *Politics and Patronage in the Gilded Age*. Madison, Wis.: State Historical Society, 1970.

Odiorne, George S. *Personnel Administration by Objectives*. Homewood, Ill.: Richard D. Irwin, 1971.

Pezdek, Robert V. *Public Employment Bibliography*. Ithaca, N.Y.: New York State School of Industrial and Labor Relations, Cornell University, 1973 (comprehensive bibliography of published materials on labor relations in government).

Roethlisberger, F. J., and Dickson, W. J. *Management and the Worker*. Cambridge, Mass.: Harvard University Press, 1939.

Rosenbloom, David. *Federal Service and the Constitution*. Ithaca, N.Y.: Cornell University Press, 1971.

Rutstein, Jacob J. "Survey of Current Personnel Systems in State and Local Governments." *Good Government*, 87, No. 1 (Spring 1971).

Siegel, Gilbert B. (ed.). *Human Resource Management in Public Organizations: A Systems Approach*. Los Angeles: University Publishers, 1972.

Stanley, David T. "Symposium, The Merit Principle Today." *Public Administration Review*, 34, No. 5 (September–October 1974).

Tolchin, Martin, and Susan Tolchin. *To the Victor . . . Political Patronage from the Clubhouse to the White House*. New York: Vintage Books, 1972.

U.S. Commission on Civil Rights. *For All the People . . . By All the People: A Report on Equal Opportunity in State and Local Government Employment*. Washington, D.C.: Government Printing Office, 1969.

Van Riper, Paul. *History of the United States Civil Service*. New York: Harper & Row, Publishers, 1958.

Zagoria, Sam (ed.). *Public Workers and Public Unions*. Englewood Cliffs, N.J.: Prentice-Hall, 1972.

Organizations and the Personnel Function

2

Personnel administration is a process which cannot be meaningfully described without consideration of organizational needs and purposes. In this chapter we will present a framework for considering the *organizational* functions of personnel administration.

■ ORGANIZATIONAL EFFECTIVENESS: THE SYSTEMS RESOURCES MODEL

It is tempting to say the effectiveness of organizations can be measured by the degree to which they accomplish their stated objectives. But what makes one organization more or less successful than another? Are there aspects of performance that can be linked to goal attainment capabilities? Is it possible to detect areas of activity that must be carried out successfully by all formal organizations if they are to accomplish their ends?

Confusion can arise from attempts to use ultimate goals (cancer prevention, flood control) as standards for judging organizational effectiveness. To avoid this confusion, we will use what Stanley Seashore and Ephraim Yuchtman call a systems resources model.[1] In their words, effectiveness is the "ability of the organization, in either relative or absolute terms, to exploit its environment in the acquisition of scarce and valued resources."[2] Notice that they say nothing about the specific goals of organizations. Their concept of effectiveness is based on the universal needs of organizations to extract essential resources from their surroundings.

The systems resources model is derived from the proposition that all organizations are open systems which continuously interact with their environments. They must take in resources from their environments if they are to survive and carry out the many activities normally associated with complex social systems. Effective organizations perform well in this regard. In systems resources terms, the locus of effectiveness lies in the quality of the transactions between an organization and its environment.

The acquisition of human and material resources is a process ultimately tied to organizational purposes. Goals are key structuring properties of organizations, and it is difficult to understand their internal operations and relationships with external agencies without knowing something about their formal and informal objectives. However, in analyzing or trying to predict the behavior of one organization or a group of organizations having similar objectives, it is important to concentrate on processes that contribute to goal accomplishment *no matter what the goals are.*

External and internal extraction

To refine the systems resources model, it is possible to specify two broad areas of organizational activity: external extraction and internal extraction.[3] Organizations can be compared with regard to their performance in both areas.

---

[1] Stanley E. Seashore and Ephraim Yuchtman, "A System Resource Approach to Organizational Effectiveness," *American Sociological Review*, 32, No. 6 (December 1967), 891–903.

[2] Ibid., 898.

[3] Daniel Katz and Robert L. Kahn, *The Social Psychology of Organizations* (New York: John Wiley & Sons, 1966), pp. 161–70.

External extraction. Organizations vary in the degree to which they are able to secure human and material resources from their external environments. Some organizations are more successful than others in influencing outside agents to contribute ideological and political support, skilled manpower, and money and material. All organizations are in the last analysis dependent on their environments for these and other scarce resources, and they must develop a capacity to deal effectively with those who hold and allocate them. The relative ability of organizations to capture resources from their external environments can be called their *external extraction capability.*

Internal extraction. Organizations also face inward in their search for resources. Employees represent a pool of psychological, physical, and intellectual energy that can be tapped to great advantage. The ability of organizations to harness these internal resources and to convert them into skilled, predictable role performances can be called their *internal extraction capability.*

External and internal extraction capabilities are by no means unrelated. High levels of employee motivation can contribute to success in convincing clients that the organization deserves support, and external support can encourage employees to stay with the organization and work harder. It is the "mix" of external and internal extraction processes which makes up the overall capacity of an organization to

FIGURE 1

Elements of organizational effectiveness

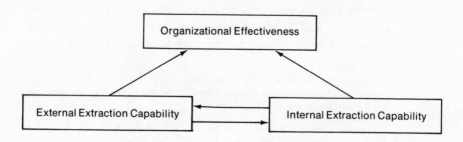

exploit its environment and therefore determines its effectiveness from a systems resources standpoint. (See Figure 1.)

■ EXTERNAL EXTRACTION: THE ENVIRONMENTS OF PUBLIC ORGANIZATIONS

The external environments of public organizations are complex and highly political, as described by Gary Wamsley and Mayer Zald:

> A public organization is part of a policy subsystem, an arena of individuals, groups, and organizations, of "relevant others" affected by and interested in a given policy. The relevant others have a role to play or an interest in influencing an area of policy for which a particular public organization has prime concern. These relevant others represent a variety of actors in and out of government: interest groups, competing public organizations, superior organizations, individuals, appropriation subcommittees, subject matter committees, and staff agencies. They may be competitive, cooperative, hostile, overseeing, reviewing, controlling, but regardless of their role they shape the mandate and the conditions of existence for a public organization.[4]

Administrators of organizations try to induce relevant elements of their organizations' environments to contribute resources and support on a regular and predictable basis. They do this by constructing and maintaining transactional relationships with "relevant others." External extraction is usually accomplished through an exchange process in which the organization produces *outputs* which are valued *inputs* to other organizations, groups, or individuals.

The outputs used by public organizations to capture support may be very general or symbolic in nature. The Federal Bureau of Investigation has garnered generous support from legislative, executive, and public groups by virtue of its image as an agency which provides essential law enforcement and national security services. Organizational outputs also may be very specific and concrete: "an agency gains external support if it offers a well-received

---

[4] Gary L. Wamsley and Mayer N. Zald, *The Political Economy of Public Organizations* (Lexington, Mass.: D. C. Heath & Co., 1973), p. 26.

product of an efficacious clientele; a clientele able to influence key, proximal others so as to enlarge the organization's share of resources and legitimacy."[5] Even a cursory
look at the policies and programs of agencies such as the
Departments of Agriculture and Labor indicates their very
close ties with organized farm and labor groups. From an
organizational standpoint, these symbiotic relationships
bear fruit in the influence that concerned interest groups
have on the budgetary process and the political calculations
of executives and legislators.[6]

The opportunities and constraints facing public organizations will be reflected in their behavior, especially their
outputs: "we cannot understand a system without a constant
study of the forces that impinge on it."[7] The emergence of
collective bargaining and equal employment opportunity
programs in the public sector illustrates how governmental
agencies attempt to adapt to changing environmental circumstances. New or changed practices of this kind can be
seen as the results of efforts to keep outputs (be they symbolic or material) in line with the needs and expectations of
those who influence or control the resource allocation
process. Thus the "logic" of many personnel policies and
practices in the public sector can be found in the political
realities and forces of the times from which they emerged.[8]
The reader is encouraged to review the several historical
stages of personnel philosophy and practice described in
Chapter 1 in this light.

Up to this point we have described in very broad terms the
transactional base of relationships between organizations
and their environments. Now we will sharpen our focus on
the environment and on the role played by personnel in
the external extraction process.

---

[5] Ibid., p. 43.

[6] Aaron Wildavsky, *The Politics of the Budgetary Process* (Boston: Little,
Brown & Co., 1964), pp. 65–74.

[7] Katz and Kahn, *Social Psychology of Organizations*, p. 27.

[8] See Paul P. Van Riper, *History of the United States Civil Service* (New
York: Harper & Row, Publishers, 1958).

Diffused and focused environments

It is useful to break down the external environment into two categories, diffused and focused. The *diffused environment* is the general sociocultural background against which organizations operate; it consists of the values, traditions, and social institutions that condition the goals and behavior of formal organizations. As such, it does not figure directly in organizational resource extraction, except to the extent that it sets limits and creates opportunities for organizations.[9]

FIGURE 2

The environment of an organization

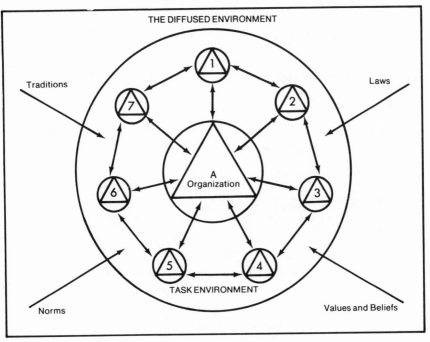

---

[9] See James D. Thompson, *Organizations in Action* (New York: McGraw-Hill Book Co., 1967), pp. 25–38.

In many societies, for example, the diffused environment precludes the use of slavery and physical coercion as ways of extracting resources.

The second category, the *focused environment*, is made up of those elements of an organization's setting that have a visible, specific, and significant impact on its goals and goal achievement capacity. These elements are other organizations and different groups and individuals. James D. Thompson calls this the *organizational task environment;* it is the most immediate and critical segment of the organization's surroundings, the area in which the transactional character of the resource extraction process becomes most apparent. The most meaningful "action" takes place in the context of the task environment.[10] Figure 2 is a representation of the relationship between a focal organization, its task environment, and the diffused environment.

■COMPONENTS OF THE TASK ENVIRONMENT

For the purposes of analysis, it will be helpful to separate the task environment into (1) suppliers, (2) consumers or clients, (3) competitors, and (4) integrators.[11] The same organization, group, or individual may act as supplier, consumer, competitor, or integrator, depending on the time and situation; these are four *modes* of behavior which need not be exclusive functions of different entities.

Suppliers
Suppliers produce and allocate various kinds of resources of value to an organization. Interest groups, legislators, and executive policymakers are potential suppliers of public, political and financial support. As such, they must be convinced that an agency's mission and performance justify the funding and staffing of its ongoing and proposed activi-

---

[10] Ibid., pp. 26–27.

[11] Koya Azumi, "Environmental Needs, Resources, and Agents," in Koya Azumi and Jerald Hage (eds.), *Organizational Systems* (Lexington, Mass.: D. C. Heath & Co., 1972), pp. 91–100.

ties. Universities, training institutions, and labor unions are examples of suppliers of personnel to meet specific staffing needs. Since they are influential with executive agencies and legislative bodies, they also affect the supply of political and financial support.

Acquiring and developing human resources. Probably the most visible external extraction function of public personnel is the acquisition of human resources (male and female workers). Public agencies rely on a wide range of technical and administrative skills which are obtainable for the most part only from their task environments. The human resource acquisition process has two basic dimensions, the first and most common of which is an organizational *maintenance* activity. Recruitment and selection procedures are geared to filling new positions and replacing employees as vacancies occur. Hence the staffing maintenance service provided by personnel offices and commissions is akin to that of a grocery store which maintains "stocks" of goods purchased routinely by customers.[12]

The second dimension of the human resource acquisition process is *adaptive*. Personnel experts participate in the design and application of techniques for anticipating and dealing with quantitative and qualitative changes in organizational requirements. The nature and scope of agency activities change over time, and the technologies they use are in many cases becoming highly complex. Therefore, the skills profiles of public organizations can shift radically over a relatively short time span, and human resource acquisition programs must be directed not only at meeting current demands but also at satisfying future needs. The maintenance of an effective personal services extraction capacity is becoming increasingly dependent on carefully planned and executed acquisition strategies.

Accurate assessments of organizational trends and of their relationship to the composition of the available labor pool are essential. Eli Ginzberg has pointed out that the environ-

---

[12] Eli Ginzberg, *Manpower Agenda for America* (New York: McGraw-Hill Book Co., 1968), pp. 1–7.

ment can no longer be expected automatically to generate people with the necessary skills and abilities—especially under conditions of rapid social and technological change. Critical shortages and surpluses have resulted from the assumption that organizational and national human resource needs will be met through the operation of a self-adjusting market. Serious social, political, and economic dislocations can take place when large numbers of people discover that their skills are out of date, no longer required, or in such oversupply that jobs are next to impossible to find. Since the consequences for organizations unable to fill key positions are equally serious from a systems resources standpoint, it is imperative that they develop and pursue task-environment-related strategies intended to prevent critical shortages from occurring. (Human resources planning is discussed further in Chapter 6.)

Influencing the labor market. The pressure to improve the fit between organizational staffing requirements and environmental resources has forced public agencies into actively attempting to manage relationships with labor-supplying elements of their task environments. One way to establish more adequate match-ups is through an analysis of the internal task structure of the organization and redesign of roles and technologies in order to maximize the capacity to use existing human resources. Some jobs can be simplified or broken down into several less complex functions, mechanized or automated systems can be installed to replace human roles where adequately trained personnel are not available, and career ladders can be restructured and lengthened to accommodate skills—upgrading training at the entry level and providing periodic on-the-job education.[13]

The other side of the coin is a sustained organizational effort to manipulate the supplier facet of the task environment. Various incentives are used to influence potential

---

[13] Ewan Clague, "Government Employment and Manpower Planning in the 1970's," *Public Personnel Review*, 31, No. 4 (October 1970), 279–82. See also Harold Suskin, "Job Evaluation—It's More Than a Tool for Setting Pay Rates," *Public Personnel Review*, 31, No. 4 (October 1970), 283–89.

suppliers to produce individuals with capabilities that meet organizational needs. At the entry level, many federal agencies fund and administer scholarships, training programs, and research projects in fields closely related to their existing or projected staffing requirements. During the race to "catch up" with the Soviet Union in space exploration and military missile technology, the Department of Defense and the National Aeronautics and Space Administration (NASA) pumped huge amounts of money into universities and colleges willing and able to reorient their educational priorities toward the physical sciences and engineering. As expected, these programs significantly increased the numbers of students pursuing careers in the sciences, engineering, and public management. By offering jobs in these areas and by creating strong financial incentives for institutions to train in these fields, the federal agencies concerned were able rather quickly to modify the character of the labor pool.[14]

Building supportive relationships with suppliers. A parallel approach is the encouragement of supportive ties with institutions able to provide midcareer training and skills development programs for public employees. Although the mechanisms used to induce outside organizations to play a supportive role are the same — financial incentives and jobs — the focus here is on gaining access to their facilities and expertise.

Today, many governmental units have formal contracts with universities, professional associations, and consulting organizations for on- and off-the-job training of their personnel. Other less formal but equally symbiotic relationships can be found on all levels of government. The city and county of Los Angeles have historically supported local institutions willing to engage in midcareer education for city and county employees; they often grant time off and cover the tuition costs of employees. Schools such as the

---

[14] U.S. Department of Labor, *Manpower Report of the President* (Washington, D.C.: Government Printing Office, 1969), pp. 161–62.

University of Southern California have responded by
building large programs in public administration and
related fields. The benefits to both sides are obvious. This
pattern of formal and informal transactions can be expected
to grow as more federal funds are channeled into training in
the states and localities. Probably the most visible example
of this trend today is the rapid development of law enforcement training programs offered on college and university
campuses.

Establishing in-house suppliers. As one writer has put it,
"the larger the number of suppliers and consumers of an
organization, the greater the autonomy of the organization."[15]
This maxim applies to the organizational problem of extracting human resources, in which the object should be to
create multiple, even redundant, sets of alternative suppliers. The techniques described above rely on the capacity
of public organizations to mesh their interests with those
of external, often nonpublic, agencies. However, there is
always the possibility that external suppliers will not be
able to generate appropriate resources or will be unwilling
to do so under "acceptable" terms. Uncertainty of this kind
can be reduced if internal sources of supply can be established and administered to suit organizational purposes.

The Federal Executive Institute (FEI), a U.S. Civil Service
Commission facility, trains federal supergrade personnel
(GS-16-18 and their equivalents). Established in 1968,
the FEI caps an extensive technical and administrative
training system that gives the federal government significant internal alternatives to external suppliers.[16] Because
this system is financed, staffed, and administered directly,
in-house resources are controllable, and their outputs can
be geared specifically to the needs of federal agencies. These

---

[15] Azumi, "Environmental Needs, Resources, and Agents," p. 98.
[16] Paul C. Buchanan (ed.), *An Approach to Executive Development in
Government: The Federal Executive Institute Experience* (Washington,
D.C.: National Academy of Public Administration, n.d.). See also Richard C.
Collins, "Training and Education: Trends, Differences, and Issues," *Public
Administration Review,* 33, No. 6 (November–December 1973), 510–11.

resources reduce dependency on outside sources and increase the probability that gaps in the external environment can be compensated for at relatively low cost. The creation by governments of organizations such as the FEI, military and police academies, and the Foreign Service Institute of the State Department is not an uncommon phenomenon, especially under conditions where their absence would leave public organizations in a state of complete dependence on external sources for personnel — sources which may not exist.

Jurisdictional specialization and intergovernmental cooperation. Local governments and most states do not have the resources necessary to build anything approaching the federal system for acquiring and developing personnel. Therefore, they employ to good advantage the strategies of jurisdictional specialization and intergovernmental cooperation.

Jurisdictional specialization in this case means that one jurisdiction, often a county, functions as a central personnel agency for all cities and towns within its area. The Onondaga County (N.Y.) Department of Personnel

> . . . prepares job specifications and classifies all governmental positions in compliance with State Civil Service Law for the governments of Onondaga County, the City of Syracuse and all school districts, towns, villages, and special districts within the County. The Department is responsible for preparing and conducting examinations, receiving and distributing examination applications and notifying applicants of test results and establishing eligible lists. The Department maintains civil service records for employees and certifies payrolls for the above local governments.[17]

Specialization of functions in this example represents a state-mandated effort to treat counties as administrative systems. All governmental units within the county are in turn treated as subsystems. Authority and resources are concentrated in the County Department of Personnel, and costly duplications of effort are avoided. Benefits to the con-

---

[17] Onondaga County, N.Y., *County Executive's Tentative Budget, 1974*, p. BC-5.

cerned subsystems are relief from the administrative and financial burdens associated with running a full-fledged personnel service, and access to coordinated countywide facilities. If governments within such a system feel that their needs for independence and flexibility in personnel matters outweigh the benefits of centralization, however, they may not relish the subsystem role.

Examples of *intergovernmental cooperation* are the pooling of resources to fund and administer joint training programs, and agreements whereby governments use each other's personnel under certain conditions. Multijurisdiction police-training systems are now being developed with state and federal aid. Regional and statewide police-training structures can be found today in many places, including Oregon, California, Michigan, New York, and the New England states.[18] Programs funded under provisions of the Intergovernmental Personnel Act of 1970, referred to in Chapter 1, contain the seeds of a far-reaching pattern of cooperation between federal, state, and local governments.

Direct sharing of personnel is most commonly reflected in joint agreements between fire and police departments. Costs are shared and participating jurisdictions retain "recall" rights, but emphasis is placed on interdependency and mutual support. One three-way police cooperation agreement states in part:

> In the event of emergency, the mayor of the municipality affected may call on the mayors of the other two municipalities for the services as auxiliary policemen of such number of personnel and such equipment as he deems essential . . . the mayor called upon shall assign to service in the requesting community such number of personnel as auxiliary policemen and such equipment as in his judgment may be released for such purpose.[19]

Such agreements allow the organizations involved to acquire additional personnel on a special-need basis. Inter-

---

[18] President's Commission on Law Enforcement and Administration of Justice, *Task Force on the Police* (Washington, D.C.: Government Printing Office, 1967), pp. 76–77.

[19] Ibid., p. 114.

organizational cooperation enables agencies to respond effectively without having to maintain their staffs at levels geared to meet exceptional rather than normal circumstances, and it also increases the probability that people with the appropriate skills will be available when they are needed. Prearranged counterpart support also reduces dependency on often less-than-satisfactory ad hoc linkages with suppliers such as volunteer groups.

Contracting. Contracting is another option open to public organizations seeking to obtain the services of trained personnel. This arrangement, which makes it possible to exploit the talents and technologies of the private sector and of other governmental units, can support and improve the extractive capabilities of public bureaucracies in several ways.[20]

Public agencies are at a disadvantage where the private sector controls the means of production and can offer better pay and benefits to highly skilled people. They can, however, tap these resources through contracts which make it possible for them to avoid the constraints set by budgets, personnel service ceilings, salary level limitations, and civil service procedures. Contracting often increases organizational flexibility and reduces dependency on traditional mechanisms for attracting, selecting, and placing personnel. By shifting managerial responsibility for staffing and supervising to the contractor, the public agency can escape the administrative costs associated with expansion to produce more services or goods.

Governments also contract with each other for services in functional areas such as law enforcement. Under a contract program, one government undertakes to provide specified services to another for a fee; that is, it agrees to act as an agent of the other government in its jurisdiction. Los Angeles County provides law enforcement services to about one third of the incorporated municipalities within the county;

---

[20] See John W. Macy, Jr., *Public Service: The Human Side of Government* (New York: Harper & Row, 1971), pp. 27–37.

and in Connecticut the state provides police services to cities on a contract basis.[21]

It appears from the available information that contract law enforcement costs a city less than if it provided its own services, mainly because of the economies large programs generate.[22] Contracting allows small cities and other under-equipped jurisdictions to use the established personnel systems and technical facilities of the city or county that is acting as the supplier. Thus it can be an effective way of assuring predictable, high-quality input relations with suppliers. However, since contract services of this kind are usually available from only one source, predictability and economy are often purchased at the expense of autonomy and flexibility; the purchasing jurisdiction loses political and administrative control over many aspects of how the program is staffed and executed. The feasibility of contractual arrangements with other governments, therefore, is likely to depend on the social and political character of the community and on the organizational function concerned.[23]

Contractual ties with the private sector may strengthen a public agency's hand in extracting resources through political means. Large corporations and labor unions often come to rely heavily on the resources they obtain through government contracts; they develop a strong vested interest in the "health" of their public counterparts. This organizational interdependence stimulates the formation of powerful political coalitions. The support of concerned contractors can usually be counted on when efforts are made to expand agency programs and to obtain approval of budgetary requests from executive or legislative suppliers.[24]

Too, contracting serves to buffer public agencies from criticism that they are overgrown and encroaching on the

---

[21] President's Commission on Law Enforcement. *Task Force on the Police.* pp. 106–7.

[22] Ibid., p. 106.

[23] Ibid., p. 107.

[24] Peter Woll, *American Bureaucracy* (New York: W. W. Norton & Co., 1963), pp. 134–35.

proper domain of private enterprise. As John Macy, Jr., notes, contracting permits large-scale expansion of public programs, while avoiding ideological attacks from groups that fear "creeping socialism" or "big government." Thus it becomes a strategy for acquiring human resources while retaining ideological acceptability.[25]

Finally, the very need for government to "buy" the services of externally controlled personnel in critical areas brings into question the adequacy of existing public personnel systems, their pay scales, and the working conditions they foster. By contracting, public management has focused attention on its inability to compete with the private sector for highly skilled personnel and strengthened its case for higher pay, more flexible personnel procedures, and better working conditions within government. A 1962 committee report to President Kennedy which specified competition from private contractors as a reason for declining competence in government research and development laboratories "became a blueprint not only for the relationship between government and contractor laboratories but likewise for a continuing effort to improve the working environment and employment conditions in government laboratories."[26]

Dealings with public employee organizations. Employee organizations are now powerful suppliers in the task environments of many public organizations. Increasingly they are likely to withhold the services of their members if they are unable to negotiate what they consider to be satisfactory agreements with management, and job actions and strikes have become common on the government scene. Whatever their causes, disruptive labor-management relations represent a failure by the organization to maintain stable extractive linkages with employee groups.

Unpredictable or hostile relationships with employee groups can be very costly to public agencies and their clienteles. This is reflected in the current emphasis on

[25] Macy, *Public Service*, pp. 27–29.
[26] Ibid., p. 33.

building viable collective bargaining arrangements, which recognizes the necessity of effective interaction with unions as suppliers of vital human resources. Personnel and labor relations offices at all levels of government are being asked to supply the technical expertise and bargaining skills necessary to establish and maintain mutually beneficial interactions with public employee organizations. Sam Zagoria points out that the number of specialists in labor relations is growing, "as chief officers of local government recognize there is as much need for expertise here as in zoning, sewage planning, or other municipal responsibilities and the impact on a city budget can be much greater."[27]

Creating and exploiting competition among suppliers. Encouraging interorganizational competition in the task environment is one strategy whereby public agencies may avoid becoming heavily dependent on any one supplier of human resources. By setting up conditions under which suppliers must actively compete for the resources being distributed by the organization, management expands its access to alternative sources of supply and may be able to drive down the overall costs of inputs. One technique of this kind is the requirement of competitive bids for contracts. Organizations dependent on certain suppliers may not only support the growth of competition among them but also may try to convert dependency into domination by capturing and including them within their zones of administrative control.

Public employers have historically exerted strong control over employee relationships with the organization through management-dominated civil service and merit systems. This is essentially a strategy to control labor supply. With the advent of widespread collective bargaining and the accompanying increase in employee organization power, the unions often have turned the tables by systematically exploiting their monopoly position as suppliers. Especially

---

[27] Sam Zagoria (ed.), *Public Workers and Public Unions* (Englewood Cliffs, N.J.: Prentice-Hall, Inc., 1972), p. 176.

at the local level of government, management has retaliated by trying to develop alternative suppliers in the form of private contractors. In this way it attempts to use the threat or reality of competition to reduce its own dependency, while emphasizing the ultimate dependency of employee organizations on their own supplier—the employer.[28]

The violent opposition to the contracting-out of public services by employee organizations is a reaction to the emergence of a potentially very competitive sector of *their own* task environments. Employee groups may make strenuous efforts to block viable competition in functional areas traditionally reserved for civil service workers because they know that if management is allowed to expand the field of alternative suppliers, its dependency status in the collective bargaining relationship will be reduced.

The unions have contested contracting arrangements by mobilizing supportive coalitions of legislators, personnel administrators, clientele groups, and other influential elements. An Office of Management and Budget (OMB) proposal to replace many military and civilian government employees on Defense Department bases with contract workers stimulated an apparent coalition between employee groups and the Pentagon, which does not want to lose its control over military personnel. Reports indicated that the Pentagon and employee organizations were sharing information in a coordinated effort to block the OMB proposal.[29]

Political interdependence and exchanges are critical. Contracting-out a service may be economically the most attractive arrangement, but it might have negative political and social consequences that make it a very costly strategy for the organization to follow. It could produce, for example, a decline in political leverage and client support.

The supplier challenge for personnel administrators. If personnel administrators are to affect the human resource

---

[28] Harry H. Wellington and Ralph K. Winter, Jr., *The Unions and the Cities* (Washington, D.C.: Brookings Institution, 1971), pp. 62–65.

[29] *Federal Times*, January 16, 1974. See also David T. Stanley, *Managing Local Government under Union Pressure* (Washington, D.C.: Brookings Institution, 1972), pp. 90–93.

extractive capacities of their organizations positively, they must be prepared to contribute meaningfully to managerial decisions regarding dealings with the supplier facet of the task environment. Personnel specialists must be equipped to think and behave strategically because

> . . . relations with suppliers, associates, and supporters are never fixed entities. Even in the worst of circumstances they are directly affected by the ingenuity and imagination of administrators. Even in the best of circumstances, the availability of resources, assistance and support, and the terms on which it is obtained, will depend on the interrelations between the organizations and the suppliers.[30]

Consumers or clients

Consumers or clients are the parts of the task environment that are subject to or use the organization's outputs. They frequently are also suppliers because they exchange money or services for these outputs, or because they are able to influence the resource allocation process at the legislative and executive levels of government through political means. While direct economic exchanges are more typical of the private sector in the United States, some public agencies do provide goods and services on a fee basis. With rare exceptions, however, public organizations depend on the political support of their constituencies far more than they do on direct economic transactions. Consequently, they tend to gear their programs and practices to the expressed needs and values of their most powerful and influential clients.[31]

Maintaining organizational prestige. The merit system, particularly the image conveyed by merit-oriented personnel procedures, provides a good illustration of how personnel administration can be used as an extractive mechanism in dealings with clients. The politically neutral norms

---

[30] Bertram M. Gross, *The Managing of Organizations* (New York: Free Press, 1964), p. 417.

[31] Norton Long, "Power and Administration," in Peter Woll (ed.), *Public Administration and Policy* (New York: Harper & Row, Publishers, 1966), pp. 42–57.

of the merit concept communicate the image of an expert, impartial public service. Agencies operating in politically charged atmospheres can find this posture highly functional when they need the support of ideologically conflicting groups inside and outside of government.

The more able an organization is to convince others that the way it does business reflects the values and expectations dominant in the social setting, the more likely it will be to garner a broad base of client support. Personnel policies and practices can play a potentially significant part in building the prestige of an organization.[32]

Protecting the organization. In addition to projecting a positive image that enhances an organization's claim to material and human resources, the personnel function can be so conducted as to protect or buffer it from attacks by outside groups.

When organizations fail to respond adaptively to meaningful changes in environmental values and norms, their prestige is likely to erode quickly. Recent criticisms of the values expressed in the operation of public personnel systems strike at their failure to meet the standard set by the norm of equal employment opportunity, and it has become increasingly apparent to public administrators that the image or fact of discrimination tends to alienate important suppliers. Although it might sound harsh to put it in these terms, it is doubtful that affirmative action programs would ever have originated from exclusively intraorganizational sources.

Personnel administrators with the task of devising and administering programs which satisfy the demands of relevant clients and suppliers are in a difficult position. They must be able simultaneously to accurately monitor the constraints and opportunities presented by the external environment and to develop organizationally appropriate responses. Not only must external interests be satisfied, but

---

[32] Charles Perrow, "Organizational Prestige: Some Functions and Dysfunctions," *American Journal of Sociology*, 66 (January 1961b), 335–41.

internal demands for competent job performance and minimal disruption must be met.

Uncontrolled environmental penetrations (in this case, the infusion of underskilled and less predictable employees) can seriously disrupt the established social and technical routines of organizations. Since the traditionally available buffering mechanisms represented by standard civil service entrance examinations and other "merit" practices are losing their social and political viability, new techniques are necessary. A partial list of relatively new buffering processes would include organizationally sponsored preentry and postentry training programs, job simplification, and training of supervisors to deal with the social and psychological tensions created by widely divergent skills, values, and expectations in the workplace.[33]

Competitors

Competitor organizations try to attract limited resources from suppliers by offering similar services or outputs. Because money, skilled personnel, and high ranking in political support are resources that more often than not are in short supply, organizations search out strategies that will maximize their competitive advantages. Vertical and horizontal expansion, administered markets, and the building of protective political coalitions are typical responses to the threat of competition for resources in the external environment.[34]

Competing for human resources. Public agencies face stiff competition from the private sector for skilled technical and administrative personnel. In this, the cultivation of supportive political coalitions is very important. Time and again, the organization's management joins forces with employee organizations, legislators, prestigious groups which

---

[33] Bernard Rosen, "Affirmative Action Produces Equal Employment Opportunity for All," in Lloyd G. Nigro (ed.), "A Mini-Symposium: Affirmative Action in Public Employment," *Public Administration Review*, 34, No. 3 (May–June 1974), 237–39.

[34] Thompson, *Organizations in Action*, pp. 28–50.

influence public policy, and concerned clientele to exert pressure on pivotal points in the decision-making process. Failures can be costly, as Robert E. Hampton, Chairman of the U.S. Civil Service Commission, noted when he predicted that a Senate vote against raising the pay of senior civil servants might lead to "serious morale problems" and cripple efforts to recruit people for these key positions.[35] In a more general sense, Hampton's comments can be seen as illustrative of the lobbying role required of those working in behalf of public personnel systems.

Attracting talented people away from competitors depends on more than simple economic parity or advantage in the labor market. There is evidence that noneconomic factors can attract highly qualified people to government service.[36] The opportunity to work at challenging and responsible jobs is an equalizer which can be offered by public agencies, which are generally unable to offer economic benefits on a par with those in the private sector. Innovative and aggressive civil service commissions and agency personnel officers can be of great help in this respect. Yet personnel administrators have been reluctant to change their traditional orientation toward personnel as a regulatory and standardizing function. The capacity to offer potential employees job security and equal treatment under merit system rules is important, but the challenges facing modern government demand "a new and better balance in the personnel regulations that are designed to insure honesty and equity, for among them are certain restrictive rules which unduly hamper the kinds of autonomy, personal growth, creativity, and innovation for which there is now a critical and growing need."[37]

Removing impediments to agency competitiveness. Agency flexibility and discretion are also significant factors in the

---

[35] *Federal Times,* March 20, 1974.

[36] See Franklin K. Kilpatrick, Milton C. Cummings, Jr., and M. Kent Jennings, *The Image of the Federal Executive* (Washington, D.C.: Brookings Institution, 1964), pp. 119–66.

[37] Ibid., pp. 267–68.

competition for human resources. The organization should be so structured as to allow it to react appropriately to environmental conditions. From a competitive standpoint, there are situations where otherwise functional personnel procedures actually work against a capacity to respond opportunistically. Situation-by-situation adaptiveness and quick action are often necessary if competitors for resources are to be beaten to the punch.

Generalized rules administered centrally, which are typical of most traditional merit systems, tend to function most effectively under conditions of relative environmental stability and predictability. When personnel resources are available and readily accessible, bureaucratic models for personnel administration work fairly well. In these cases, secure extractive relationships allow organizations to follow standardized and somewhat passive recruitment patterns. However, in situations that combine resource scarcity and competition, a capacity to "tailor make" responses is usually required. In practice this means that the authority and skills necessary to make appropriate decisions regarding a wide range of personnel matters have to be located as close as possible to the problem at hand, most likely at the agency or subagency level. (Chapter 3 discusses decentralization of the personnel function.)

Another method of improving the adaptiveness and hence the competitiveness of organizations is to increase the flexibility of personnel rule systems. Rigid, narrowly defined rules administered by control-oriented personnel agencies and offices are frequently cited by public managers as a major barrier to effectiveness.[38] All complex organizations rely for their existence on intricate structures of formal and informal rules. It is the functionality of specific rules — not the need for rules — that is the central issue for personnel administration. As Charles Perrow observes, "The greatest

---

[38] Frederick C. Mosher, "Features and Problems of the Federal Service: The Management of Merit," in Wallace S. Sayre (ed.), *The Federal Government Service* (Englewood Cliffs, N.J.: Prentice-Hall, Inc., 1965), reprinted in Robert P. Golembiewski and Michael Cohen (eds.), *People in Public Service* (Itasca, Ill.: F. E. Peacock, Publishers, 1970), pp. 397–400.

problem with rules is that organizations and their environments change faster than the rules."[39] A very real problem for personnel administrators is to keep personnel policies and procedures in line with the internal conditions and external demands faced by management on a day-to-day basis.

The external extraction needs and problems of a research bureau, police department, welfare office, or hospital may be very different in important respects. If uniform personnel strategies were imposed on all of these organizations, these variations could not be accommodated. One practical way of avoiding the rigidities of a monolithic personnel process is to expand the range of legitimate options open to an agency, thus increasing the probability that effective responses will be feasible. Depending on the situation of the agency, it can choose to use one or all of the options open to it. Organizations operating in predictable, noncompetitive contexts could opt for relatively standardized sets of "response rules," while others could adapt to unpredictability, fluidity, and competition by responding to environmental "cues."[40]

Integrators

Integrators mediate or control aspects of the relationships between an organization and its suppliers, clients, and competitors.[41] Broadly speaking, integrators make and administer rules governing task environment interactions. Examples of integrators include the courts, regulatory commissions and boards, and administrative agencies which monitor and supervise certain interorganizational relations.

Legislative bodies, civil service commissions, and control agencies such as the OMB frequently act as integrators in matters affecting the personnel operations of public organizations. They control funds and personnel levels and promulgate rules governing relationships between man-

---

[39] Charles Perrow, *Complex Organizations, A Critical Essay* (Glenview, Ill.: Scott, Foresman, & Co., 1972), p. 31.

[40] Thompson, *Organizations in Action*, p. 71.

[41] Azumi, "Environmental Needs, Resources, and Agents," p. 99.

agement and employees. Their support obviously is often critically important to agency personnel administrators. Where integrators can help create a stable and predictable environment for an organization, the organization does well to try to build a supportive coalition with them. Coalitions with key integrators can be very useful because they usually have the legal or administrative authority to stabilize and structure the terms under which organizations transact with one another. Both private- and public-sector administrators have long recognized the value of friendly relationships with integrators. If allowed to do so, organizations will make every effort to "capture" relevant integrators. The complaint that many industries have taken over the regulatory commissions originally created to control them is a reflection of this phenomenon.[42]

The U.S. Civil Service Commission as an integrator. Like its counterparts on the state and local level, the U.S. Civil Service Commission plays the role of an integrator in its capacity as a primary maker of personnel policy. Not unexpectedly, the Commission is at the center of a large field of organizational interests which individually and in combination attempt to influence its policies, programs, and procedures. Included in this complex policy arena are: (1) the President, (2) OMB, (3) several congressional committees, (4) the federal courts, (5) veterans' groups, (6) minority groups, (7) employee organizations, (8) professional associations, (9) citizen and consumer lobbies, and (10) the many departments, bureaus, and agencies of the government.[43]

Because of its function as a rule maker, the Commission comes under strong pressure to satisfy the desires of these groups. Departmental administrators, who are well aware of the impact Commission policies can have on their autonomy and resource extractive capabilities, struggle continu-

---

[42] Samuel P. Huntington, "The Marasmus of the ICC: The Commission, The Railroads, and the Public Interest," in Woll, *Public Administration and Policy*, pp. 58–90.

[43] Michael Cohen, "The Personnel Policy-Making System," in Golembiewski and Cohen, *People in Public Service*, pp. 123–37.

ously to get its support and protection. They have consistently argued that the Commission should assume the role of a consultant to and defender of agency personnel administration and not act as a "policeman" or regulator of agency activities. The historical debates over "protectionist" versus "positive" personnel policies, centralized as opposed to decentralized authority, and the more recent disputes over minority employment goals and quotas have focused on the Commission's behavior as a major integrator in the federal personnel system.

In the opinion of some critics, Commission-agency cooperation may not be altogether functional or always in the public interest, but the resource extraction process pushes the agencies to seek such a relationship. Over the course of the past 30 years, the federal executive has succeeded in redefining the Commission's role, and by 1963, the President was able to state that "The management of Federal personnel matters is a kind of partnership in which the agencies and the Commission share responsibility for the well-being and development of the Federal personnel system."[44]

The courts as integrators. Courts on all levels of government have historically played an integrative role in public personnel systems, especially with respect to the rights and obligations of management and employees. This subject is dealt with in detail in Chapter 11; suffice it to say here that new judicial rulings have substantially changed the structure of power within the environment of the personnel administrator.

Integrators in the labor-management relations field. As collective bargaining has spread in the public sector, there has been a parallel development of integrators to regulate labor-management transactions. Public employment relations boards administer the bargaining statutes, determine

---

[44] U.S. Civil Service Commission, "Department-Commission Relations: The President's Formal Position," in Golembiewski and Cohen, *People in Public Service*, p. 494.

bargaining units, supervise representation elections, and mediate and adjudicate conflicts. They are of value to both agency management and union leadership in providing stable and predictable processes for collective bargaining, facilitating third-party interventions, and keeping both sides within the bounds of good-faith bargaining.

Because such integrators are so important to both sides, it is not surprising that they are the targets of strenuous efforts by management and labor alike to control their membership, legal authority, and procedural guidelines. The intense political activity that surrounds and pervades legislative and executive attempts to establish these boards is predictable and normal in this context.

In contrast to earlier times, management cannot now assume that its biases will be reflected in the charters given to integrators and expect that they will automatically defend its traditional powers. This new environment places added responsibilities on personnel administrators; first, they must have the expertise and knowledge necessary to represent management's interests effectively in the political processes which lead to the formation of these integrators, and second, they have to be able to work with them, once established. In David T. Stanley's words:

> . . . a weak or inattentive management group can have its powers significantly reduced through successive concessions to aggressive unions. Management needs to maintain its strength in the employment bargain. It can do so first by sheer competence—by being properly organized and staffed for labor relations. Second, *management's prerogatives should be spelled out in legislation, executive orders, and union agreements.* (Italics ours)[45]

Integrators work within the parameters set by law or executive orders, and it is important that these guidelines do not undermine agency efforts to build stable, productive relationships with employee organizations. In many jurisdic-

---

[45] David T. Stanley, "The Effect of Unions on Local Governments," in Robert H. Connery and William V. Farr (eds.), *Unionization of Municipal Employees*, Proceedings of the Academy of Political Science (New York: Columbia University Press, 1970), pp. 53–54.

tions, legal-administrative domination of the relationship is no longer feasible or desirable, but balance is essential. Personnel administrators trained and experienced in public-sector labor relations can do much to defend agency interests and exert legitimate influence on the policymakers who create and administer labor relations boards. In light of the organizational drive to capture integrators, positive action by personnel administrators in behalf of their organizations is a virtual necessity in the interorganizational climate that has been stimulated by collective bargaining in the public sector.

■ BOUNDARY SPANNING THROUGH PUBLIC PERSONNEL ADMINISTRATION

As has been noted, many public organizations face task environments of growing complexity. Rapid technological, economic, political, and social change has pressured them to develop a capacity for adaptiveness in their responses to environmental conditions. Increasingly, the organization's effectiveness in external resource extraction depends on administrators who are strategically aware and able to deal with the constraints and opportunities of situations as they are presented.

Public personnel administration, which is geared to helping agencies meet their human resources needs, is being asked to expand its horizons beyond the internal organization and to engage the problems of managing relationships with the external environment. The development and maintenance of profitable human resource linkages is becoming a primary dimension of the public personnel administrator's role. Personnel administration that for all practical purposes stops at the organization's boundaries is no longer adequate, because the complexity and interdependence of modern society do not allow a purely intraorganizational viewpoint.

The personnel administrator of today must be prepared to bridge the division between the internal and external environments of organizations and work to bring them into productive alignment. Internal arrangements and procedures must be designed and redesigned to exploit possibilities as they arise, and the organization must apply its resources and skills to the task of influencing its environment. Contributing meaningfully to this important process is one of the basic challenges of modern public personnel administration.

The chart in Figure 3 is a map of the organization terrain

FIGURE 3

Map of Organization's Terrain

involved. The triangle in the middle represents the organization and its core technology, goals, and human resources needs. Surrounding the organization is a boundary zone in which it comes together and interacts with its task environment. Within this zone is a series of linking strategies, processes, and structures which permit the organization to extract resources from the various sectors of the task environment shown in the outer ring of the chart. Although they are impossible to show in the figure, overlaps, multiple interdependencies, and cross-cutting interactions among factors of the environment can be expected in real-world situations. Even without indicating these, however, the figure helps define the systems integration role of the public personnel administrator.

■ INTERNAL EXTRACTION: MEDIATING RELATIONSHIPS BETWEEN THE ORGANIZATION AND ITS MEMBERS

The other side of the personnel administrator's role is helping to create conditions within the organization which improve its capacity to extract resources from its own members. This aspect of the personnel function demands considerable expertise in the processes whereby human needs and expectations can be meshed with the behavioral and technical demands of formal organizations. To the organization, internal extraction is a problem in the design of social, psychological, and technical systems which will maximize the contributions people make to the accomplishment of organizational ends. Internal resource extraction rests on a foundation consisting of a web of formal and informal incentives which taken together constitute the organization's side of a transactional relationship with its employees.

Organizational incentives: The inducements-contributions equation

Personnel administration is most often associated with techniques for providing and administering formal incentives. The most common incentives are wages and salaries, but the term "incentive" has a far broader meaning:

An *incentive* is a *stimulus* which incites action. In its broad usage "incentive" is applicable to any inducement, material or non-material, which impels, encourages, or forces a person to perform a task to accomplish a goal. *A psychological reaction is the primary effect of an incentive. Its secondary effect is behavior.*[46]

Organizations use incentives of many kinds to stimulate and reinforce behaviors that contribute to the performance of organizational tasks and to the attainment of program goals. Specifically, sought-after behaviors include competent and predictable role performance; coordinated and cooperative interpersonal and group efforts in the pursuit of system objectives; conformance to the organization's norms, rules, and policies; and active support of its viewpoints and goals. Positive (rewarding) and negative (punishing) incentives are used for these purposes.

The most successful incentives systems are those that offer rewards matching the felt needs and expectations of the employee groups affected. The essence of any incentives system, therefore, is the effort to bring inducements, needs, and expectations into alignment. The objective is to apply incentives that make it rewarding for employees to behave in ways that directly or indirectly contribute to the pool of resources available for *organizational* uses. In this viewpoint, internal extraction is a process energized by mutually profitable exchanges between the organization and its membership. As George C. Homans has expressed it, "The open secret of human exchange is to give the other man behavior that is more valuable to him than it is costly to you and to get from him behavior that is more valuable to you than it is costly to him."[47]

The premise of the inducements-contributions equation is that both interacting parties seek to emerge from the process with a profit of some kind. Profit is "the difference between the value of a reward a man [or organization] gets

---

[46] William G. Scott, *Organization Theory: A Behavioral Analysis for Management* (Homewood, Ill.: Richard D. Irwin, 1967), pp. 284–85 (italics in original).

[47] George C. Homans, *Social Behavior: Its Elementary Forms* (New York: Harcourt Brace & World, 1961), p. 62.

by emitting a particular unit-activity and the value of the reward obtainable by another unit-activity, foregone in emitting the first."[48] In other words, profit equals reward minus cost $(P = R - C)$.

Cost is the value, actual or anticipated, of an action *not taken*. For example, a decision is made to spend a million dollars on a management training program (unit-activity), rather than putting the money into new high-speed electronic data processing equipment (foregone unit-activity). In this case, profit would be calculated by subtracting the anticipated value of the EDP equipment (cost) from the value attributed to the results of the training program (reward). If costs are deemed to be higher than rewards, a loss results. In this illustration, the organization would find it difficult to estimate the value of the training program in dollar terms, but other indicators such as productivity, job satisfaction, and turnover would be used.

The concept of perceived profit is equally useful in considering the relationships between individuals and organizations. For the individual, the organization must be seen to be providing rewards which in combination outweigh the costs tied to behaving in ways required to obtain those rewards. The organization, on the other hand, must see the rewards to it associated with these elicited behaviors as worth more than the costs tied to stimulating them. If either side perceives an overall loss, the relationship will be broken off or an effort will be made to change the terms of the exchange. Employees will seek employment elsewhere if they believe their services are not adequately rewarded in comparison to what they could get from another organization. If they cannot move or feel that leaving would be too costly, they may simply reduce their day-to-day contributions to a level where some sort of balance or profit is achieved. As individuals or in groups, employees also seek to have the organization improve the incentives it offers. Organized labor has always directed its efforts toward improving the inducements side of the inducements-contributions equa-

---

[48] Ibid., p. 63.

tion. The recent interest of public management in productivity bargaining indicates its concern with the contributions side.[49]

Those acting on behalf of the organization will systematically manipulate incentives and expectations in order to develop inducements-contributions mixes which produce substantial profits. If it is to construct an effective incentives structure, management must be able to recognize and tap basic, pervasive needs and expectations in the work force. The problem is to define as accurately as possible the rewards-costs profile of the individual or group concerned and then to understand its relationship to organizational resources and needs.

The difficulties involved should not be minimized. Individuals have motivational patterns which are different, complex, and shifting. Their reactions to organizational conditions can vary widely, and it is risky to make assumptions in this area. A long history of research on the relationships between technological, social, and psychological factors and such contributions-related variables as morale, job satisfaction, and productivity has revealed an enormously complicated picture. In one writer's words,

> Organization and management theory has tended toward simplified and generalized conceptions of man. Empirical research has consistently found some support for the simple generalized conception, but only some. Consequently, the major impact of many decades of research has been to vastly complicate our models of man, of organizations, and of management strategies.[50]

In theory, and only in theory, the "perfect" incentives system would fully exploit the motives of each individual employee. A serious attempt to realize this goal, however, would inject a degree of complexity and variability that would be unmanageable for operating organizations. A rela-

[49] See Chester A. Newland, "Personnel Concerns in Government Productivity," in Chester A. Newland (ed.), "Symposium, Productivity in Government," *Public Administration Review*, 32, No. 6 (November–December, 1972), 807–15.

[50] Edgar H. Schein, *Organizational Psychology* (Englewood Cliffs, N.J.: Prentice-Hall, Inc., 1965), p. 60.

tively programmed and broadly applicable set of inducements is far more desirable from an administrative standpoint. Organizations can also accept adequate as opposed to
maximal contributions because they face chronic resource
shortages, especially in light of what can be done with those
that are available. This scarcity makes the costs of highly
individualized inducements packages prohibitive; the ex-
penditure of money, time, and expertise would not be justified when viewed *in relation to its capacity to raise extracted
contributions beyond levels attained through far less costly
means.*[51]

Controlling master variables

Public personnel administration concentrates on the development and implementation of rational mechanisms for
extracting internal human resources. To the degree possible,
the techniques employed should fit within a means-ends
framework that promotes organizational purposes, and
predictability of results and administrative economy are
prime considerations. Effectiveness in achieving these objectives depends on management's ability to control a set of
interrelated master variables. These variables are those
social-psychological conditions, managerial practices, and
resource allocations that management can manipulate with
relative certainty about their impact on employee behavior
as it relates to organizational requirements and goals.

With respect to these master variables, public personnel
specialists have two roles. First, they can help line managers
in isolating material and nonmaterial factors influencing
worker behavior and in taking appropriate corrective actions
when necessary; this is essentially a consultative role.
Second, they can facilitate effective internal human resource
extraction by assuring that personnel policies and practices
meet certain criteria: they should (1) be consonant with
knowledge about the nature of the work force, (2) adequately
reflect managerial needs, (3) promote technical efficiency,

---

[51] Robert A. Dahl and Charles E. Lindblom, *Politics, Economics, and Welfare* (New York: Harper & Row, Publishers, 1953), pp. 164–68.

and (4) support favorable social and psychological conditions within the organization. The personnel administrator thus functions as an expert in the design and implementation of human resources management systems which can provide the organization with the capacity to extract internal resources.[52]

These two roles are enacted within the parameters set by the extent to which management (including the personnel administrator) is able to control two types of master variables: (1) the nature of the organization's human resource base, and (2) the social and technical characteristics of the organization itself.

Controlling the human resource base. Organizations rely on a series of filters and checkpoints to maintain control over the character of their work force and to facilitate the integration of the worker with the technical and social-psychological fabric of the organization. Many of these techniques are in the traditional domain of personnel administration and are discussed in detail in the chapters to follow. They include: (1) recruitment procedures aimed at individuals and groups having desirable skills, attitudes, and expectations; (2) pre-entry testing and evaluation to determine skills levels and conformity to organizational norms; (3) placement policies designed to match people to positions; and (4) performance evaluation systems which make it possible to monitor behavior and to remove or transfer employees who fail to meet the demands of their positions. In the final analysis, these and other screening techniques have one overriding purpose: to control relevant characteristics of the human resource base and thereby increase the predictability of its responses to organizational demands and incentives.

It is highly improbable that even the most sophisticated recruiting and filtering systems will provide organizations with employees possessing all of the desired characteristics. Internal changes and imperfect selection contribute to this error factor, and the recruitment pool simply may not con-

---

[52] Douglas McGregor, *The Human Side of Enterprise* (New York: McGraw-Hill Book Co., 1960), pp. 163–75.

tain a perfect population. Organizations develop formal and informal ways of compensating for imperfect control at the entry level. Training is a widely used compensator; skills can be changed or improved through training experiences conducted or sponsored by the organization. Penalties are used to discourage "deviant" behavior and rewards to encourage "proper" behavior. Attitudes and expectations are often modified by experiences within the organization, and socialization to group norms is a powerful influence. Thus organizations act as schools in which new perceptions are developed and patterns of behavior are learned.[53]

Controlling the sociotechnical nature of the organization. The capacity to control the human side of the member-organization relationship is limited, except for prisons, mental institutions, and other highly coercive organizations. The external environment sets constraints on managerial prerogatives through values and traditions that are related to how people should be treated, and it gives rise to viewpoints and expectations which must be accommodated. In both the public and private sectors, management does not have a free hand in personnel matters. Some of these constraints are the products of legislation, executive decisions, and court rulings concerning societal priorities and the rights of individuals and groups. Others flow out of pervasive socio-economic changes which are felt in the form of new or different attitudes and needs. Thus organizations must also be able to adjust to uncontrollable and changing features of their environments.

To adapt successfully, organizations must also adjust their social and technological structures and processes. Social aspects of the organization include administrative arrangements, leadership styles, decision processes, and the psychological "climate" of the workplace, all of which should act as positive rather than negative factors in motivating employees to make contributions. Technical variables relate to the operating technology of the organization—the ma-

---

[53] Katz and Kahn, *Social Psychology of Organizations*, pp. 48–58.

terials used, how they are processed, and the physical and mechanical procedures employed. There have been indications that technology and the physical, social, and emotional conditions it creates have a very real impact on how employees feel about their work and how they relate to the organization.[54]

The social and technological dimensions of organizations are interrelated, and each affects the other. A particular technology may severely restrict the capacity of an organization to offer social and psychological rewards to its membership. Assembly-line technologies have been linked to alienation and job dissatisfaction because they require employees to work in social isolation at repetitive, intrinsically monotonous jobs. Yet research has revealed that automated, continuous-process technologies (as in the oil and chemical industries) do not cause alienation; the explanation seems to be that in this case workers can interact socially and concentrate on solving nonroutine problems.[55] While technology does not *determine* how organizations will function socially, it is a powerful conditioning factor that should be recognized.[56]

Although some of the technologies in government agencies are highly routinized, most are not industrial in nature. The technologies found in medicine, education, and scientific research appear to function well in a variety of administrative and social systems. The problem for the vast majority of organizations is to find ways of blending technology and social arrangements into desirable rather than undesirable patterns.

■ THE DIAGNOSTIC AND DESIGN CONTRIBUTIONS OF PERSONNEL SPECIALISTS

Discussion of the two general categories of master variables — the human resource base and the sociotechnical system —

---

[54] Michel Crozier, *The Bureaucratic Phenomenon* (Chicago: University of Chicago Press, 1964), pp. 13–55.

[55] Robert Blauner, "Technology, Integration, and Alienation," in Azumi and Hage, *Organizational Systems*, pp. 116–19.

[56] David Silverman, *The Theory of Organizations* (New York: Basic Books, 1970), pp. 100–125.

makes it easier to define the contributions personnel specialists can make to internal human resource extraction.

First, personnel administrators can develop methods of more clearly defining and evaluating the technical (formal) and behavioral (informal) demands of positions. The techniques of position classification and job evaluation are good examples of how the formal aspects of positions can be clarified. Techniques for evaluating informal requirements are less developed but probably no less important.[57] The evaluation of incentives is a closely related activity. Personnel administration has tended to focus on formal, extrinsic incentives (wages and fringe benefits), and more attention should be given to informal, intrinsic incentives and disincentives (social and psychological aspects) of specific tasks.

Second, personnel specialists have a continuing role in the design of systems to attract, select, and place employees who are most likely to perform satisfactorily and respond favorably to organization inducements. Contemporary personnel administration is far more advanced in its capacity to screen and place employees on the basis of technical qualifications than it is in predicting responses to the social and psychological climates of organizations and their subunits. Although some research suggests that organizational control could be improved through the use of behavioral tests and selection criteria, little has been done to validate them extensively within public agencies.[58]

Third, personnel administrators can take the lead in developing methods of monitoring relationships between employees and the organization. It has been proposed that supervisors conduct regular "audits" of employee perceptions and needs in order to detect and eliminate job-related dissatisfactions which can lower productivity and morale.[59] Such audits could aid management by pinpointing

---

[57] Everett G. Dillman, "A Behavioral Science Approach to Personnel Selection," *Academy of Management Journal*, 10, No. 2 (June 1967), 185–98.

[58] Nesta Gallas, "The Use of Sociometric Tests in Personnel Selection," *Public Personnel Review*, 23, No. 2 (April 1962), 100–106.

[59] Rensis Likert, "Measuring Organizational Performance," *Harvard Business Review*, 36, No. 2 (March–April 1958), 41–49.

problems caused by working conditions and by identifying performance gaps attributable to the incentives structure of the organization.[60] The efficacy of incentives could be evaluated in the light of the motivational profiles of different groups of employees. Feedback obtained through such studies would provide a basis for the planning and execution of more effective policies.

Fourth, building on this diagnostic capability, personnel administrators can follow up by suggesting and helping carry out needed changes in the social and technical characteristics of organizations. This is essentially a systems design function. Trained personnel specialists could work with management to manipulate sociotechnical variables which are to some degree subject to administrative control, with the objective of creating working conditions conducive to employee productivity.

Traditionally, efforts to improve productivity in public agencies have emphasized technological factors (automation, physical plant modernization) and the improvement of administrative efficiency through reorganization of formal structures. However, contemporary approaches also recognize the importance of social and psychological interventions. The field of *organization development* deals with motivation and behavior as they relate to: (1) the psychological dimensions of jobs, (2) different supervisory styles, (3) group dynamics and leadership, (4) decision-making procedures, (5) intergroup relations, (6) administrative practices and authority patterns, and (7) the communication and interpersonal skills of managers.[61]

Purposeful interventions are possible in these and other areas of organizational life. Job enlargement and enrichment are being explored as means of meeting needs for meaning-

---

[60] Gerald Zaltman, Robert Duncan, and Jonny Holbek, *Innovations and Organizations* (New York: John Wiley & Sons, 1973), pp. 2–3, p. 55.

[61] See Warren G. Bennis, *Organization Development, Its Nature, Origins, and Prospects* (Reading, Mass.: Addison-Wesley Publishing Co., 1969), and Samuel A. Culbert and Jerome Reisel, "Organization Development: An Applied Philosophy for Managers of Public Enterprise," *Public Administration Review*, 31, No. 2 (March–April, 1971), 159–69.

ful, challenging work.[62] Supervisors are being trained in human-relations-oriented leadership approaches, based on research findings that trust and supportive relationships are powerful inducements.[63] Employees who expect or need responsibility seem to respond positively to participative decision-making processes and group-based problem solving.[64] Training in open communication and honest inter-

FIGURE 4

Master Variable Control Grid

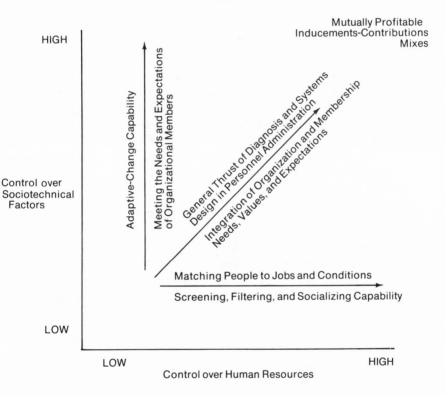

[62] Frederick Herzberg, *Work and the Nature of Man* (Cleveland: World Publishing Co., 1966).

[63] Rensis Likert, *New Patterns of Management* (New York: McGraw–Hill Book Co., 1961), pp. 97–139.

[64] Paul Blumberg, *Industrial Democracy: The Sociology of Participation* (New York: Schocken Books, 1969), pp. 123–38.

personal relations may help managers improve the psychological atmosphere of the workplace.[65]

In sum, organizations are far from helpless or unchangeable. Given understanding, a willingness to change, and the necessary skills and resources, changes in internal arrangements can be made which will improve the capacity of organizations to utilize the talents and energies of their employees. Indeed, there is a strong likelihood that tomorrow's personnel administrator will be expected to have the ability to engage in organization development programs.[66]

The professional abilities of public personnel administrators are likely to develop along the lines indicated in Figure 4. Specialists are working in both control areas, but the broader perspective requires a capacity to see their interrelations, limitations, and potential. The horizontal axis represents the capacity to control the nature of the human base; the vertical axis indicates control over sociotechnical variables. The effectiveness of incentives programs is directly linked to the capacities of organizations to exert significant control over elements of one or both of these master variables.

In much the same way that they must deal strategically with the external environment, personnel administrators must systematically consider the constraints and opportunities represented by internal factors in the organization. This diagnosis must then be translated into action through procedures intended to exert effective leverage on critical control points. The end product, hopefully, will be a greater capacity to integrate job-centered incentives with the needs, values, and expectations of employees.

BIBLIOGRAPHY

Bertalanffy, Ludwig von. *General Systems Theory: Foundations, Development, Applications.* New York: George Braziller, 1969.

---

[65] W. Warner Burke and Warren H. Schmidt, "Primary Target for Change: The Manager or the Organization?" in Warren H. Schmidt (ed.), *Organizational Frontiers and Human Values* (Belmont, Calif.: Wadsworth Publishing Co., 1970), pp. 151–69.

[66] Culbert and Reisel, "Organization Development," p. 164.

Bertalanffy, Ludwig von. "General System Theory—A Critical Review," in Joseph Litterer (ed.), *Organizations, Systems, Control, and Adaptation.* Vol. 2. New York: John Wiley & Sons, 1969.

Black, Guy. *The Application of Systems Analysis to Government Operations.* New York: Frederick A. Praeger, 1968.

Buckley, Walter (ed.). *Modern Systems Research for the Behavioral Scientist.* Chicago: Aldine Publishing Co., 1968.

Buckley, Walter. *Sociology and Modern Systems Theory.* Englewood Cliffs, N.J.: Prentice-Hall, Inc., 1967.

Burns, Tom, and G. M. Stalker. *The Management of Innovation.* 2d ed. London: Tavistock, 1966.

Churchman, C. West. *The Systems Approach.* New York: Dell Publishing Co., 1968.

Easton, David. *A Systems Analysis of Political Life.* New York: John Wiley & Sons, 1966.

Hare, Van Court, Jr. *Systems Analysis: A Diagnostic Approach.* New York: Harcourt Brace & World, 1967.

Johnson, R. A., F. E. Kast, and James E. Rosenzweig. *The Theory and Management of Systems.* 2d ed. New York: McGraw-Hill Book Co., 1967.

Katz, Daniel and Robert L. Kahn. *The Social Psychology of Organizations.* New York: John Wiley & Sons, 1966.

Klir, George J. (ed.) *Trends in General Systems Theory.* New York: Wiley-Interscience, 1972.

Laszlo, Ervin. *The Relevance of General Systems Theory.* New York: George Braziller, 1972.

Likert, Rensis. *New Patterns of Management.* New York: McGraw-Hill Book Co., 1961.

Optner, Stanford L. (ed.) *Systems Analysis: Selected Readings.* London: Hammondsworth (Penguin), 1973.

Price, James L. *Organizational Effectiveness: An Inventory of Propositions.* Homewood, Ill.: Richard D. Irwin, 1968.

Rice, A. K. *The Enterprise and Its Environment: A System Theory of Management Organisation.* London: Tavistock, 1963.

Schein, Edgar H. *Organizational Psychology.* Englewood Cliffs, N.J.: Prentice-Hall, 1965.

Scott, William G., and Terrence R. Mitchell. *Organization Theory: A Structural and Behavioral Analysis.* Rev. ed. Homewood, Ill.: Richard D. Irwin, 1972. Chap. 4.

Siegel, Gilbert B. "Human Resource Management as an Organization System Function." In Gilbert B. Siegel (ed.), *Human Resources in Public Organizations, A Systems Approach.* Los Angeles: University Publishers, 1972.

Sutherland, John W. *A General Systems Philosophy for the Social and Behavioral Sciences*. New York: George Braziller, 1973.

Thompson, James D. *Organizations in Action*. New York: McGraw-Hill Book Co., 1967.

Van Gigeh, John P. *Applied General Systems Theory*. New York: Harper & Row, Publishers, 1974.

Wamsley, Gary L., and Mayer N. Zald, *The Political Economy of Public Organizations*. Lexington, Mass.: D. C. Heath & Co., 1973.

Wiener, Norbert. *The Human Use of Human Beings: Cybernetics and Society*. Rev. ed. New York: Doubleday Anchor Books, 1954.

Responsibility
for Personnel
Administration

3

The decisions made in fixing responsibility for carrying out any undertaking are vital ones which involve more than efficiency. Both *who* is given a share of the responsibility and *how much* responsibility is granted are power determinants which can have decisive consequences for the preservation of democratic control. Responsibility is assigned both to organizations and individuals, and the administrative structures and officials charged with responsibility for particular functions constitute the "establishment." The personnel administration establishment in government is currently distrusted by many people, as much and even more so than the governmental bureaucracy as a whole. In this environment, the aura of tradition behind present arrangements is much less a legitimizing factor than in long periods of the past.

■ THE TRADITIONAL RESPONSIBILITY MODEL

As mentioned in Chapter 1, the Pendleton Act (1883) centered responsibility for implementation of the merit system in a commission which, whether viewed as independent or semi-independent, was not at the beck and call of the President. Essentially this was a compromise decision; the Chief Executive was to bear part of the responsibility and have some control, but he was not to be allowed to undermine the merit system. The three-man Civil Service Commission was bipartisan, with not more than two of the members to be adherents of the same political party. Yet the commissioners were to serve indefinite rather than fixed and overlapping terms, as evidence of the faith that Presidents could be trusted to make good appointments.[1]

The responsibility of department heads was viewed very simply: they were to be controlled in all personnel actions by the merit-policing Civil Service Commission. No serious conflict was seen between effective departmental use of personnel resources and the Commission's policing responsibility.

The practical consequence of the Pendleton model was to create a divorce between executive responsibility and personnel administration. Once the merit principle was cemented and the requirements of executive leadership became much greater, pressures to change this original model were inevitable.

■ PROPOSALS OF ROOSEVELT'S COMMITTEE ON ADMINISTRATIVE MANAGEMENT

Some 40 years ago, Franklin D. Roosevelt's Committee on Administrative Management made one of the clearest expositions of the principle of executive responsibility for personnel administration:

> Personnel administration is an integral part of general administration; the specialized personnel agency of highest

---

[1] Since passage of Public Law 854, approved July 31, 1956, the commissioners have served for six-year, staggered terms. President Eisenhower made the chairman of the Commission his adviser on personnel management, an arrangement later terminated, and Congress was concerned that the role of the Commission in protecting against spoils was being weakened. See Senate Committee on Post Office and Civil Service, *Administration of the Civil Service System*, 85th Cong., 1st sess. (Washington, D.C.: Government Printing Office, 1957).

rank should therefore be closely attached to the President's office. The principle of division of labor requires that personnel administration be given the undivided attention of professionally qualified persons; but the responsibility for developing adequate and constructive policies, standards, and activities throughout the Executive Branch of the Government cannot be segregated from general administration and separately discharged without disadvantage both to the administration of the personnel function and to general administration.[2]

The Committee proposed that the Civil Service Commission be abolished and replaced by a Director of Personnel appointed by the President and reporting directly to him. There also would be a Civil Service Board with purely advisory functions which through its investigations and reports would serve as the watchdog of the merit system. The Board, consisting of distinguished citizens drawn from a wide cross section of American life, was to be appointed by the President, with Senate confirmation. One of its responsibilities was to be to select a nonpolitical board of examiners to administer a competitive examination for the position of personnel director and certify the three highest ranking candidates to the President, who would select one.

Roosevelt's Committee was much influenced by the corporate model, in which the personnel function is in the direct line of control by the executive head, like other management tools such as finance and planning. The Committee rejected the contention that a plural body was needed for policymaking and appellate functions, arguing that a single administrator, with the help of the advisory board, could develop well-balanced policies and that special appeals bodies could be created both within the central personnel agency and the line departments to hear appeals, with adequate safeguards of independence and impartiality.

The Senate approved these proposals but the House rejected them, fearing that elimination of the Commission

---

[2] Floyd W. Reeves and Paul T. David, *Personnel Administration in the Federal Service*, President's Committee on Administrative Management (Washington, D.C.: Government Printing Office, 1937), p. 37.

would lead to partisan abuses and seriously weaken the protective function of the central (governmentwide) personnel agency. A bill proposed by Senator Joseph Clark of Pennsylvania in 1958[3] resurrected important elements of the FDR plan, but it did not progress, and Congress has not since given serious consideration to similar schemes. So long as presidential power and a resurgence of spoils are feared, the corporate model will be considered inappropriate.

■ THE MODEL STATE CIVIL SERVICE LAW, 1953

In 1953, the National Civil Service League and the National Municipal League sought to distill the best lessons of the past on the subject in the form of a Model State Civil Service Law.[4] Since by this time personnel administration was increasingly being viewed as an arm of management, it is not surprising that the model law significantly reflected the executive responsibility principle.

A State Personnel Department was provided for, the executive head to be a Director of Personnel, with the Department also including a three-man Civil Service Commission. The governor was to appoint the commissioners to staggered six-year terms, with no requirement for bipartisanship, and would also appoint the director of personnel upon the recommendation of the state civil service commission.

The commission's powers were to be:

1. To approve or disapprove the civil service rules, including classification and compensation plans, submitted by the director of personnel.
2. To hear employee appeals, principally in disciplinary cases.

---

[3] See *Congressional Record*, January 16, 1958, vol. 104, No. 7, pp. 475–76, for Clark's explanation of the bill.

[4] Model State Civil Service Law, prepared by the National Civil Service League, 1825 K. Street, N.W., Washington, D.C. 20006, and the National Municipal League. Reproduced in Felix A. Nigro, *Public Personnel Administration* (New York: Holt, Rinehart & Winston, 1959), pp. 445–61.

3. To advise the governor and the director on personnel problems.
4. To represent the public interest in the administration of the merit system.
5. To make investigations of the functioning of the personnel system and recommend changes to the director.
6. To prepare annual and special reports to the governor on the personnel system.

The principle of executive responsibility is reflected, first, in giving the chief executive (the governor) the power to name the commissioners. This was the usual practice in state governments in 1953, as it is today, but even now, in a majority of American cities, counties, and districts, the governing body has executive as well as legislative duties and appoints the civil service commissioners by majority vote.[5]

In many state and local jurisdictions, the personnel director is named by the civil service commission rather than the chief executive, to provide "greater independence of the personnel system."[6] It is this concept of isolation from the chief executive which was rejected in the 1953 model law, with the reasoning that the executive's support is essential for the strength of the personnel function. In the early days of civil service reform, strong executive leadership was not needed because the problems facing government were much simpler then. By 1953 many chief executives had come to support improved government personnel as "good politics," so the drafters of the Model Law argued that it should be made easier for them to exert their influence. Yet the possibility that some might seek to undermine the merit system was not overlooked in the 1953 draft. Staggered terms were provided for the commissioners, and bipartisanship was rejected because it had never been demonstrated that "one brand of partisanship offsets an-

---

[5] Winston W. Crouch, *Guide for Modern Personnel Commissions* (Chicago, Ill.: International Personnel Management Association, 1973), p. 34.
[6] International Personnel Management Association, *Guidelines for Drafting a Public Personnel Administration Law* (Chicago, 1973), p. 11.

other."[7] The members of the commission could be removed by the governor only for cause after a public hearing; similarly, the director of personnel could be removed by the commission only for cause after a commission hearing.

The 1953 model law proved persuasive and was followed closely by many state and local governments instituting civil service programs. This was a middle ground between complete executive control of the personnel function and virtual insulation of that function from the chief executive. The director of personnel was to be "experienced in the field of personnel administration," but the commission would infuse the viewpoints of citizen groups, guard against any narrow professionalism on the part of the director of personnel and his or her staff, and maintain constant vigilance against any return to spoils.

■ RECOMMENDATIONS OF THE MUNICIPAL MANPOWER
COMMISSION, 1962

In its 1962 report on personnel administration in urban governments, the Municipal Manpower Commission, a prestigious study group sponsored by the Ford Foundation, was very critical of civil service commissions. It found that, because of the existence of the commissions, *"the selection, hiring, promotion and discipline of personnel, a fundamental element of management in any enterprise, is in too many urban governments artificially separated from and independent of the chief executive."*[8]

Essentially this study group saw no need for civil service commissions in "mature urban units . . . those that have grown up politically and administratively." The 1953 model law was no solution at all because, although the commissions varied in degree of independence, they limited the chief executive's freedom to "hire, develop, discipline and dismiss" the personnel he directed and supervised. Additionally, the commissions were frequently so biased in favor of the employees they made it impossible for administrators

---

[7] Section 5. *A Model State Civil Service Law*, 1953.
[8] Municipal Manpower Commission, *Governmental Manpower for Tomorrow's Cities* (New York: McGraw-Hill Book Co., 1962), p. 64.

to discipline and otherwise manage the work force effectively. These were strong criticisms, but they expressed sentiments long held by many executives at all levels of government. Accordingly, the Municipal Manpower Commission recommended that the commissions be abolished or limited to advisory functions except in jurisdictions lacking "maturity," where they could be continued to carry out "functions apart from personnel management" such as hearing appeals against "personal or political favoritism."[9]

This recommendation had little impact in terms of a reduction in the number of civil service commissions with more than purely advisory functions. Many observers deeply sympathized, however, with the basic theme that the commissions impeded effective management. Many others believed that the real problem was that administrators simply wanted unbridled authority in personnel matters.

■ A MODEL PUBLIC PERSONNEL ADMINISTRATION LAW, 1970

In 1970, the National Civil Service League — the same organization that had drafted Senator Pendleton's bill for him — prepared a new model law in which it recommended the abolition of independent civil service commissions. This model stated: "Most public jurisdictions have reached the point where sound administrative practices as well as a sense of political fair play demand that the chief elected official be given greater authority over the personnel function if we are to continue to charge him with the ultimate responsibility of administering the jurisdiction." The League considered that the so-called protective role of the commissions was often exaggerated and that in fact the commissions frequently reflected "political expediency rather than the requirements of good personnel administration."[10]

The new Model Public Personnel Administration Law provides for a personnel department, to be headed by a director of personnel appointed by the chief executive and

---

[9] Ibid., pp. 65, 108.
[10] National Civil Service League, A Model Public Personnel Administration Law (Washington, D.C., 1970), p. 5.

serving at his or her pleasure, like any other department head. A seven-man citizen personnel advisory board, appointed by the chief executive and confirmed by the legislative body, would advise on all aspects of personnel administration. Its members could be removed by the chief executive for cause only after an opportunity to be heard publicly on the charges. Finally, there also would be a hearing officer, appointed by the citizen personnel advisory board, who would hear employee appeals from adverse employer actions such as dismissals, demotions, and suspensions and then make recommendations to the chief executive for appropriate action on the appeals. The hearing officer would be tenured but could be removed by the chief executive for cause after a public hearing.

The National Civil Service League still strongly supports the merit principle but considers obsolete the administrative machinery and much of the procedures it recommended to Pendleton.[11] The International Personnel Management Association, the professional organization of personnel workers at all levels of government, opposes "unfettered control" by the chief executive. It believes that organizational arrangements are means, not ends, and that in some circumstances the independent civil service commission serves well, in others the "management controlled personnel system" is more appropriate.[12]

A National Civil Service League survey in 1970 showed that in one third of the 560 largest units of state and local government, the "traditional independent civil service commission existed." A League study made in 1974 to determine the impact of its new model law indicated that about 8 percent of these governments had replaced the commissions with "a citizen oversight group without rule-making authority."[13]

---

[11] See Jean J. Couturier, Pro, and Harold E. Forbes, Con, "The Model Public Personnel Administration Law: Two Views," *Public Personnel Review*, 32, No. 4 (October 1971), 202–14.

[12] International Personnel Management Association, *Guidelines for Drafting a Public Personnel Administration Law*, pp. 4, 7.

[13] Jean J. Couturier, "A Citizens' Action Success Strategy for Social Reform: Case Study of a 'Model Law,'" *Good Government*, 91, No. 3 (Fall 1974), 22.

■ THE IMPACT OF COLLECTIVE BARGAINING

The first appreciable decline in the power of civil service commissions came with the recent rapid spread of collective bargaining.[14] As public employees have increasingly put their hopes for better employment conditions in collective contracts rather than civil service, the commissions have lost prestige. With very few exceptions the commissions do not represent management in negotiations for salaries and fringe benefits, and they usually are not in a position to influence the management position at the bargaining table greatly. Their role under the civil service law of recommending the pay plan becomes far less important than it was in pre-collective-bargaining days. Furthermore, when contracts provide for final-step binding grievance arbitration, as they increasingly do, the commissions no longer represent for employees the appeals body of last resort, save for the courts. While adverse actions such as dismissals usually are not subject to binding arbitration at present, before long they may be, as employee pressures for such provisions increase.

In truth, collective bargaining creates conditions which strengthen the case for executive control of the personnel function. Although the union usually does not negotiate directly with the chief executive, it negotiates with a management team which is close to him and knows what he will and will not approve. Chief executives must directly control management's side of the negotiations because so much is at stake — the possibility of strikes and in any case the wage bill, and hence the tax rates, of the community.

This is why the National Civil Service League's proposal to abolish the commissions may seem like a clean-cut solution to those who have been looking for ways of adapting the complicated arrangements in government to collective bargaining.[15] The elimination of the commissions would not

---

[14] See Jerry Lelchook and Herbert J. Lahne, *Collective Bargaining and the Merit System*, U.S. Department of Labor, Labor-Management Services Administration (Washington, D.C.: Government Printing Office, 1972), pp. 53–63.

[15] See John F. Burton, "Local Government Bargaining and the Management Structure," *Industrial Relations*, 11, No. 2 (May 1972), 123–40.

mean the end of the merit system. Rather, because in many jurisdictions the director of personnel is either the chief negotiator or a member of the management team, responsibility for the personnel function would be focused more clearly.

A proposal to create three agencies

To achieve accommodation of collective bargaining with the merit principle, B. Helburn and N. D. Bennett believe that three separate agencies are necessary. They argue that there should be two laws—one dealing with the merit system and the other with collective bargaining—and provision for a third agency for centralized negotiations and staff services.[16]

The coverage of the first law would be limited to whatever is necessary for preservation of the merit principle. Reviewing the literature, Helburn and Bennett conclude that merit procedures (examination and ranking according to ability) should apply only to personnel movements into, within, and outside the organization, certainly to appointments and promotions. The jurisdiction of the merit system agency (apparently they have a commission or board in mind) would no longer extend to general personnel and employee relations matters such as compensation, fringe benefits, position classification, training, and grievance procedures.

The second law would fix responsibility for administering the collective bargaining program by assigning it either to any existing agency with similar responsibilities for the private sector or to a new agency created for the public program. It would decide disputes as to the scope of negotiations, but, since the merit system as strictly defined in the first statute would not be negotiable, the desired accommodation should be assured. If the collective bargaining agency made a ruling which the employer or the union considered as threatening the merit principle, an appeal could be taken to the merit system agency. Ultimately, the courts would

---

[16] B. Helburn and N. D. Bennett, "Public Employee Bargaining and the Merit Principle," *Labor Law Journal*, 23, No. 10 (October 1972), 618-29.

have to decide unresolved conflicts between the two agencies on negotiability questions.

A third agency, apparently to be created by a third law, would be responsible for centralized negotiations where feasible and for staff services to management in personnel and labor relations. This apparently would be the operating personnel department.

This proposal is thought-provoking, not because it is likely to be adopted in its entirety by many jurisdictions but because it pinpoints the significant issues in accommodating collective bargaining with the merit systems and suggests the implications for organization arrangements. Many people who would not accept Helburn and Bennett's "strict" definition of merit at the same time would agree with them as to what should and should not be negotiable. Grievance procedures, for example, concern justice and the employee's rights and thus are an essential of merit, yet in our opinion they can safely be made subject to negotiation.

When personnel directors negotiate for management and represent it in contract administration, they clearly are a part of management; in collective bargaining, there is no role ambiguity. Conflicts will always exist between personnel departments and line officials, but the management identity between the two groups may be closer under collective bargaining. The charge that "personnel" lines up with the employee is apt to be made less often when there is collective bargaining, although this, of course, does not mean that the personnel office should be expected to oppose any employee request that is resisted by a supervisor. Civil service commissioners may appreciate not being forced into such close identification with management but, since they are appointed by the chief executive, they nevertheless are viewed by the unions and many of the employees as a part of management.

Unions monitor contract enforcement and may serve on joint safety, training, and other committees with management. Therefore, they become an important part of the organization for personnel administration. Not without justification, union leaders often claim that stewards, in investigating grievances, are assisting the personnel office.

■ RESPONSIBLE GOVERNMENT AND THE ESTABLISHMENT

In the report of Robert Vaughn for Ralph Nader on the U.S. Civil Service Commission there is a line of reasoning related to the present concern about making government more responsible which leads to proposals for radical changes in the Commission.[17] This line of reasoning has elements in common with the union criticisms noted above, but it is based on a view of the administrative branch as a whole.

Vaughn's thesis is that the bureaucracy wields enormous power which it exercises irresponsibly. Special interests dominate agency policymaking; the honest and courageous employee who speaks up and criticizes agency policies is fired, and there are many cases of employees being treated unfairly by agency managements. The individual must look to the Commission and its Board of Appeals and Review (BAR) for justice, but the Commission and the BAR often do not provide justice in their appeals decisions because of "inability and unwillingness to see beyond the management viewpoint." According to Vaughn, the Commission does not side with the abused employee because to do so would create a "deep and continuing conflict with its principal clientele groups—the managers and personnel officers of Federal agencies." In general, it does not see its role as correcting the irresponsible behavior of agency managements in personnel matters. The solution, Vaughn suggests, is to increase the independence of the Commission within the executive branch, at the same time removing the appeals function from it and creating an Employee Rights and Accountability Board outside the executive

---

[17] See House Committee on Post Office and Civil Service, 92nd Cong., 2nd sess., *Legislative Oversight Review of the Civil Service Commission* (Washington, D.C.: Government Printing Office, 1972), testimony of Robert Vaughn, pp. 4–78.

branch.[18] (The Commission has made certain changes in the appeals system which are described in Chapter 10.)

The Commission has made a thorough, point-by-point refutation of the Vaughn charges,[19] but our purpose is not to analyze the report and the Commission's refutations in detail. Rather, it is to show the particular connection made by one group of critics between unrestrained bureaucratic power on the one hand and alleged failings of the personnel system on the other. Obviously, the remedy for irresponsible bureaucracy is only partially in organizational arrangements. If agency managements behave in the "lawless" way described by Vaughn, some very fundamental changes in the whole environment of government will have to be made.

■ THE CENTRAL PERSONNEL AGENCY AND LINE DEPARTMENTS

Most of the preceding discussion has dealt with the central personnel agency, and little has been said about its relationships with line agencies. Personnel offices, of course, exist in the line agencies and, depending upon the need, are also found in bureau and other subdivisions, as in the federal government. Whether or not a line agency or one of its subdivisions has a personnel office (if it is small, it may not), someone in the agency is designated to handle personnel matters and maintain liaison with the central personnel agency. This raises the question of the extent to which the central personnel agency should delegate its authority to the line agencies.

Until World War II, the U.S. Civil Service Commission functioned largely on a centralized basis, requiring prior approval of many agency transactions. The war demanded speed in hiring, and the government grew so big that the

---

[18] Ibid., pp. 12, 15. See Robert Vaughn, *The Spoiled System: A Call for Civil Service Reform*, Washington, D.C.: Public Interest Group, 1972.

[19] United States Civil Service Commission, *Analysis of the Nader Reports* (Washington, D.C.: October 4, 1972).

Commission gave much more authority to the agencies to make appointments and take other actions, subject to Commission postaudit. Since the war, the Commission has extended this decentralization program to the point that, for some years now, the agencies have acted on their own in most personnel matters, following Commission guidelines and subject to Commission postreview. The Commission has an extensive evaluation (inspection) program under which agency personnel decisions are periodically audited and, if necessary, ordered canceled.

Whenever authority is delegated, there is the possibility of its misuse, intentional or otherwise.[20] The realistic question is whether a policy of requiring prior approvals is feasible—and in a jurisdiction as huge as the federal service, it obviously is not. Relationships between the Commission and the agencies were often much strained during the period when the Commission functioned on a centralized basis. Although there inevitably will always be disagreements and some friction between the Commission and the agencies, they have carried their "team" relationship to the point where some critics consider it to be too cozy. The Commission regularly consults with the agencies and their personnel directors through an Interagency Advisory Group, which, in the opinion of one union official, "has entrenched its power so deeply that today it has become the de facto board of directors of the Federal civil service structure, with substantial influence on policy and program formulation."[21] This official said that his union had made certain proposals relating to the grievance and appeals system which Commission representatives had initially favored but then rejected because the Interagency Advisory Group objected. There is a great need for empirical research to ascertain the practical effects of decentralization and other personnel policies, and, in the absence of such research, such criticisms as these cannot

---

[20] See Gladys M. Kammerer, "Revolution by Decentralization," *Public Personnel Review*, 13, No. 3 (July 1952), 141.

[21] House Committee on Post Office and Civil Service, *Review of the Civil Service Commission*, pp. 111–12.

be evaluated. Our purpose is simply to indicate how the nature of the criticisms on the centralization-decentralization issue has changed.

In state and local governments, there also are pressures for decentralization of personnel authority, particularly in the larger jurisdictions like New York City, where, in early 1975, a State Charter Commission recommended essentially the same division of responsibilities between the central personnel agencies and the line departments as in the federal service.[22] Complete delegation of recruitment and selection is not considered feasible in small and medium-sized jurisdictions, since it is much more economical to have a single examining unit, for example. Yet line agencies can collaborate in the examination process, as in making suggestions about kinds of tests and questions, and authority can be delegated to them in position classification and other areas. Some such decentralization has taken place, but the fear of providing an opening for spoils remains an important deterrent factor (and a justified one in some cases).[23] There are many examples of interdepartmental councils of agency personnel officials which meet regularly with representatives of the central personnel agency to discuss mutual problems.

■ SERVICE TO THE LINE OFFICIAL

Finally, there is the problem of how best to organize the personnel staff to provide the most effective service to line officials. This problem exists in both the central personnel agency and the departmental personnel offices.

Traditionally, service has been provided by specialists or specialist groups representing certain aspects of the personnel program, such as recruitment, classification,

[22] Glenn Fowler, "Personnel Policy of City Assailed, Charter-Study Panel says Overcentralized System Results in Poor Service," *New York Times*, March 23, 1975.

[23] See Norman J. Powell and Marilyn Magner, "Relations of Operating Agencies to the Examining Process," *Public Personnel Review*, 18, No. 3 (July 1957), 156–59.

training, and employee relations. Under this arrangement, line officials proposing a single personnel action often must deal with several different personnel specialists, first the classification man, then a recruitment representative, and so on. These conferences with multiple representatives of the personnel staff are time-consuming and often have contributed to poor relations with the line organization.

Under the generalist plan, a single representative of the personnel staff is given a certain jurisdiction in terms of organization units or occupations, and within that jurisdiction deals with line officials on *all* personnel matters. The line official has a chance to establish a close working relationship with the personnel representative, and the latter can develop versatility. Since there are limits to the range of specialized knowledge any one personnel technician can acquire, a small corps of specialists in the different personnel fields is maintained in the personnel director's office to provide advice, upon request, to the generalist.

The generalist plan has been successfully used by the California State Personnel Board and some other central personnel agencies, as well as by some departmental personnel offices.[24] While this plan could not be expected to solve all relationship problems between the personnel office and line officials, it represents a total approach, rather than the fragmented one for which personnel administration has been much criticized.

BIBLIOGRAPHY

Bart, Peter, and Milton Cummings, Jr. *The Transfer of the Kansas State Civil Service Department.* ICP Case Series, No. 31. University, Ala.: University of Alabama Press, 1956.

Couturier, Jean. "The Model Public Personnel Administration Law: Two Views — Pro." *Public Personnel Review,* 32, No. 4 (October 1971).

---

[24] See Frederick C. Mosher, *Reorganization of the California State Personnel Board,* Interuniversity Case Program, No. 32 (Indianapolis: Bobbs-Merrill Co., Inc., 1961), and James E. Stafford and Don Domm, "The Generalist Approach to Personnel Administration," *Public Personnel Review,* 31, No. 4 (October 1970), 254–60.

Forbes, Harold E. "The Model Public Personnel Administration Law: Two Views—Con." *Public Personnel Review*, 32, No. 4 (October 1971).

Hampton, Robert E. "What Is Our Role: The Basic Question." *Civil Service Journal*, 13, No. 3 (January–March 1973).

House Committee on Post Office and Civil Service. *Legislative Oversight Review of the Civil Service Commission*. 92nd Cong., 2nd sess. Washington, D.C.: Government Printing Office, 1972.

House Subcommittee on Post Office and Civil Service. *Hearings on S. 3888 and S. 1638*. 86th Cong., 1st sess. Washington, D.C.: Government Printing Office, 1958 and 1959.

International Personnel Management Association. *Guidelines for Drafting a Public Personnel Administration Law*. Chicago, 1973.

Lang, Theodore. *Public Personnel Councils*. Personnel Report No. 583. Chicago: International Personnel Management Association, 1958.

League of California Cities. *A Suggested Personnel System*. Berkeley, Calif., 1956.

Mosher, Frederick C. *The Reorganization of the California State Personnel Board*. ICP Case Series, No. 32. University, Ala.: University of Alabama Press, 1956.

National Civil Service League. *A Model Public Personnel Administration Law*. Washington, D.C., 1970.

Nigro, Felix A. *Public Personnel Administration*. New York: Holt, Rinehart, & Winston, 1959. Chap. 2.

Page, Thomas (ed.). *The Public Personnel Agency and the Chief Executive—A Symposium*. Chicago: International Personnel Management Association, n.d.

Reeves, Floyd W., and Paul T. David. *Personnel Administration in the Federal Service*. President's Committee on Administrative Management. Washington, D.C.: Government Printing Office, 1937.

Shaw, William A. "Independent Civil Service Commissions and Executive Power." *Public Personnel Review*, 14, No. 3 (July 1953).

Careers
and the Structure
of the Service

4

A career is vital in every life because it connotes advancement and success. Later in this chapter we will give our ideas as to the essential elements in career systems, with particular reference to filling the higher positions in the civil service. First, however, a few comments on careers in general are in order.

"Dead-end" jobs deal death to the career concept. Far too many such jobs have always existed in the American public service, but this escaped public attention for some time. Now there is growing emphasis on restructuring positions and building career ladders which in effect can become escape routes, particularly for the "large numbers of people locked into low-level routine jobs."[1] The structure of individual jobs and of the service as a whole—particularly the grouping and grading of positions—has an important bearing on the career possibilities of *all* employees. This structure typically is encrusted with tradition, but with

---

[1] Jean Stewart, "Job Restructuring . . . One Road to Increased Opportunities," *Civil Service Journal*, 13, No. 4 (April–June 1973), 30.

proper analysis and effort it can be changed to eliminate dead-end jobs and others with very restricted promotional opportunities.

Although it is the responsibility of the employee to exert himself to realize his potential, the government cannot claim to have a career system if the employee is expected to determine career opportunities and to make a career for himself *unaided.* He should not, for example, have to conduct his own private searches to determine promotional possibilities, through luncheons and other means of pursuing contacts.

It cannot be said that a career system exists if employees are not protected from unfair treatment for political or other reasons. At the same time, such a system does not exist when its entire rationale is to protect employees from the competition of others and from risk-taking in general. There are numerous examples of alleged career systems in which advancement is wholly or predominantly on the basis of time-serving, and only those within the organization unit or other narrowly defined area are allowed to compete for promotion. Typically, in such systems employees suffer no penalty in terms of advancement or other recognition if they shun challenging new assignments, whether for fear of failure or because of apathy; indeed, the employer is often unimaginative and does not offer them such opportunities.

A viable career system is one in which management's conception of its requirements for flexibility and efficiency are always subject to recognition of the human needs of its personnel. In its enthusiasm for career planning, management may at least unconsciously come to look upon employees as "items" to be moved from one location to another on organization charts or otherwise manipulated in *its* interests. This is why competent, risk-taking civil servants often are suspicious of proposed new career schemes. They suspect, sometimes with good reason, that there are pitfalls in these schemes which could damage rather than benefit their individual careers.

■THE BRITISH CIVIL SERVICE SYSTEM

A comparison between the British and the American civil service systems can provide an excellent basis for analyzing the career concept. Knowledge of the British Civil Service was considerably broadened with the publication of a report named after its chairman, Lord Fulton, in 1968.[2] It should be noted, however, that the findings and recommendations of the Fulton Committee have been challenged in important respects.[3]

The Fulton view of civil service

The Fulton Committee found that the structure of the British civil service still derived closely from that set forth in the Northcote-Trevelyan report of 1854.[4] Northcote and Trevelyan recommended a division of the service into intellectual and routine work, with university graduates to be recruited for the former and nongraduates for the latter. They particularly had in mind filling the top administrative posts with the best products of the universities. Acceptance of the Northcote-Trevelyan view essentially gave Britain a public service divided into a higher and a lower class of work.

After World War I, the Administrative, Executive, and Clerical classes were established, with recruitment to each geared to completion of designated levels of educational preparation: university for the Administrative Class, secondary school for the Executive Class, and a lower level of education for the Clerical Class. When it became necessary to employ large numbers of specialists (scientists, engineers, architects, doctors, lawyers, and other professional workers), the same principle was followed of dividing each occupational group into higher and lower classes, such as Scientific

---

[2] See *The Civil Service*, vol 1, *Report of the Committee 1966–68, Chairman: Lord Fulton* (London: Her Majesty's Stationery Office, Cmnd. 3638, June 1968).

[3] See John Garrett, *The Management of Government* (Harmondsworth, Middlesex, England: Penguin Books Ltd., 1972), pp. 47–57.

[4] Reprinted in full in Appendix B of *The Civil Service*, vol. 1, pp. 108–18, and in *Public Administration*, 32 (Spring 1954), 1–16.

Officer, Experimental Officer, and Scientific Assistant. Fulton found 47 general service classes, which existed in all or a substantial number of departments (all the previously-mentioned classes fall in this category). There were also more than 1400 departmental classes, which had members employed in one department only. Each general service and departmental class had its own grading structure and pay scale; each functioned to protect the interests of the incumbents but also, with few exceptions, limited their career possibilities to positions in the particular class only.[5]

The Northcote-Trevelyan thinking had placed the emphasis upon categorization by attributes of individuals, rather than detailed analysis of job duties. Position classification, as practiced with so much attempted precision in the United States, was not attempted. Members of the same occupation were sometimes placed in different classes, and a further heresy existed: there often was "no discernible difference in content between work done at the lower levels of one class and the upper levels of the one beneath it."[6] In Fulton's eyes, this was unfortunate because of two assumptions: (1) any job could be accurately identified as belonging to "one or other of the classes," and (2) the position in question was most appropriately filled by selection from members of that class only. Each class tended to "regard the posts that its members usually fill as its own preserve, guaranteeing a career structure with a fixed number of posts at various levels," and the staff associations zealously guarded this "territory" for their members.[7]

Some movement between classes took place but it was restricted, and very few specialists could obtain administrative posts. It was clear that specialists were not viewed as capable of making a contribution to administration; in most ministries, in fact, administrators and specialists were organized in separate units as parallel hierarchies. In a motorway construction organization, the administrative division, after receiving the advice and project plans of the

[5] See *The Civil Service*, Vol. 1, p. 65.
[6] Ibid., p. 66.
[7] Ibid., p. 67.

specialist division, would make the decisions on routes, costs, contracts, and expenditures. The engineers and other specialists were deprived of the opportunity to participate in policy determinations on the projects as a whole, and they were denied access to the minister. Decision making was awkward because of the need for numerous conferences between representatives of both hierarchies and, worse, ministers might even make crucial decisions relying on advice from administrators who had not understood the recommendations of the specialists.[8]

Although Fulton found that a substantial proportion of those in the Administrative Class had been promoted from the Executive Class, many of these promotions had taken place during and directly after World War II; the annual number of such promotees to Assistant Principal (beginning grade of the Administrative Class) was only about six. Upward mobility into higher administrative posts for those without university training was thus very limited, contributing to the view of the Administrative Class as closed and undemocratic.

Reasoning that the essence of a true career system was the guarantee (dependent upon ability) of unrestricted upward and lateral movement, both within and between departments, Fulton concluded that Britain did not have such a system. Apart from the rigidities created by the structure of the service, other essentials of a dynamic career service were lacking. Late entry (i.e., after experience outside the government) was very limited, as was movement from government into the private sector. Most civil servants spent their entire careers within the service, which explains why they had "little direct and systematic experience of the daily life and thought of other people."[9]

The entire service was still based on the "cult of the

---

[8] The Civil Service, vol. 2, Report of a Management Consultancy Group, Evidence Submitted to the Committee under the Chairmanship of Lord Fulton, 1966–1968 (London: Her Majesty's Stationery Office, 1968), pp. 56–59, 104–10. See also V. Subramanian, "The Relative Status of Specialists and Generalists: An Attempt at a Comparative Historical Explanation," Public Administration, 46 (Autumn 1968), 331–40.

[9] The Civil Service, vol. 1, p. 12.

amateur" or "generalist" or "all-rounder." Northcote and
Trevelyan had argued that it was a much wiser policy to
recruit young persons with first-class minds directly from the
universities rather than individuals who had tried private
employment and gained some work experience. Unlike the
sponsors of the Pendleton Act in the United States, they did
not believe in "practical" tests for public employment.
Actually, by their time the amateur tradition had been firmly
established in English life;[10] they simply applied it to a new
scheme of competitive recruitment for the public service.
The trouble, in Fulton's view, was that while society was
now much more complex, the amateur approach persisted.
In its extreme form, the civil servant felt he demeaned himself if he developed very detailed knowledge about a particular subject; indeed, he had to exercise care in this
respect, for, if he showed such inclinations, he might be
denied promotion. To be "promotable" one had to transfer
frequently (every two or three years) to new posts in order to
develop the knowledge of the government machine that is
valued by superior officers.

Fulton's verdict was that by and large members of the
Administrative Class did not have a proper conception of
their responsibilities in the modern state, which provides so
many specialized services to its citizens. Not only did they
fail to develop knowledge in depth of the programs to which
they were assigned, but they were mostly interested in being
"advisers on policy matters to people above them rather than
in managing the administrative machine below them."[11]
The work of administration was mostly assigned to members
of the Executive Class; for example, they were the managers
of regional and local offices, and they generally were in
charge of government accounting, negotiation and management of contracts, automatic data processing, organization
and methods work, and departmental training. The responsibilities of government had grown so much that the top
administrative positions required people who could manage

---

[10] See Ernest Barker, *The Development of Public Services in Western
Europe, 1660–1930* (Hamden, Conn.: Archon Books, 1966), p. 32.
[11] *The Civil Service*, vol. 2, p. 86.

very large blocks of work, who were administrators rather than advisers. The amateur approach had deemphasized specialized training in management, and there was very little such training for members of both the Administrative and Executive classes.

Fulton's recommendations

Among Fulton's principal recommendations were the following:

1. The abolition of the class structure derived from Northcote-Trevelyan and the use instead of American-style position classification, with a continuous grading system into which all positions could be fitted after job evaluation.
2. The merging of the Administrative, Executive, and Clerical classes into a single Administration Group.
3. Selection of employees to fill administrative posts on the basis of demonstrated capacity, regardless of their points of entry into the service.
4. Management training for both administrators and specialists.
5. Establishment of a Civil Service College.
6. Much more emphasis on personnel management and on career planning for all employees.

Under Harold Wilson, who had been tutored at Oxford by Fulton, the Cabinet approved the elimination of the old classes in principle, and later, in January 1971, the 206,723 members of the Administrative, Executive, and Clerical classes were merged into a single Administration Group. In January 1972, unified grading was adopted for all grades down to and including the undersecretary level, some 700 positions in all, but since then unified grading has not progressed. This is largely because of disagreements between the First Division Association and the Society of Civil Servants, which represent the members of the former Administrative and Executive classes, on the one hand, and the Institution of Professional Civil Servants, which represents the specialists, on the other. Although it is not clear how many specialists would compete for promotion to administrative posts under unified grading, the administrators are concerned that there would be enough such competition to reduce their normal promotion prospects. They argue that Fulton exaggerated the lack of movement from class to class, and all that is needed to accomplish Fulton's objective of an open service is the merging of the former classes, with new occupational groups logically established and career management firmly introduced to promote more movement within and between such groups. The British recruiting literature now emphasizes that *every* qualified person will be considered for *every* opening, indicating that such career management will be offered.

Throughout the tenure of Prime Minister Edward Heath (1970–74), there was skepticism about his government's enthusiasm for unfreezing the old class distinctions. The Assistant Principal grade has been replaced by a new entry grade of Administration Trainee, for which internal candidates with at least two years of experience in the civil service compete with graduating university students. The Administration Trainees are, however, divided into a *fast* and a *main* stream, and the suspicion persists that in the selection for the fast stream, university graduates will be preferred over internal candidates.

With the establishment of the Civil Service College there has been a vast increase in management training. This is the most visible contribution of Fulton to date.[12]

There have been many criticisms of the validity of Fulton's findings and recommendations. The picture of the Administrative Class as dilettantish and ineffectual has been labeled false. Fulton, it should be said, praised the British civil service as a whole for its competence and dedication. He criticized it as a personnel system he frankly deemed archaic.

A quick and superficial American reaction to Fulton's findings would be that "their" system was proved wrong and they recognize that ours is "right." Actually, the Fulton

---

[12] See Felix A. Nigro, "What Has Happened to Fulton?" *Public Administration Review*, 33, No. 2 (March–April 1973), 185–87, and "Robert Sheldon on the Civil Service," *Whitley Bulletin*, 54, No. 4 (April–May 1974), 51–55.

Committee makes more complimentary references to the French than to the U.S. civil service. Preparation of higher civil servants in France is commented on very favorably, among other reasons because it provides for *polytechniciens* (equivalent to Fulton's designation of specialist), whose preparation includes training in economics and managerial disciplines and who thus have a background for administration as well as in professional fields such as engineering.[13]

■ AMERICAN EFFORTS TOWARD A CAREER SERVICE

Civil service became a reality in the United States in 1883 with the passage of the Pendleton Act, as noted in Chapter 1. As introduced by Senator George Hunt Pendleton, the bill contained a provision for limiting outside recruitment to the lowest grade. This was so repugnant to the Senate that Pendleton proposed an amendment to delete it, which was "accepted without even the formality of a roll call."[14] The British principle of appointment through competitive examinations was endorsed by Congress, but the idea of a closed service, with entrance limited to the bottom rungs of career ladders, was dismissed. At all levels of government in this country there has always been a great deal of lateral entry to the intermediate and top grades, and maximum age limits have been very high or nonexistent. There also has been much movement between government and private employment, in line with the country's history of mobility and its respect for the freedom of the individual to prove his ability to any employer. This allowance for movement, however, raised the question of how the career concept could be implanted in government if many employees did not spend all or the major part of their lives in the public employ. It was suggested that government employment was a mere episode, not a career, for many.

---

[13] *The Civil Service,* vol. 1, pp. 135–36. See also Brian Chapman, *British Government Observed* (London: Allen & Unwin, Ltd., 1963), p. 26.

[14] Paul Van Riper, *History of the United States Civil Service* (New York: Harper & Row Publishers, 1958).

In addition to questioning the constant shuttling in and out of public service, there was much concern about the prevailing practice in government of recruiting for specific jobs rather than providing for a progression of increasingly more responsible positions. The Pendleton Act had set this precedent by its emphasis on "practical tests," which was fully in line with the American preference for pragmatism. There has always been flexibility in this pragmatism, however, and the sentiment for recruitment for careers, not individual jobs, gained support as the need to attract talent to the public service became evident.

The stimulus of the New Deal

With the advent of the New Deal in the 1930s, the times became more propitious for the career idea. As large numbers of college graduates were employed in the new agencies and programs, the challenge of government employment grew throughout the nation. In 1935 the report of the Commission of Inquiry on Public Service Personnel, appointed by the Social Science Research Council to study personnel practices in the public service, was published. The Commission, which examined practices in various parts of the country and held public hearings, compiled voluminous testimony about poor personnel practices in government. It recommended that the public service, instead of being "minutely classified into pigeon holes, for which the civil service commission tries to find men who exactly fit each compartment," be divided into career ladders for which "young men are normally selected to start on the bottom rung." These ladders would "rise from different points depending upon the kinds of service," with "opportunity . . . provided for advance at different rates of speed and for transfer from one ladder to another."[15]

Although the Commission recommended normal entrance to the bottom rungs, it did not propose a British-style closed service, since both upward and horizontal mobility were to be guaranteed. Like many other Americans, its members

---

[15] Commission of Inquiry on Public Service Personnel, *Better Government Personnel* (New York: McGraw-Hill Book Co., 1935), pp. 4–5, 27–28.

were concerned that young people were not being attracted
to public service as they were in Britain.

Prior to the New Deal, college graduates in professional
fields such as agriculture, geology, engineering, and forestry
had been entering government and making careers for themselves, but the public service generally was not promoting
the career concept and making positive efforts to attract
college students. Many Americans were impressed by the
British Administrative Class because it reserved the administrative posts for college graduates and offered them the
possibility of rising to the top career position, that of Permanent Undersecretary.

In the American public service, engineers, scientists, and
other specialists usually obtained the administrative posts,
but their preparation and outlook were considered too
narrow. It was not argued that they should be denied the
opportunity to compete for such posts, as in Britain. The
concern was that the requirements of the administrative
function as such were not being stressed, and management
training programs for specialists or anyone else generally
did not exist.

Teachers of government were generally unable to indicate
to students any possibilities for administrative careers in
government, and they were among the most anxious that
such career patterns be established. Increasingly, the need
for generalists was being recognized, but in this context the
term "generalists" did not mean amateurs or all-rounders
as described in the Fulton report. Syracuse University and
a few other learning institutions pioneered with public
administration programs, but the graduates of these programs were primarily employed in housekeeping staff services such as personnel and finance. Actually, these are management specialties, so generalist could be considered a
misnomer in this sense. Nevertheless, these students were
not graduates of the engineering, architectural, forestry, and
other professional schools which had been supplying trained
personnel for government. Universities also began to offer
programs to broaden the outlook of graduates of these professional schools who had been promoted to administrative

posts. Here the purpose (often stated) was to convert specialists into generalists, but again the intention was not to make them all-rounders. As the reader can readily see, much caution should be exercised with the use of the two words, generalist and specialist.

Recent U.S. developments

Efforts by the U.S. Civil Service Commission to provide a clear route in government for college students were climaxed by the Federal Service Entrance Examination (FSEE), introduced in 1955 and replaced in 1975 by a similar examination, the Professional and Administrative Career Examination (PACE). In recent years, from 6,000 to 12,000 positions have been filled annually through this examination, which is open to all college majors except engineers, physicists, chemists, accountants, and a few other technicians. The PACE recruit is not limited to personnel, budget, and other staff jobs; the broad field of program administration is also open to him, in housing, urban development, recreation, labor, business regulation, and numerous other substantive programs of government. Through PACE and other recruitment techniques, about 20,000 trainees are hired each year, practically all for entrance-level professional, administrative, and technical positions.[16] The agencies also make good on what Henry Reining, Jr., calls the "career contract"[17] by providing development programs for the recruits. There are still many problems to be solved in improving college recruitment and career management of recruits, but the situation is vastly improved in comparison to the 1930s.

One fundamental change is that the federal government as employer now accepts responsibility for the career development of its employees. The funding and the help given may seem much too inadequate, but prior to passage of the Government Employees Training Act of 1958 the agencies were not required to provide any type of training program.

---

[16] See U.S. Civil Service Commission, *Mandate for Merit*, 1972 annual report (Washington, D.C.: Government Printing Office, March 1973), p. 28.

[17] Henry Reining, Jr., "The FSEE: The University Point of View," *Public Administration Review*, 16, No. 1 (Winter 1956), 11–14.

Personnel officers themselves sometimes told employees they should "pay for their own training." Perhaps the most obvious change in federal personnel administration is the acceptance of in-service training.[18] President Lyndon Johnson's Executive Order 11348, issued on April 20, 1967, increased the government's training commitment; agencies now must periodically review *each* employee's training needs in relation to career objectives.[19] Considering the very large number of federal employees, this is a massive commitment. So is a provision in the Equal Employment Opportunity Act of 1972 which requires the agencies to establish training and education programs for upward mobility of the thousands of employees in low-level jobs.[20]

Most federal executives have backgrounds as specialists in the professions. In the three highest General Schedule grades, about 42 percent are scientists and allied professionals and another 18 percent are from law and other professions; the vast majority are managers (82 percent) and supervisors (14 percent), with only 4 percent nonsupervisory workers.[21] Training programs for federal executives are no longer a rarity, but it is recognized that both private industry and the military "do a better job of finding, molding and placing their executive talent for the more demanding positions."[22] The Office of Management and Budget and the Civil Service Commission are cooperating in efforts to stimulate the agencies to develop imaginative career executive programs, but, as the chairman of the Civil Service Commission reported to the President in 1973, many agency leaders are indifferent and give low priority to executive development.[23]

---

[18] See Henry D. Kallen, "Training in the Federal Service – 170 Years to Accept," *Public Administration Review*, 19, No. 1 (Winter 1959), 36–46.
[19] Executive Order 11348, Providing for the Further Training of Government Employees, April 20, 1967.
[20] Section 717(b), Public Law 92–261, 92nd Cong., H.R. 1746, March 24, 1972.
[21] See House Subcommittee on Manpower and Civil Service, *The Federal Executive Service* (Washington, D.C.: Government Printing Office, 1972), pp. 24–25.
[22] "OMB: 'Operation New Executives,'" *Federal Times*, May 23, 1973.
[23] "Letter of Rebuttal . . . From OMB," *Federal Times*, June 6, 1973.

If by generalist is meant someone with management skills plus broad experience in and understanding of program administration and the role of government in society, then it can be said that present programs of executive development in public agencies do try to make generalists out of specialists. Program knowledge is not deemphasized, although certainly the objective is to broaden the executive's perspective. Much depends on the provision of broad, planned work experience, and there has hardly been enough of this.

There is an awareness that in the United States the training of specialists is still much too narrow. Harlan Cleveland believes that "our scarcest resource appears to be men and women who have the incentive to grow beyond their specialized fields, who have some understanding of the administrative process, who are challenged rather than repelled by complexity."[24] He notes that the Gardner Report of 1957, coming after the first Russian Sputnik, found the shortage of "gifted generalists" the real problem and predicted that they would increasingly be drawn from "the ranks of those whose education and experience have included *both* depth and breadth — who have specialized but not allowed themselves to become imprisoned in their specialty."[25]

When the Intergovernmental Personnel Act (IPA), mentioned in Chapter 1, was first considered in Congress, Senator Edmund S. Muskie said, "When we examined the potential of State and local governments to attract bright, young people for careers in public service, we found a discouraging picture. . . . Career development systems, including the chance for job mobility, inservice training, and promotions were minimal except in the larger jurisdictions."[26] This was in 1967; in 1962 the Municipal Manpower Commission had reported that "this country's local govern-

---

[24] Harlan Cleveland, *The Future Executive: A Guide for Tomorrow's Managers* (New York: Harper & Row Publishers, 1972), p. 72.
[25] Ibid., p. 74.
[26] Senate Subcommittee on Intergovernmental Relations, *Intergovernmental Personnel Act of 1967, Intergovernmental Manpower Act of 1967.* (Washington, D.C.: Government Printing Office, 1967), p. 2.

ments are doing little to develop the persons who must bear vital responsibilities."[27] These characterizations were for the country as a whole, with its thousands of governmental units; there were jurisdictions which had made important progress in attracting college students to career service but, in truth, as Muskie noted, they were the exceptions. Passage of the IPA in 1970 therefore offered great possibilities for the development of career service in state and local governments.

In recent years, civil service career system advocates in the United States have not recommended limiting entry to bottom rungs. Increasingly, in fact, the concept of careers has stressed mobility and lateral movement between levels of government and the private sector. The emphasis has been on avoiding pigeonholing and other barriers to career opportunities. It is recognized that provision for lateral entry in and of itself does not mean that government employment will be considered merely a temporary episode; John Macy points out that "In practice, the great bulk of the professional and administrative personnel enter the system at a job level specified for recent college graduates or for those entering employment with higher degrees."[28] If career opportunities are provided in government, able young persons will be attracted to it and can be expected to spend much if not all of their lives in the public employ. Interestingly, there is concern in Britain that, in terms of national needs, its civil service may draw an unduly high proportion of young talent away from the private sector. This indicates the opposite danger – one not likely to occur in the United States.

■ THE PROPOSAL FOR A
FEDERAL EXECUTIVE SERVICE

In February 1971, President Richard M. Nixon recommended to Congress the adoption of a plan proposed by the

---

[27] Municipal Manpower Commission, *Governmental Manpower for Tomorrow's Cities* (New York: McGraw-Hill Book Co., 1962) p. 73.

[28] John W. Macy, Jr., *Public Service, The Human Side of Government* (New York: Harper & Row Publishers, 1971), p. 43.

Civil Service Commission for improving career management in the higher civil service. The plan, which provided for establishment of a Federal Executive Service (FES), was not approved by Congress but still has many supporters. Examination of the Civil Service Commission's documentation supporting the proposal[29] reveals the problems involved in career service planning.

There has been no effective system, governmentwide or within most executive agencies, for determining future needs for executives and for making detailed plans to meet these needs. Legislation for new programs is debated and approved without any consideration of the implications in terms of requirements for executives, and program and financial plans are not supported by "appropriate" analyses of these requirements. Control of executive resources is greatly hampered by the numerous personnel systems and statutory restraints governing the filling of executive positions and the deployment of their incumbents. For example, the separate pieces of legislation enacted by Congress authorizing "supergrade" positions (grades 16–18 of the General Schedule) may require that the appointees be assigned only to certain designated programs, despite the fact that needs change and the talent may be urgently required elsewhere in the agency.[30] Since no arm of the executive branch has been given responsibility for "monitoring the total results of executive manpower requirements,"[31] there is no assurance that agencies have neither too many nor too few executives and that they are utilizing them effectively. Within most agencies, career fields and promotional ladders have not been clearly identified, the quality of executive performance is not adequately assessed, and there frequently is great difficulty in identifying and developing executive talent.

The FES would include all civilian executives in GS–16–

---

[29] See "Documentation, The Federal Executive Service," *Public Administration Review*, 31, No. 2 (March–April 1971), 235–52.

[30] House Subcommittee on Manpower and Civil Service, *Federal Executive Service*, p. 128.

[31] See "Documentation," 241.

18 and certain other executives in the same salary range under other pay systems, an estimated 7,000 in all. ("Executive" henceforth refers to this group.) The agencies would review their executive requirements annually and submit their requests for executive positions to the Civil Service Commission, which, jointly with the Office of Management and Budget (OMB), would analyze these requests. Then the Commission would authorize the positions it considers necessary and report these authorizations to Congress. Barring disapproval by Congress within 90 days of this submission, the authorizations would become effective. Thus for the first time there would be servicewide, co-ordinated review and action on agency executive manpower requests.

Members of the FES would be placed in two categories: career and noncareer. The career category would consist of individuals "whose general employment outlook and expectations are oriented toward Federal service generally";[32] most would be from within the government, although a small number might come in by lateral entry from the outside. Noncareer executives would be those "whose relationship to the agency head require an interdependence based on such factors as program philosophy, political agreement or personal confidence,"[33] and their employment would likely be temporary. As part of its examination of agency needs, the Commission, after consultation with OMB, would authorize a career/noncareer ratio for each agency. Governmentwide, the number of noncareer executives would not be permitted to exceed 25 percent of the FES, the Commission's estimate of the present distribution. The agency ratios would be included in the Commission's submission to Congress and also would become effective within the 90-day period if Congress did not disapprove. Since there is no real distinction in the present duties of career and noncareer executives, their assignments in the FES should be interchangeable, permitting career executives to qualify

---

[32] Ibid., 244.
[33] Ibid., 243.

for advancement to the top posts. They are now generally barred from these posts, although some who have been offered and have accepted such appointments have thus lost their career status.

Position classification would not apply to the FES. Employees therefore would be deployed from position to position without the present danger of "downgrading" if the classifiers find the new job assignments less responsible. Position classification is unsound for higher level executives because the job becomes bigger or smaller depending on the executive's talents, and there are great differences in level of achievement, a factor position classifiers cannot take into account. Agency heads would determine the salaries of FES members, within a broad range approximating that encompassed by GS–16–18; this would make possible faster and more substantial salary increases. To avoid salary escalation, the Commission, after conferring with OMB, would establish an average FES salary, applicable to all agencies, which could not be exceeded by any one agency without specific authorization.

Those serving in executive assignments at the time of legislative enactment of the FES would have the choice of entering it without Qualifications Board review or continuing in their present positions without loss of any rights. Those entering the FES afterward would be subject to all provisions of the Service, including prior approval by Qualifications Boards appointed by the Commission and consisting of highly qualified experts from inside and outside the civil service. Noncareer executives would be selected by agency heads without Qualifications Board approval and would serve at their pleasure, as at present.

Employment of each FES career executive would be in accordance with a three-year contract, subject to renewal without the requirement of further Qualifications Board approval. Career executives accepting appointment to the FES could resign from it at any time, transfer to any agency or employment group excluded from FES coverage, and transfer to the FES in another agency. They could be dismissed under adverse-action procedures applicable to all employees, but not as part of a reduction in force or reorganization. If the agency did not offer contract renewal, or the executive declined it, an appointment at the GS–15 level would have to be offered, with the executive retaining his or her FES salary for two years. Since present supergrade employees could decline appointment to the FES, for some years there would be a dual personnel system. Commission Chairman Robert Hampton, responding frankly to a question during hearings of the House Subcommittee on Manpower and Civil Service, said that he doubted an executive declining appointment could be promoted: "All positions to which he could be promoted would be under FES; the only way he could take one would be to join the FES."[34]

FES members would be required to serve in the positions and geographical locations where they were needed. They could, however, appeal to the Civil Service Commission if they felt a transfer would impose undue hardship, in line with their right to appeal to the Commission any agency action which they consider constitutes a violation of their contracts. Denial of contract renewal would not, however, be a part of these appeal rights.

Reactions to the proposal

During the hearings on the Federal Executive Service conducted by the House Subcommittee on Manpower and Civil Service in 1972, representatives from agency management, the Civil Service Commission, and the Office of Management and Budget all strongly recommended the FES. Spokesmen for the affected employee organizations were either much opposed or were unwilling to support the proposal without major changes.

The Secretary of Health, Education, and Welfare, Elliott L. Richardson, and Undersecretary of the Treasury Charles E. Walker contended that the FES would introduce much-needed flexibility in the use of executive personnel and that it would improve rather than adversely affect the present status of executives. Representatives of the Government

---

[34] House Subcommittee on Manpower and Civil Service, *Federal Executive Service*, p. 54.

Employees Council, AFL–CIO; the American Federation of Government Employees; the National Federation of Federal Employees; the National Federation of Professional Organizations; the Federal Professional Association; and the National Society of Professional Engineers all were concerned about the lack of appeal rights in contract non-renewal. They feared that the FES could be manipulated for political reasons and that agency heads would deny contract renewals to executives they did not like, no matter how competent. The entire plan, with its interchangeability of assignments for career and noncareer executives, wide discretion for agency heads in setting compensation, and elimination of position classification was viewed as damaging rather than benefiting the present situation of executives in the federal service. It was also maintained that much of the flexibility sought by management already existed if only it were used, and, in any event, systematic executive manpower planning could be developed without changing to a contract basis of employment.

The hearings brought out once again the crucial factor of *trust*. Employee leaders do not doubt the sincerity of many management representatives, nor do they question the need for flexibility in the use of executives. Nevertheless, past experience makes them skeptical that such increased discretion for agency heads would not in the end provide much more opportunity for political manipulation. During the hearings, OMB Associate Director Frank Carlucci was asked if, when he was in the Office of Economic Opportunity, he had discovered that some OEO executives favored having local community action programs run by "political activists." He said, "I would like to think we have weeded most of these people out. Had we something like the Federal Executive Service, we could have moved a lot more efficiently on it, I can assure you."[35] At present, career officials cannot be weeded out easily because they have appeal rights and must be proved inefficient or guilty of gross misconduct. Holding policy views that differ from those of the

---

[35] Ibid., p. 71.

administration in power is not a justifiable basis for removal action. Yet the problem remains that career officials with such different views are "locked in" their positions and could successfully sabotage administration policies.

National Civil Service League Chairman Bernard Gladieux supported the FES at the hearings but also emphasized that "requirements for evidence of party regularity have been greatly broadened and made much more absolute by the present administration." He would accept the good faith of the administration despite this record and hoped that it "would accept the FES as a replacement for its political clearance practices with respect to civil service."[36] What he apparently meant was that with FES the administration could more easily assure responsiveness to its policies— but this brings us back to the ineradicable question of trust. The hearings took place before the Watergate disclosures, which obviously greatly reduced the level of trust.

The FES proposal passed the Senate in 1972 but failed in the House. A similar plan recommended by Nixon to Congress in the summer of 1974 was not acted upon. This plan omitted the three-year contract feature.

One of the arguments for the FES was that, with its prospects of more challenging assignments and better salary recognition for outstanding achievement, more college students would be attracted to federal career service. Comptroller General Elmer B. Staats, himself an outstanding career man, thought otherwise, because of the uncertainties of contract renewal. He said, "The relatively secure tenure of Government employment which allows talented employees to achieve high levels of responsibility is . . . a major factor in inducing such persons to accept Government employment and remain in it in preference to work in private industry where earnings may be much higher."[37] The impact on the service as a whole of any plan for a special corps in the higher grades is always a difficult question, and in some ways it is unanswerable.

[36] Ibid., pp. 115, 117.
[37] Ibid., p. 38.

■ESSENTIALS OF A TRUE CAREER SYSTEM

The discussion above of the British and American civil service systems makes clear that recruitment, compensation, promotion, training, performance evaluation, and other personnel policies all decisively affect the realization of career service. These topics are dealt with in detail in subsequent chapters of this book. To conclude this chapter, here are what we consider to be the essentials of a true career system:

1. Every qualified person within the particular governmental jurisdiction should be considered for every open position.
2. There should be adequate provision for lateral entry but not so much as to deny career opportunities to those already employed by the jurisdiction.
3. The jurisdiction should provide training and career management programs to help all employees achieve their career objectives.
4. The system should place in administrative posts those who have in-depth knowledge of the substantive programs in which they will have responsibility—or who have the interest and capacity to gain such knowledge—and who also are good managers or can become good managers.
5. The recruitment program and the total personnel system should attract able young persons to career service in government, including careers as specialists (engineers, lawyers, scientists, and other professionals); as program administrators; and as management specialists, as in personnel, budget, and finance.

BIBLIOGRAPHY

Birkenstock, John, Kurtz, Ronald, and Phillips, Steve, "Career Executive Assignments—Report On A California Innovation," *Public Personnel Management*, 4, No. 3 (May–June 1975).

Brown, R. G. S. *The Administrative Process in Britain.* London: Methuen, 1971 (distributed in U.S. by Barnes & Noble, New York), Chaps. 3 and 4.

Caiden, J. E. *The Commonwealth Bureaucracy.* Melbourne, Australia: Melbourne University Press, 1967.

Chapman, Brian. *The Profession of Government.* London: Allen & Unwin, 1959.

The Civil Service, vol. 1, *Report of the Committee 1966–68. Chairman: Lord Fulton,* London: Her Majesty's Stationery Office, Cmnd. 3638, June 1968.

The Civil Service, vol. 2, *Report of a Management Consultancy Group, Evidence Submitted to the Committee under the Chairmanship of Lord Fulton, 1966–1968,* London: Her Majesty's Stationery Office, 1968.

Cleveland, Harlan. *The Future Executive, A Guide for Tomorrow's Managers,* New York: Harper & Row, Publishers. 1972, Chap. 3.

Commission of Inquiry on Public Service Personnel, *Better Government Personnel.* New York: McGraw-Hill Book Co., 1935.

Cooley, A. S. "The Permanent Head." *Public Administration* 33, No. 3 (September 1974) (Australia).

Gregoire, Roger. *The French Civil Service.* Brussels: International Institute of Administrative Sciences, 1965.

Headey, B. "The Civil Service as an Elite in Britain and Germany." *International Review of Administrative Sciences,* 38, No. 1 (1972).

House Subcommittee on Manpower and Civil Service. *The Federal Executive Service.* Washington, D.C.: Government Printing Office, 1972.

Kuruvilla, P. K. "The Career Concept in the Canadian Public Service." *International Review of Administrative Sciences* 39, No. 1 (1973).

Mosher, Frederick C. *Democracy and the Public Service.* New York: Oxford University Press, 1968. Chap. 5.

Nigro, Felix A. "Two Civil Service Systems — Alike Yet Different." *Good Government,* 90, No. 2 (Summer 1973).

Reimer, Everett. "Modern Personnel Management and the Federal Government Service." in Wallace Sayre (ed.), *The Federal Government Service: Its Character, Prestige, and Problems.* New York: The American Assembly, Columbia University, 1954.

Ridley, Fred F. (ed.) *Specialists and Generalists.* London: Allen & Unwin, 1968.

Classification
and Pay

5

Classification and pay, which are among the most important elements in career service planning, are considered more fully in this chapter.

■ CLASSIFICATION SYSTEMS

Classification can be based on *jobs* or on *people* (those occupying the jobs). In the United States, the basis has been jobs; position classification took hold in the early part of the 20th century and became virtually a religion which still has many devout followers (deservedly so, for historical reasons). *Position classification* also prevails in other countries such as Canada, Costa Rica, Panama, and the Philippines. In Britain, Western Europe, and most other nations that have personnel systems, however, *rank classification*, based on the characteristics of those holding particular kinds of jobs, is in effect.

Position classification is closely linked to the scientific management movement, which called for discovering the "one best way" of carrying out a particular work operation.[1]

[1] See V. Seymour Wilson, "Scientific Management and Personnel Policy in North American Administrative Systems," *Public Administration*, 51 (Summer 1973), 183–203.

Detailed analysis of job duties was essential in identifying the precise nature of each task and determining the skills required to execute it. This insistence on dissection of work activities into their smallest component parts was extended to job analysis.

The immediate goal of position classification was to fill each job with individuals who met the production requirements for that job only. The forward orientation in scientific management was aimed at bigger and bigger output, not selecting workers for their career potential. Frederick W. Taylor and his disciples emphasized structure of jobs and organizations, not the characteristics of people. It is no coincidence that the two consulting firms awarded contracts to prepare and install some of the first classification plans in state and municipal governments were headed by men with an engineering background—E. O. Griffenhagen and J. L. Jacobs. The position classification "science" which developed inevitably was characterized by recognition of numerous narrow classes of positions rather than a moderate number of broad classes grouping many kinds of jobs. The telephone-directory dimensions of position classification plans have frequently been noted.

Historically, position classification, with its stern objectivity, was a weapon in the fight against spoils. If jobs were carefully studied and qualification requirements precisely stated, politicians could not succeed with referrals of unqualified persons. If the position was what counted, it was easier to thwart the "people" influence of politicians.

■ CLAIMS FOR POSITION CLASSIFICATION

Several justifications—all very logical—were made for position classification as the pillar of the personnel system. It was said that examinations could not be properly constructed unless jobs had first been analyzed and sorted into classes of positions. (In position classification lexicon, a *class of positions* consists of all jobs which are sufficiently equal in duties, responsibilities, and qualification requirements to justify holding the same examination for filling vacancies in the class.) If no attempt were made to analyze and group positions, each individual job would have to be treated separately, leading to many inconsistencies. One appointing officer would establish qualifications for filling a job, following his own ideas on the matter, even though they might be very different from those of another supervisor attempting to recruit for exactly the same kind of opening. In fact, both might only have a very hazy idea of what the position required. Several different examinations might be given for jobs so similar that a single examination should have been given.

Similarly, it was claimed, defining lines of promotion would be next to impossible without position classification because no one could be sure of the exact relation of one job to another. Indeed, the examining staff, working in the dark, might even establish lower qualifications for more responsible positions in the same line of work. Numerous different, misleading titles would be given to jobs which were essentially the same, thus confusing budget as well as personnel procedures. If positions were not studied and classified, there would be no standard against which employee performance could be measured. Too, if duties were not known in detail, training needs could not be accurately diagnosed. Finally, unless positions were placed in classes, equal pay for equal work could not be guaranteed. (Classification and compensation plans are tied together, with every class of positions which is distinguished assigned to one of a number of salary grades, each grade having the same pay scale.)

In practice, these claims proved overstated. Position classification does bring order into the recruiting and examining programs, but test construction experts usually need much more information than that given in the *class specifications* (typically the title, a summary of the characteristics of the class, examples of duties, and minimum qualifications of training, experience, knowledge, and skills). The title structure is clarified; even in today's worst-maintained plans elevator operators are not frequently titled clerks and vice versa, as J. L. Jacobs found in his 1931 report on classification and compensation plans in Philadelphia.[2]

Since the emphasis in position classification is on describing requirements of individual jobs, the establishment of promotional ladders as part of a true career system is generally not considered a responsibility of the position classification analyst. Position classifiers divide the service into occupational groupings and establish series of classes of positions reflecting differences in the responsibility and difficulty of jobs in the same line of work (e.g., junior, senior, and principal clerks), but the analyst is a specialist in positions and does not usually think in terms of careers. The isolation of position classifiers from the rest of the personnel function has been a sad result of this specialization, but the same has been true of other kinds of personnel specialists. The professed use of class specifications in performance evaluation and in determining training needs has been pure rhetoric; if such use has existed, it has been minimal. The information in the specifications provides the merest beginning point for these purposes.

The principal use of position classification has been in salary standardization through its tie-in with the compensation plan. Most employees think of position classification as a compensation-fixing device rather than a multiple-purpose tool of personnel management—and, based on the record, they are justified in so thinking.[3]

Notwithstanding its failure to serve purposes claimed for it, position classification unquestionably helped make personnel administration more orderly and aided in eliminating the gross salary inequities of a time when pay rates were set according to no plan at all. Further, we do not want to give the impression that many line managers, personnel directors, and classification technicians themselves did not want to make position classification serve broader purposes.[4] The

---

[2] City of Philadelphia, *Classification and Compensation Plans*, 1931.

[3] See House Committee on Post Office and Civil Service, *Report on Job Evaluation and Ranking in the Federal Government*, 91st Cong., 1st sess., House Report No. 91-28. (Washington, D.C.: Government Printing Office, 1969), p. 13.

[4] See Merrill J. Collett, "Re-thinking Position Classification and Management," *Public Personnel Review*, 32, No. 3 (July 1971), 171-72.

fact is that their views did not prevail, although in recent years what is known as *position management* has been adopted by many public agencies. Basically, this means structuring jobs and thus the administrative organization to provide for better utilization of personnel, elimination of dead-end jobs, development of "clear-cut ladders of progression for groups of employees, as well as for individuals,"[5] elimination of duplication of work, and greater efficiency in general. Position management basically is the responsibility of line officials, but the personnel office can assist by making suggestions based on information obtained through classification surveys and other personnel processes.[6] Traditionally, personnel people were considered to have no business making such suggestions; many of them did not want to be "tainted" by getting too close to program managers who, they suspected, simply wanted approval of blown-up job descriptions.

■ RANK CLASSIFICATION

In rank classification, the kind of work performed and the level of responsibility are important in the class distinctions made, but job analysis is not employed on any precise basis. As Roger Gregoire explains,

> A civil servant is primarily a member of a corps; he is thus qualified to hold a series of positions classified at the same level, although the work may vary considerably with each of them; his assignment to one of these positions is a decision of secondary importance which is quite separate from his appointment, and, should he be transferred from that position to another in the same grade, his situation will remain unchanged.[7]

Since the British system is still primarily based on rank, it is a good example of this type of classification. The classes in

---

[5] Harold Suskin, "Job Evaluation—It's More Than a Tool for Setting Pay Rates," *Public Personnel Review*, 31, No. 4 (October 1970), 287.

[6] See Carl F. Lutz and Albert P. Ingraham, "Design and Management of Positions," *Personnel Journal*, 51, No. 4 (April 1972), 234–240.

[7] Roger Gregoire, "The Civil Service in Western Europe," *Public Personnel Review*, 17, No. 4 (October 1956), 289.

Britain are much broader than in the United States. To illustrate, there are two clerical classes: the General Clerical Class and the Clerical Assistant Class. Within the former, there are two grades, Clerical Officer and Higher Clerical Officer, but few departments use the latter grade. There is only one grade in the Clerical Assistant Class.[8] (The British definitions of class and grade are obviously different from ours.) In many of our public jurisdictions a half dozen or more different levels of clerical workers are recognized, and such specialized classes as tax, police, and identification clerks have sometimes been established. The British also have eight scientific classes covering *all* kinds of scientists; under position classification, dozens of classes would be created for chemists, physicists, biochemists, and numerous other kinds of scientists employed by government. As a final example, the British now have three classes of Executive Officers assigned to a wide variety of jobs which in the United States would be placed in numerous different classes in finance, purchasing, supply, and general administration.

In Britain, members of the same class are often assigned to unequal work, as noted in Chapter 4. Interestingly, while the Fulton Committee's Management Consulting Group recommended "more precise assessment and grading of the content of jobs,"[9] it expressed approval of "fluid complementing," an arrangement for such classes as the scientific ones where the number of positions at certain levels is "not determined by inspection and evaluation of each job but in terms of agreed percentages of the total complement of posts at the three levels." This permits the "promotion of an officer who remains engaged upon the same work; his personal contribution is expected to be greater but the job itself does not change."[10] Yet this same consulting group recommended job evaluation based on factor ranking (the factors being important elements of job content such as the education and experience required, discretion exercised, and the number

---

[8] See *The Civil Service*, vol. 2, *Report of a Management Consulting Group, Evidence Submitted to the Committee under the Chairmanship of Lord Fulton, 1966–1968* (London: Her Majesty's Stationery Office, 1968) pp. 30–35.
[9] Ibid., p. 32.
[10] Ibid., p. 53.

and kinds of subordinates supervised).[11] This suggests that
they did not want to eliminate rank classification completely,
or possibly that they did not foresee the full extent of the
change job evaluation would make in long-established
British practices.

The Fulton Committee's reasoning in recommending job
evaluation and unified grading may not have been technically sound. Its evidence that the class structure derived
from the Northcote-Trevelyan report of 1854 (see Chapter 4)
made effective career management very difficult is convincing, but its conclusion that job evaluation and unified
grading were necessary to correct this situation is not. As
M. J. Flores and J. B. Heath point out, there is a difference
between job analysis and job evaluation; the former is necessary for career management, and the latter is not.[12] Critics
of Fulton have argued that unified grading is not necessary
for unfreezing the old class distinctions. According to Flores
and Heath, while there is some dissatisfaction with pay dif-
ferentials in Britain, there is nothing seriously wrong with
the pay structure. They write that

> . . . in the civil service valuing how much jobs are worth, and
> paying people accordingly, would create several types of
> problems. Perhaps the most important is that currently civil
> servants are not paid strictly according to the jobs they do,
> but rather according to their *rank* in a class (that is, the civil
> service pay structure is one based on *people*, not on jobs).[13]

Job evaluation as recommended by Fulton's consulting
group would make necessary many narrow classes, which is
alien to the British tradition, and it is difficult to see how the
British could live with such a situation in their public
service.

Use of the rank principle in the United States
Rank classification would be a feature of the proposed
Federal Executive Service, which was discussed in Chapter
4. The Civil Service Commission's policy was at one time

---

[11] Ibid., p. 92.
[12] M. J. Flores and J. B. Heath, "The Fulton Report: Job Evaluation and
the Pay Structure," *Public Administration,* 48 (Spring 1970) 15–22.
[13] Ibid., 17.

limited to recognizing the "impact of the man on the job," as stated in a circular issued in August 1960. The gist of this circular was to remind the agencies that through outstanding performance the employee could make his job so much more responsible as to warrant its reclassification to a higher grade. The Commission made clear, however, that "the impact of the man on the job is reflected in the classification *when* and *because it actually makes the job materially different than it otherwise would have been.*" The Commission had already introduced the "quality graduate concept" whereby, for example, a "superior" bachelor degree candidate was deemed qualified for GS–7, instead of GS–5. The circular justified this as being based on "informed predictions as to . . . job content." Because of their ability, quality graduates could be expected to perform above the minimum entrance level and the other graduates to perform at the entrance level "for at least some undefinable period."[14] This reasoning demonstrates how reluctant the Commission was to support the rank principle as such.

One of the recommendations of the Job Evaluation and Pay Review Task Force, established by the Civil Service Commission in accordance with legislation passed by Congress in 1970, was the development of a "Personal Competence Ranking System" for certain occupational categories or occupations such as attorneys, health services, scientists and engineers in research and development, teachers, and the Foreign Service. The Task Force noted that "The skill, training, experience, creativity, and judgment of individuals in these occupations result in highly personal and substantial contributions to their jobs. This effort is not readily evaluated by normal techniques of job evaluation."[15] The individuals would be ranked on the basis of occupational credentials and other capabilities by panels of peers or superior officers. The Commission has approved in principle the Task Force's recommendation for the factor-ranking method of job evaluation instead of position classifica-

---

[14] *Federal Personnel Manual*, Letter No. 511–1, August 19, 1960.
[15] "Report to the President on Job Evaluation and Pay," *Civil Service Journal*, 12, No. 4 (April–June 1972), 13.

tion, with its narrative standards.[16] It has not yet made its decision on personal competence ranking.

Actually, some rank classification has long existed under position classification, even for some lower level jobs. Secretarial positions are frequently classified according to the rank of the boss, but some secretaries to junior executives perform much more difficult work than secretaries to senior officials.[17] If the position classifier tried to change this, offended officials might oppose the entire classification project, a possibility which is not at all farfetched.

In social work, higher classifications are sometimes established simply to reflect the superior training of employees. Unless supervisory responsibilities are exercised, caseworkers will normally be assigned to the same general type of work. Some will have had training at graduate schools of social work, while others will have only the undergraduate degree. The incentive to obtain the graduate training is to earn more, so pressure is brought on the classifier to take into account the qualifications of the person. The basic casework job is the same, but it is argued that the caseworker with the superior training does a more professional job of interviewing and serving the needs of welfare clients. Sometimes two levels of caseworkers are agreed to by the classifiers, who admittedly in such cases are forced by the strength of the opposition to deviate from the principle of duties classification.

Similarly, such groups as teachers and attorneys have been placed in very broad classes with the distinctions based more upon qualifications and reputation than duties. Public school teachers' salaries have long been based largely on their professional background as measured by years of graduate work. The skill of trial attorneys varies so much that the

---

[16] See "Of Job Factors and Benchmarks," *Civil Service Journal*, 13, No. 3 (January–March 1973), 12–13. For an explanation of job measurement systems, see Milton Rock (ed.), *Handbook of Wage and Salary Administration* (New York: McGraw-Hill Book Co., 1972), pp. 2–86.

[17] See Julius E. Eitington, "Why Classify Secretarial Positions?" *Personnel Administration*, 15, No. 5 (September 1952), 33, and Eitington, "Injecting Realism into Classification," *Personnel Administration*, 15, No. 2 (March 1952), 31–35.

classification analyst may decide to follow the recommendations of the head of the legal department, for a storm of opposition would result if the positions of the weakest and the most effective attorneys were placed in the same class.

■ THE ROLE OF EMPLOYEE ORGANIZATIONS IN CLASSIFICATION

In Britain there is a long history of joint negotiation and consultation between the government and the employee organizations on personnel policies. When the Fulton Committee report was published, the government made it clear that consideration of Fulton's recommendations "would be carried out in the closest consultation with the Staff Associations."[18] A Joint Committee of the National Whitley Council was established for that purpose, and the decisions on implementation of the Fulton report, including those on classification and pay structure, are made in this body.

In the United States there is no machinery similar to the Whitley Council, although much more consultation between the Civil Service Commission and the employee organizations now takes place. At all levels of government, the determination of classification standards and the classification of individual positions have been considered management prerogatives. In most state and local jurisdictions with collective bargaining legislation for public employees, classification of positions is excluded from the scope of bargaining, as it is under Executive Order 11491 as amended, which governs the federal program.[19]

The firm belief that position classification is a science, certainly an objective system, makes the idea of union participation an anathema to many personnel technicians.

---

[18] Civil Service National Whitley Council, *The Shape of the Post-Fulton Civil Service* (London: Her Majesty's Stationery Office, March 1972), p. 1. For an explanation of the Whitley Council structure, see H.M. Treasury, *Staff Relations in the Civil Service* (London: Her Majesty's Stationery Office, 1965).

[19] See United States Federal Labor Relations Council, *Labor-Management Relations in the Federal Service, Amendments to Executive Order 11491 with Accompanying Report and Recommendations* (Washington, D.C., 1975).

They believe that if classification standards and individual classifications were bargained, the decisions reached would reflect power factors and the process would become very unscientific. The unions, which would push for higher classifications, would not worry about distorting the classification plan or creating pay inequities so long as their demands in a particular negotiation effort were accepted. Different unions might represent the same kinds of workers in different bargaining units, and settlements could create many inconsistencies in classification as well as pay and fringe benefit matters.

To many union leaders, job evaluation—whether of the position classification or the factor-ranking variety—is far from scientific. They claim that many positions are improperly classified and too often classification technicians base their decisions on pure hunch. They also say there is no reason to think that unions would want to create distortions and inequities with their bargaining demands, and the unions have competent research staffs to supply the necessary expertise in classification matters to its negotiators. Some employee organizations can accurately say that they had a leading role in the passage of position classification legislation in the first place. The experience in the private sector is often cited; it is held that equitable classification relationships exist in many companies where job evaluation plans are negotiated and individual classifications are subject to the grievance procedure.

There may be a stronger justification for negotiation of classification standards than of individual classifications. The Tennessee Valley Authority (TVA) has a continuing Joint Classification Committee composed of four TVA representatives appointed by the director of personnel and an equal number of representatives of the Tennessee Valley Trades and Labor Council named by its president. Its functions include: (1) approval of requested classification changes in the wage schedules, such as establishment or elimination of classes and changes in titles and the relative level of a class, (2) approval of qualification and classification standards for trades and labor jobs, and (3) settling problems concerning classification of the duties and responsibilities of trades and labor classes. The committee's decisions are binding upon the TVA and the council if approved by the director of personnel and the council president. Management allocates the positions to classes, and an employee who is dissatisfied with his classification can invoke the grievance procedure. The Council can insist on final resolution of the grievance by binding decision of an impartial referee.[20]

The American Federation of Government Employees (AFGE), which has the largest membership of any union in the federal service, and the AFL–CIO have proposed creation of a National Standards Board to establish, review, and approve classification standards. It would consist of six members, three representing all unions with exclusive recognition on the basis of proportional representation and the remaining three the government. Former AFGE President John F. Griner also recommended establishment of a three-member Classification Review and Appeals Board, one member to represent the unions, one the government, and the third the general public. This board, to be located within the Civil Service Commission, would oversee the classification program and review and decide appeals on standards approved by the National Standards Board.[21]

Under the Connecticut collective bargaining law, classification matters can be bargained. In the City of Hartford, labor agreements have required that any new class of positions be subject to union negotiation in order to establish a mutually acceptable salary before establishment of the class. In addition, disagreements over the classification of individual positions are subject to arbitration by the State Board of Mediation and Arbitration rather than resolution by the city's Personnel Board. Hartford Director of Personnel Robert D. Krause, whose merit credentials are very strong, is quoted as saying that "it could be argued that the State

---

[20] See Felix A. Nigro, *Management-Employee Relations in the Public Service* (Chicago: International Personnel Management Association, 1969), p. 186.

[21] House Committee on Post Office and Civil Service, *Legislative Oversight, Review of the Civil Service Commission* (Washington, D.C.: Government Printing Office, 1972), p. 114.

Board of Mediation and Arbitration has upheld merit factors as much as the City's Personnel Board, if not more."[22]

If unwillingness to agree to negotiation of classification standards and to binding grievance arbitration of disputed individual classifications is based on fears of endangering merit principles, these fears may be unjustified. When the new public personnel administration matures, negotiation or at least collaboration with the unions on classification standards, along with binding arbitration of disagreements over individual classifications, may well be accepted procedures. Much, of course, will depend on union attitudes and performance.

■ PAY POLICY

Henry Parris has identified three possible approaches to fixing compensation for public employees: (1) to pay as little as possible so as to relieve the burden on the taxpayer, (2) to pay enough more than the private sector in order to set a good example, or (3) to pay rates comparable with those in the private sector.[23] In both Britain and the United States, the third policy is the one now generally followed as a matter of principle. In Britain the guideline, as stated in the Priestly Report of 1955, is "fair comparison with the current remuneration of outside staffs employed on broadly comparable work, taking account of differences in other conditions of service."[24] In this country, the principles stated in the Federal Pay Comparability Act of 1970 call for "equal pay for substantially equal work" and comparability with "private enterprise pay rates for the same levels of work."[25] Because the British classification system is different, "equal

---

[22]Sterling Spero and John M. Capozzola, *The Urban Community and Its Unionized Bureaucracies, Pressure Politics in Local Government Labor Relations* (New York: Dunellen, 1973), pp. 206–7.

[23] Henry Parris, *Staff Relations in the Civil Service* (London: Allen & Unwin, 1973), p. 81.

[24] *Report of the Royal Commission on the Civil Service, 1953–55*, Cmd. 9613, 1955.

[25] Section 2(a), Public Law 91–656, 91st Cong., H. R. 13000, January 8, 1971.

pay for equal work" has not been the battle cry there as it has in the United States.

In the United States, government has been at a disadvantage in salary competition with private employers for several reasons. First, until recently it was not generally accepted that government should pay comparable rates for white-collar workers; it was considered "normal for public servants to make a financial sacrifice."[26] The payment of prevailing wages for blue-collar workers has a long history; as the price level rose after World War II blue-collar pay tended to stay competitive with private rates, but white-collar worker pay fell further and further behind. Second, legislators naturally did not want to authorize compensation higher than their own, and politically it was very difficult for them to raise their own salaries. Third, when they authorized increases, legislators usually were more generous with those in the lower brackets. They sympathized more with the "underdog"; besides, the lower paid employees were much more numerous and frequently were a potent political force. As a result, pay for top executives was poor by comparison with that offered in industry. Fourth, pay rates usually could not be changed without legislative action, whereas private companies, except for the rare times in American history when wage controls have been in effect, can raise them whenever they want.

Recent innovations in the U.S. federal service

In 1962 Congress passed a Salary Reform Act which stated that "Federal salary rates shall be comparable with private enterprise salary rates for the same levels of work."[27] This applied to white-collar workers; rates for blue-collar workers had long been set on the basis of periodic surveys by local wage boards of private industrial rates for comparable positions. White-collar pay was so far behind that Congress in 1967 passed another law authorizing the President, without

---

[26] Elmer B. Staats, "Experience of the Federal Government in Maintaining Equivalency with Private Sector Pay," paper presented at the Conference on Public Employment, Syracuse University, October 26, 1972, p. 9.
[27] Federal Salary Reform Act of 1962, Public Law 87–973, 87th Cong.

requirement of Congressional approval, to bring federal pay up to private rates, "as nearly as practicable," in two big pay adjustments.[28]

This same legislation also established a Commission on Executive, Legislative, and Judicial Salaries to make recommendations to the President on the salaries of members of the House and the Senate, federal judges, and incumbents of positions in the Executive Schedule.[29] The Executive Schedule includes the positions of Cabinet secretaries, other agency heads, deputy secretaries, undersecretaries, chairmen, and other members of regulatory commissions, some bureau heads, general counsels, and certain other noncareer officials. The highest General Schedule pay, for Grade 18, cannot exceed that for the lowest level of the Executive Salary Schedule. Members of this Commission were appointed every fourth fiscal year, three by the President, two by the President of the Senate, two by the Speaker of the House, and two by the Chief Justice of the Supreme Court. After considering the Commission's report, the President included his own recommendations in "the budget next transmitted by him to Congress," and they went into effect unless within 30 days either house of Congress enacted legislation disapproving them in whole or in part. The intention, of course, was to prevent criticism that the legislators were raising their own pay.

In the Federal Pay Comparability Act of 1970, Congress delegated to the President the salary-fixing authority for General Schedule and Foreign Service employees. The President is assisted by an agent he designates, presently the Chairman of the Civil Service Commission and the Director of the Office of Management and Budget (OMB); the legislation also establishes a Federal Employees Pay Council and an Advisory Committee on Federal Pay. The Council consists of five members from three employee organizations representing substantial numbers of employees under the statutory pay systems; they are appointed by the President's

---

[28] Sec. 212, Postal Revenue and Federal Salary Act of 1967, Public Law 90–206, 90th Cong., H.R. 7977, December 16, 1967.

[29] Ibid., Sec. 225.

agent. There are three members of the Advisory Committee, all from outside the government; the President appoints them after receiving recommendations from the director of the Federal Mediation and Conciliation Service and "other interested parties" of persons noted for their impartiality and knowledge of labor relations and pay policy.

Each year the President's agent, after reviewing the Bureau of Labor Statistics (BLS) annual survey of private enterprise white-collar rates and also considering the views of the Federal Employees Pay Council and of representatives of other employee organizations, recommends to the President "appropriate adjustments in rates of pay." The President's Advisory Committee reviews the agent's report to the President, considers any further views submitted to it by employee organizations and others, and makes its own recommendations to the Chief Executive. The President then adjusts the pay rates, which go into effect on or after October 1 of the applicable year, but if the President believes it inappropriate to make the pay adjustment because of "national emergency or economic conditions affecting the general welfare," he can send an alternative plan to Congress. This plan goes into effect within 30 days of transmittal unless either house passes a resolution of disapproval.

The BLS labels as "dramatic" the application of the pay comparability principle.[30] When the Salary Reform Act of 1962 was passed, the average pay gap with private pay was 11 percent, from a low of 18 percent at GS-3 to a high of 38.2 percent at GS-17. In 1970, the average gap was 6 percent, but this was closed six months later by a pay increase. Between 1962 and 1970, federal pay increased 58 percent, private rates 42 percent.

There are policy as well as statistical problems in making the surveys of private rates which serve as the basis for comparability adjustments. The purely statistical tasks are: (1) drawing a scientific sample of establishments which represent all those within the scope of the survey, (2) ensur-

---

[30] Thomas W. Gavett, "Policymaking and the Role of Labor Statistics," *Monthly Labor Review*, 94, No. 9 (September 1971), 39.

ing that data collected meet survey requirements, such as correct occupational matches and concepts of wages, and (3) tabulation of the data. The nonstatistical decisions are related to (1) the reference data of the survey, (2) minimum size of establishments included, (3) industries and geographical areas covered, and (4) whether the objective should be to produce national, regional, or local findings.[31] The Federal Employees Pay Council presents its views on such policy questions, as does a Federal Prevailing Rate Advisory Committee under the new legislation for determining blue-collar rates. Under the latter legislation, the Civil Service Commission prescribes "practices and procedures" for determining the rates; the employee organizations holding exclusive representation for the largest numbers of prevailing rate employees have five seats on the 11-member Advisory Committee, the other members being drawn from agencies where the bulk of blue-collar employment is concentrated, particularly the Defense Department.[32]

Largely because of disagreements on the policy questions indicated above, there have been many conflicts between union and management representatives over both white- and blue-collar pay. Presidents Richard Nixon and Gerald Ford on various occasions sought to delay pay increases in order to restrain inflation, but they failed because the comparability principle is now an established part of the Washington scene. With inflation increasing as it has, these conflicts have been sharp, but they are inevitable in any case.

Since top General Schedule pay cannot exceed that of the lowest level in the Executive Schedule, and since salaries in the latter schedule by law could not be changed more than once every four years, until the fall of 1975 the $36,000 ceiling for GS employees remained the same as when rates were adjusted in 1969 as the result of the recommendations of President Johnson's Commission on Executive, Legislative, and Judicial Salaries. Because of the time lapse, the four-year cycle made it necessary, when adjustments were made, to

---

[31] Ibid.
[32] Public Law 92–392, 92nd Cong., H.R. 9092, August 19, 1972.

grant huge increases to Congressmen, judges, and top officials, thus causing taxpayer resentment; the cost of the 1969 raises was about $23 million annually.

Since Nixon delayed his salary recommendations for Congressmen, judges, and Executive Schedule employees until submission of his 1975 budget early in 1974, Congress was unwilling to anger the voters by increasing its salaries in an election year.[33] Finally, in the summer of 1975, Congress passed and Ford approved legislation providing that in the future Congressmen, judges, and Executive Schedule officials would receive annually the same percentage increases granted employees under the comparability legislation. By that time, the number of Executive Schedule officials with salaries frozen at $36,000 had increased to more than 14,000, and Chief Justice Burger had vigorously protested the inadequacy of judicial salaries. The new legislation was approved by only one vote in the House, indicating the continuing fears of voter retaliation.[34]

Federal pay scales for white-collar workers in the same salary grades are uniform, without regard to geographical variations in the cost of living. The BLS 1971 survey showed that, in the GS–5 range, the lowest locality rates for the ten federal occupations surveyed was "far below the national average—by as much as 50 percent." The highest locality rates were above the national average by 25 to 58 percent. Since "the national average is the basis for setting federal pay, "in some localities all grade 5s would be significantly overpaid . . . while in other localities all grade 5s would be significantly underpaid."[35] Furthermore, levels of work are compared rather than occupations, so some federal employees are paid more and some less than those in the same occupations employed by private companies in the same community. Again illustrating with the GS–5 grade level, the 1971 BLS survey revealed that the average private enter-

[33] Richard L. Madden, "Federal Pay Raise Barred by Senate," *The New York Times*, March 7, 1974.

[34] Marjorie Hunter, "House Clears Way for Increases in Pay for Congress, Judges and Executives," *The New York Times*, July 31, 1975.

[35] Staats, "Equivalency with Private Sector Pay," p. 20

prise salary for the ten federal occupations surveyed was $9,129, yet the averages ranged from $7,400 for secretaries to $10,900 for engineers. On the basis of the national average, six occupational groups would be overpaid and four would be underpaid.[36] A locality system has been considered unfeasible because federal white-collar workers are scattered throughout almost all of the nation's more than 3,000 counties, but the General Accounting Office is restudying this question, along with other aspects of present federal pay practices.

The Job Evaluation and Pay Review Task Force established in 1970 recommended several different job evaluation and compensation systems. In three of these systems — one for nonsupervisory trades and crafts employees, another for nonsupervisory clerical, office machine, and technician workers, and a third for protective employees — locality rates would be paid. (Nonsupervisory trades and craft employees are already covered under the local wage board system mentioned earlier.) In other systems (such as for the Federal Executive Service, supervisors and managers, and administrative, professional, and technical personnel) nationwide uniform rates would apply. Under the proposed systems, positions in occupations classified in the same grade would in some instances be placed in different salary scales.[37]

Compensation practices in state and local governments

Prior to the Federal Salary Reform Act of 1962, some state and local governments had more progressive pay policies in some respects than the national government did. Their governing bodies reviewed pay rates annually or biennially and authorized the adjustments considered necessary to make the rates more competitive. In a few states, like California and Michigan, the legislature had delegated to the executive branch the authority to make revisions in the pay scales; in some state and local jurisdictions, executive pay had risen well above the federal levels. In recent years,

---

[36] Ibid., pp. 19–20.
[37] "Report to the President on Job Evaluation and Pay."

some states (e.g., Michigan and Oklahoma) have established commissions to make recommendations on executive, judicial, and legislative salaries. In Michigan, these recommendations go into effect unless overruled by a two-thirds vote of the legislature; in Oklahoma legislative pay does not require action by the legislature. For the country as a whole, however, state and local salaries have been far less adequate than federal pay, and the "rigidity of the salary setting mechanisms of many State and local governments" often delays "an adequate response to the realities of the labor market" and contributes to "major recruitment problems, especially in the search for professional, administrative, and technical personnel."[38]

The biggest change is determination of pay rates and fringe benefits through the collective bargaining process in a now sizable number of state and local governments. Under Executive Order 11491 as amended, pay and fringes are not subject to negotiation in the federal service. They are negotiated in the Postal Service, on the basis of special legislation — the Postal Reorganization Act of 1970.[39]

Salary increases and recognition of performance

One of the most troublesome problems has been how to provide adequate recognition for superior performance within a particular grade level. An employee's performance is often superior but, under position classification concepts, the job remains correctly classified. Pay scales in the public service have a narrower spread than in many private firms; this spread can be broadened somewhat, but not very much if the grade-level distinctions are to be maintained. Typically, in the public service within-grade increases are modest in amount and awarded, in fact, principally on the basis of seniority, no matter what the official policy states. Even when extra-meritorious increases are given, they usually are limited to one in number, and the employee's total pay is not increased very much.

---

[38] Michael E. Carbine, "Public Employees Feel Growing Pains," *Manpower*, 1, No. 10 (November 1969), 18.
[39] *Postal Reorganization Conference Report No. 91–1363*, House of Representatives, 91st Cong., 2nd sess., August 3, 1970.

Some state and local governments are now paying bonuses for either individual or group performance. In Philadelphia, a base wage is paid to water meter workers regardless of individual or group production levels, but "production above predetermined norms brings added earnings for the worker in proportion to the extra tasks accomplished." Supervisors in the water meter division receive bonuses of up to 35 percent of their base pay for reducing unit costs over the previous three-month period. St. Petersburg pays a bonus to the trash collection crew that each month achieves the best "compaction ratio" (the greatest weight of trash hauled per total number of trips to the dump). In the Pennsylvania State Bureau of Employment Security there is a piecework compensation plan for individual workers, while supervisors "receive bonuses proportional to both the productivity of their subordinates and the total production of the unit."[40]

In the case of professional, administrative, and technical workers, such quantitative measures of performance either are not available or would be misleading. It is difficult to see how for such workers exceptional performance can be rewarded without some such salary scheme as that proposed for the Federal Executive Service. As to those whose performance is mediocre, it is pointed out that "many private companies permit time-interval step increases only up to the midpoint of the grade and require stiff performance standards for steps within grade above that level."[41]

The impact of collective bargaining on compensation

The opinion of Columbia University's American Assembly that pay and fringe benefit comparability is more likely to be achieved through collective bargaining than through civil service procedures was cited in Chapter 1. Some taxpayer groups, newspapers, and other segments of the community now contend that public compensation has risen excessively by comparison with private enterprise, and unionization and collective bargaining have been an important contributing

---

[40] John M. Greiner, "Employee Incentives in Local Government: Monetary Performance Rewards," *LMRS Newsletter,* 4, No. 9 (September 1973), p. 5. Labor Management Relations Service, Washington, D.C.

[41] Staats, "Equivalency with Private Sector Pay," pp. 21–22.

factor to this rise. As yet, there is a paucity of hard research data on this; a comprehensive Brookings Institution study is under way but has not yet been completed.

In one analysis of the impact of collective bargaining in government, Paul T. Hartman of the University of Illinois uses *before* and *after* 1966 as the dividing point, since in his opinion before 1966 collective bargaining was rare in local governments and strikes were generally forbidden. Between 1960 and 1966, local government compensation generally kept up with average increases in wages and salaries, municipal rates rising annually by about 5 percent. From 1966 to 1969, although the average annual increase in all wages and salaries, for both the private and public sectors, was about 7 percent, it was 8.2 percent for teachers, 8.3 percent for firefighters and policemen, and slightly less than 8 percent for all municipal employees.[42]

Hartman believes collective bargaining was partly responsible for this difference. Citing shortage of labor as the "alternative explanation for rapidly rising relative salaries" most preferred by economists, he notes that teacher shortages had about disappeared by the end of the decade. Hartman compared nonunionized and unionized school districts with 6,000 or more students in 1968 (the total sample being 400 of the approximately 1,400 districts with this size enrollment in the country) and found that in 1969–70 entry-level salaries were higher in the unionized districts: about 4.5 percent higher for teachers with bachelor's degrees and about 4.3 percent higher for those with master's degrees. At the top of these two scales the differences were greater, about 12 and 15 percent, respectively. Hartman emphasizes that the "main movers" in annual salary increases are market forces; "the rises in the nationwide general level of wages and salaries, accelerated recently by inflation, would have pulled or pushed the salaries of teachers, even without collective bargaining." He estimates that perhaps two thirds

---

[42] Paul T. Hartman, "Wage Effects of Local Government Bargaining," in *Proceedings of the International Symposium on Public Employment Relations* (Albany, N.Y.: New York State Public Employment Relations Board, 1971), pp. 192–97.

of the teacher salary increases in 1966–69 would have occurred even without unions.[43]

A BLS survey made during 1970 and 1971 of government and private enterprise salaries in 11 large municipalities revealed that the municipal scales were generally better for equivalent work in office clerical, data processing, and maintenance and custodial work.[44] In its first national survey of employee benefits for full-time workers in U.S. municipalities, the Labor Management Relations Service (LMRS) found that cities expended a higher percentage of working-time pay for fringe benefits than private industry did. The composite average for the cities was 28.2 percent for general personnel and 33.8 percent for policemen and firemen, the percentage for private industry being 27.4[45] In its second national survey, the LMRS reported that the fringes for general municipal personnel had increased to 31.9 percent of pay in 1973, and for police and fire personnel to 35.5 percent of pay. During the same time period, private fringes had climbed at an even faster rate of 11.7 percent per annum.[46]

Developments in New York State illustrate the concern about union negotiation of fringe benefits. There are eight public retirement systems in the state, including several for New York City employees. Although pensions had been subject to negotiation, settlements providing benefits different from those stated in the state law for particular pension systems had to be approved by legislative amendment of the statute. Pension costs increased so greatly that a moratorium on further legislative approval of new contract provisions was called, and a Permanent Commission on Public Employee Pension and Retirement systems was appointed to make a comprehensive study.

[43] Ibid., pp. 194, 197.

[44] Stephen H. Perloff, "Comparing Municipal Salaries with Industry and Federal Pay," *Monthly Labor Review*, 94, No. 10 (October 1971), 46–50.

[45] Labor Management Relations Service, National League of Cities, United States Conference of Mayors, National Association of Counties, *First National Survey of Employee Benefits for Full-Time Personnel of U.S. Municipalities*, Washington, D.C.

[46] Labor Management Relations Service, *Second National Survey of Employee Benefits for Full-Time Personnel of U.S. Municipalities*, Washington, D.C.

In its report, released in January 1973, this commission said that, in terms of net disposable income after retirement, long-service public employees actually received benefits which, together with social security, provided them with a larger income in retirement than what they received when employed. It also reported that, according to a 1971 study by the U.S. Chamber of Commerce in which 885 companies reported, pension payments averaged 5.5 percent of payrolls, but the cost of New York State public employee pension plans ranged from approximately 20 to over 40 percent of payrolls. It was also revealed that in New York City some union contracts provided for the City to make special annuity fund payments to several employee associations and unions — payments in addition to those made by the City to the particular public retirement systems.[47] The commission recommended a single uniform public employees retirement plan with scaled-down benefits for all employees hired after July 1, 1973, it being impossible to cover existing employees because of a provision in the state constitution. It also recommended that pensions no longer be negotiable.[48]

The commission's recommendations were not accepted by the legislature, which established its own seven-member select committee to study pension reform proposals.[49] In July 1973, the legislature, over the strong opposition of the employee organizations, enacted a law providing for four different pension categories, based on kind of occupation, with reduced benefits for employees hired after July 1, 1973.[50] This legislation prohibited changes in public employee pension benefits until April 1, 1976, after which changes could only be made after negotiations on a coalition basis. The commission was required to present recommendations for coalition bargaining by December 1, 1973.

[47] Report of the Permanent Commission on Public Employee Pension and Retirement Systems, New York, January 30, 1973, pp. 8, 14–17, 20–21.
[48] M. A. Farber, "Uniform State Pension Plan Proposed," New York Times, January 31, 1973.
[49] Alfonso A. Narvaez, "Issue and Debate in the Legislature, Reform of Public Employe's Pension System," New York Times, July 24, 1973.
[50] Alfonso A. Narvaez, "Unions Score Newly Voted Pension Bill and Vow to Retaliate at Contract Talks," New York Times, July 28, 1973.

The commission recommended combining all public employees in the state into two statewide coalitions, one consisting of all police officers and firefighters and the other comprising all state and local public employees. Recommendations resulting from coalition negotiations would be submitted to the legislature for necessary legislation. Once enacted, the changes in retirement benefits would be considered a term and condition of employment subject to collective negotiations under the Taylor Law, the state's public worker collective bargaining statute. No action was taken in 1974 by the legislature on the commission's proposals, but some action will have to be taken before April 1, 1976, as required by the 1973 legislation.[51]

Although coalition bargaining would eliminate "leapfrogging," the tactic whereby individual unions demand as much and more than another union obtains in its settlement, Arvid Anderson, head of New York City's Office of Collective Bargaining, believes that its wisdom on a statewide basis is dubious and warns that "a monolithic structure of one 'employer' and 'one union coalition' will submerge legitimate interests and ignore different needs of public employers and employees."[52]

In his testimony before the select committee, Anderson argued that it would be a mistake to remove pensions from the bargaining table because "the drive to improve pensions will not go away because the Legislature declares there should not be bargaining on this subject." Pension disputes would simply be transferred to the legislature, with unlimited pension bills being filed; furthermore, the unions would seek to compensate by increasing the "pressure for bargaining on wages and other fringe benefits which, in turn, will result in increased pension costs for present employees under existing formulas, thereby resulting in no reduction in employment costs."[53] The legislature could maintain much

---

[51] Letter to Felix A. Nigro, from John Pertusi, Office of Collective Bargaining, New York City, February 25, 1975.

[52] Statement of Arvid Anderson, Chairman, Office of Collective Bargaining, New York City, June 21, 1973, before Select Committee on Pensions, p. 5.

[53] Ibid., pp. 2, 3.

more effective control through selective approval or disapproval of negotiated pension benefits. After all, neither public management at the bargaining table nor the legislature is compelled to accept a particular pension provision.

Some public employee leaders argue that private pension systems are grossly inadequate, so it is unfair to use them as a basis for comparison. The same argument is made with respect to private pay for certain kinds of work. On the other hand, there is evidence that in some jurisdictions some kinds of public workers have more than caught up with reasonable private rates for equivalent work.[54] Much more research is needed on the effect of collective bargaining on pay rates, as well as more hard thinking about the policies government should follow in compensating its employees.

BIBLIOGRAPHY

Baruch, Ismar. *Position Classification in the Public Service.* Chicago: International Personnel Management Association, 1941.

U.S. Civil Service Commission, *Job Evaluation and Pay Review Task Force,* vol. 1, *Findings and Recommendations.* Washington, D.C., 1972.

House Committee on Post Office and Civil Service. *Federal White-Collar Comparability Process.* 93rd Cong., 2nd sess. Washington, D.C.: Government Printing Office, 1974.

House Committee on Post Office and Civil Service. *Report on Job Evaluation and Ranking in the Federal Government.* 91st Cong., 1st sess., House Report No. 91–28. Washington, D.C.: Government Printing Office, 1969.

Labor-Management Relations Service. *First and Second National Surveys of Employee Benefits for Full-Time Personnel of U.S. Municipalities.* Washington, D.C.

Leich, Harold H. "Rank in Man or Job? Both!" *Public Administration Review,* Spring 1960.

National Commission on Productivity. *Managing Human Resources in Local Government: A Survey of Employee Incentive Plans.* Washington, D.C., 1973.

---

[54] Raymond D. Horton, *Municipal Labor Relations in New York City, Lessons of the Lindsay-Wagner Years* (New York: Frederick A. Praeger, 1973), pp. 101–3.

Nigro, Felix A. *Public Personnel Administration.* New York: Holt, Rinehart, & Winston, 1959. Chaps. 3 and 4.

Parris, Henry. *Staff Relations in the Civil Service.* London: Allen & Unwin, 1973.

Powell, Norman J. *Personnel Administration in Goverment.* Englewood Cliffs, N.J.: Prentice-Hall, Inc., 1956. Chaps. 14 and 15.

Reports of the Permanent Commission on Public Employee Pension and Retirement Systems. New York, January 30, 1973, November 1, 1973, and December 1, 1973.

Richter, Frederick F. *A Summary of the Job Evaluation and Pay Review Task Force Report.* Washington, D.C.: Classification and Compensation Society.

Warner, Kenneth O., and J. J. Donovan (eds.). *Practical Guidelines to Public Pay Administration.* Chicago: International Personnel Management Association, vol. 1, 1963, vol. 2, 1965.

Wilson, Seymour V. "Scientific Management and Personnel Policy in North American Systems." *Public Administration,* 51 (Summer 1973).

Recruitment

6

Traditional personnel administration was characterized by a confident belief in the abundance of human resources and the ready availability of an ample supply of applicants for public service jobs. This confidence bred complacence, so that any active search for candidates was the exception rather than the rule.

■ MANPOWER PLANNING

By the 1960s it was clear that the nation faced an indefinite, perhaps permanent, period of scarcity of human resources and critical shortages in many kinds of work. Leaders in both the private and public sectors urged the implementation of manpower planning, a concept which calls for forecasting specific personnel needs over a substantial number of years; intensive analysis of the skills, interests, and other characteristics of existing employees; and development of action plans for filling the anticipated future positions with qualified individuals through new hires and training of present personnel. Catchy phrases have been used to convey the importance of manpower planning (such as having the right people available at the right time in the right jobs), but it is clear that under present conditions the concept is no fad, but rather is essential to the survival of any organization.

John W. Macy, Jr., gives some examples of recruiting mistakes caused by failure to devote proper attention to key aspects in human resource planning. The feasibility of program plans depends on careful estimates of the personnel needed, yet "the statement of manpower requirements" for the project to land a man on the moon by the end of the sixties was, according to Macy,

> a minor item in the plan presented to President Kennedy. He was assured that there would be no problem in securing essential personnel. But through the attraction of exciting work and higher salaries, scarce skills were drawn away from other areas of research and engineering. In one of the early forecasts, the requirement of the space program for Ph.D. mathematicians was estimated at a number in excess of the total national supply for the year in question.[1]

The skills requirements of positions should be accurately analyzed, and overly high qualification standards should not be employed in recruiting. Yet when the managers of the Atomic Energy Commission's Los Alamos project set forth requirements for initial staffing of the security guard force, they determined that

> all security guards should be college graduates who received the highest rating on a competitive examination designed for such graduates. Several hundred young men were selected in accordance with these standards, only to find that standing guard in remote areas of the laboratory or directing traffic in the company town was not the career expression of their collegiate preparation. Both morale and performance suffered, the cost of physical security was excessively high, and a complicated redesign of standards and restaffing of the operation, which took nearly ten years to achieve, became the only means of correcting the original error.[2]

In the early sixties the U.S. Civil Service Commission began to stress the personnel officer's responsibility to advise on the human resource implications of management deci-

---

[1] John W. Macy, Jr., *Public Service, The Human Side of Government* (New York: Harper & Row, Publishers, 1971), p. 52.
[2] Ibid., p. 51.

sions. By the seventies the Commission's instructions to the agencies explicitly recognized "manpower planning as an integral part of agency personnel management responsibilities."[3] The Commission has been publishing *Federal Workforce Outlook Reports* containing detailed, year-by-year projections of future employment levels in the largest white-collar occupations represented in the federal service, as well as data on current turnover and hiring patterns. The reliability of the manpower forecasts depends upon the accuracy of the information provided by the agencies on their future work plans. The Commission's experience makes clear that it is essential for these work plans to be "developed as part of an effective multi-year agency program planning and budgeting system."[4]

In a paper published in mid-1973, H. M. Clark, the Commission's Manpower Analysis Officer and chairman of the Interagency Advisory Group Committee on Manpower Analysis and Planning, wrote that the federal government did not have effective manpower planning. The annual budget system limited planning to just one year; besides, agency work-force projections were based "on existing workload/worker relationships to expected workload changes, with the average grade and salary of the current work force being carried over to the next budget period with little or no change." These projections ignored long-term trends toward a "higher proportion of high skill occupations in the workforce" and did not consider the "impact on work-force skill-level composition . . . of changes in agency policy or practice in filling . . . vacancies." They gave "no basis for determining whether or not it will be feasible to actually provide the proposed work force on the schedule specified." Based on a requirement in the Legislative Reorganization Act of 1970, federal agencies now are planning their programs on a five-year basis, with the budget for fiscal 1974 projecting governmentwide expenditures for fiscal 1975. To

---

[3] Harry L. Clark, "The Emerging Role of Manpower Planning," *Civil Service Journal*, 11, No. 2 (October–December 1970), 13.
[4] Ibid.

Clark's knowledge, this is the "first publicly-issued, official projection of U. S. Government expenditures for a period beyond the single budget year in the entire history of the nation." If detailed work-force plans specifying both the occupations and skill levels of workers expected to be employed during each phase of the planning period are developed, if a governmentwide policy is issued defining manpower planning functions and providing guidelines for assessing agency performance in this area, and if effective selection standards and training programs for manpower planners are instituted, he believes there will be "extremely rapid, even revolutionary improvement in the near future."[5]

The District of Columbia survey of manpower planning systems

With funding by a grant from the U.S. Civil Service Commission under the Intergovernmental Personnel Act, in late 1972 the District of Columbia made a nationwide questionnaire survey of manpower planning systems in 775 state and local governments, federal agencies, and private corporations. According to the District's report,[6] such systems generally include three major components:

1. A computerized information system providing summary data by occupation on employment, labor turnover, vacancies, and wages.
2. Methodologies to make short-and long-range projections of employment levels, additional manpower requirements, training needs, and retirements.
3. Sets of action programs offering alternative procedures to cope with manpower problems.

The findings,[7] based on replies from the 354 respondents to the survey, were as follows:

---

[5] Harry L. Clark, "Manpower Planning in the U.S. Government: Where We Are," July 17, 1973. Written for publication in French in the *Yearbook of the International Institute of Public Administration*, Paris.

[6] District of Columbia Government Personnel Office, *Manpower Planning: The State of the Art*, April 1973 (reproduced by National Technical Information Service, U.S. Department of Commerce, Springfield, Va. 22151).

[7] Ibid., pp. i, ii, and 9.

1. 118 respondents (33.3 percent) had developed and were using at least one of the three components.
2. Close to 40 percent were developing "additional manpower planning tools."
3. 15 of the respondents had "comprehensive and relatively sophisticated manpower planning systems."
4. About 90 percent of the federal agencies, 43 percent of both the private corporations and state governments, and 22 percent of the local governments were "implementing modern manpower planning techniques."
5. Although the survey data suggested that the larger the employer (in terms of number of employees) the greater the possibility of existence of a manpower planning system, a sizable number of smaller employers also had such systems.
6. An average of six employees and 1.5 years were required to develop one or more components of their systems.
7. Most of the systems had been functioning for less than three years and were manned by central office staffs of one to ten persons, usually including a program manager, a manpower analyst or specialist, a computer systems analyst, and a secretary.
8. Almost 70 percent of the systems were attached to personnel offices.
9. 67 percent of the systems were organizationwide in scope.

Computers are a very important tool in manpower planning and research because of their tremendous data storage and retrieval capacities and ability to handle large volumes of data, as in the maintenance of employee skills inventories with an enormous amount of information on each individual. John Hindricks notes that "machine capabilities make it possible for the personnel researcher to evaluate an almost infinite number of interrelationships in an organization's manpower data in an effort to gain a better understanding of the factors affecting this resource."[8]

---

[8] John R. Hindrichs, "The Computer in Manpower Research," *Personnel Administration*, 33, No. 2 (March–April 1970), 39–40.

In the D.C. survey, 80 percent of the respondents were using or developing computerized manpower information systems, usually "built on top of" computerized personnel systems which "collect, store, provide, and update information necessary for the day-to-day operation of a personnel office," such as position inventories and listings of employees eligible for retirement. The manpower information system produces analytical reports which show trends and relationships, thus facilitating better informed decisions on action programs. Material in these reports could include simulation of internal transfer and promotional patterns, statistical tables on labor turnover and vacancy rates by occupational group, or correlations between employee age and length of service by occupation. Of the 118 respondents with manpower planning systems, 40 were employing techniques to estimate future manpower needs, and another 29 were preparing to do so. Forty to 50 percent of the state governments, corporations, and federal agencies, but only 16 percent of the local jurisdictions with such systems, were regularly making manpower forecasts. More than three-fourths of those making projections were predicting future levels of total employment, and two-thirds were forecasting retirements or total manpower requirements (the sum of estimated replacements and new hires). Three of five were estimating future employment in selected occupations, and two of five were "using techniques to anticipate training needs." The most common time period for the projections was one to five years, with a substantial number of two-, three-, and ten-year forecasts also being made.[9]

Three categories of action programs were distinguished in the survey:

> (1) stressed — recruitment, selection and placement, training and development, and promotion; (2) stressed somewhat — compensation, job mobility and career ladders, organization planning, program-budget-manpower coordination, and retirement; and (3) mentioned but not stressed — job restructuring, staffing standards, and manpower utilization.[10]

---

[9] District of Columbia Government Personnel Office, *Manpower Planning*, pp. 14, 16–17.

[10] Ibid., p. 19.

Significantly, the respondents reported serious problems in gaining acceptance of the manpower planning techniques and reports. Some program managers simply do not believe the projections and resist the recommended action programs. Note the following comment by one respondent:

> A basic problem in manpower planning is to sell the concept that alternative program plans must be evaluated on the basis of their manpower implications, just as they now are evaluated based on their budgetary and political implications. Manpower should not be the sole criteria for evaluation of program alternatives, but as long as we ignore manpower in our basic program choices, we will continue to suffer the kind of skill wastes we presently have.[11]

A conclusion of the D.C. survey was that the evidence suggested that much of the manpower planning activities reported represented "rather limited efforts, instead of the comprehensive systems described in recent literature."[12] An article published in late 1969 in *Manpower*, monthly journal of the Labor Department's Manpower Administration, reported that 95 percent of all municipal governments lacked formal manpower development plans.[13] A state government official aptly states that policymakers at the highest levels should "give manpower its rightful place in our scheme of things instead of regarding it as a sort of afterthought. Personnel people must be involved much earlier in program and fiscal planning involving manpower, and also be included in planning how the work of the agency gets done."[14]

■THE HERITAGE OF THE PAST

Historically, civil service recruiting has been characterized by many negative and unimaginative practices, some of which persist in many jurisdictions. Since recruiting was for individual jobs, not careers, examination announcements did

---

[11] Ibid., p. 12.

[12] Ibid., p. 5.

[13] Michael E. Carbine, "Public Employees Feel Growing Pains," *Manpower*, 1, No. 10 (November 1969), 18.

[14] See "Personnel Opinions," *Public Personnel Review*, 32, No. 1 (January 1971), 59.

not attract many of the ablest college students. Furthermore, examinations were given *after* rather than *before* graduation, with delays of some weeks or months before offers could be made, so that many high school and college graduates accepted prompter employment in private enterprise. In publicizing openings, the main reliance was placed on printed announcements sent to local post offices, U.S. Employment Service facilities, college placement centers, veterans organizations, and similar places where they were posted on a routine basis or even thrown into the wastebasket. The announcements were typically dull, with much of the content devoted to legal requirements repeated word for word in every announcement. Though they were expensive to print and failed to attract applicants, they were used anyway.[15] Some state and local jurisdictions did make effective use of paid advertisements in newspapers and magazines, but it was not until October 1957 that the U.S. Civil Service Commission gave permission for federal agencies to place such ads.

Typically, examinations had a fixed closing date, a self-imposed limitation which was very damaging because it made it necessary to refuse the applications of good candidates who for one reason or another could not meet the deadline filing date. Since the life of the resultant eligible list often was several years, during which time no new names could be added, before long the registers came to include only the names of the less desirable eligibles. Very restrictive minimum qualifications of age, physical characteristics, employment background, and training were used, without demonstrable relationship to ability to do the job. The recruiting area was also sharply restricted in many jurisdictions by the legal requirement of local residence. Payment of travel expenses for interview was exceptional; indeed, examination filing fees were sometimes imposed, thus putting some of the cost on the candidates. Despite the success of

---

[15] See Senate Subcommittee on Federal Manpower Policies, 83rd Cong., 1st sess., *Personnel Recruitment and Employment Practices in the Federal Government*, Senate Document No. 37 (Washington, D.C.: Government Printing Office, 1953), p. 12.

many private companies with college recruitment, this area was largely neglected by government and there were relatively few internship and work-study programs.

Two examples of the legacy of poor recruiting practices

How these negative recruiting practices linger on is strikingly demonstrated in the two cases of corrections work and police careers.

Corrections. In October 1969, pursuant to the Correctional Rehabilitation Study Act of 1965, the Joint Commission on Correctional Manpower and Training issued its final report,[16] based on a survey of every adult and juvenile federal and state correctional institution and every state-level probation and parole agency in the country. The Commission also studied a national sample of local-level probation agencies, made surveys of relevant college and university programs, and commissioned Louis Harris and Associates to make three national opinion surveys, including an attitude survey of correctional employees.

A major finding was that "Recruitment of correctional personnel is ordinarily carried out in an uncoordinated and haphazard manner. Most applicants seem to be of the drop-in, write-in, or referred-by variety. Correctional agencies seldom seek applicants actively, and there is no established mode of entry into the correctional system."[17] Only 26 percent of correctional employees were under 34 years of age, almost half were 30 or older when they entered the field, and only 16 percent had been recruited "directly from classrooms," evidencing the need to join the "world of education with that of corrections in order to provide a constant flow of young and enthusiastic manpower into the field." Minority groups and women were underrepresented, particularly in the middle and top management ranks. Although more than six in ten correctional workers were "almost always satisfied with their jobs," half felt they did not have much

---

[16] Joint Commission on Correctional Manpower and Training, *A Time to Act* (Washington, D. C., 1969).
[17] Ibid., p. 12.

freedom in doing their work, and one-third were reluctant to recommend corrections as a career to young people.[18]

Corrections was a closed system, promotional opportunities usually being limited to those within a single agency or department, with little lateral entry being allowed. Most correctional agencies were rejecting applications of those under 21 or over 45, thus eliminating "two excellent recruitment pools: young persons aged 18 to 21 who are often ready to start a career and, with training and educational opportunities, could hold responsible positions in a few years; and older men and women who have desirable qualifications and experience." The mandatory retirement age often was 62 or 65, prematurely cutting off many valuable staff members. Physical requirements, such as for height, weight, vision, and hearing, were frequently unrelated to the work performed, unrealistic, and inflexible. The physically handicapped were usually barred from consideration. In jurisdictions under civil service, written tests were used which were scheduled and administered at infrequent intervals, and eligibility lists were subsequently closed for a year or more. Residence requirements and prohibitions on hiring persons with criminal records also hampered recruitment.[19]

The educational background of correctional employees studied ranged from less than high school to Ph.D. status. College graduates had degrees in many different subjects, only a small minority having concentrated in social work or criminology-corrections. There was no "well-defined link to any level or discipline of the educational system." College graduates with B.A.s in history who somehow manage to get into correctional work and those with masters' degrees in social work were equally likely to be institutional counselors. The prevailing standards for educational preparation of probation and parole officers and others working primarily with individual offenders were unrealistic. Formulated by national professional organizations and endorsed by some federal agencies, these standards called for a master's degree

---

[18] Ibid., pp. 12, 14–15.
[19] Ibid., pp. 17, 18.

in social work or comparable academic study, but graduate school output of such degree holders was much too limited. Yet college counselors were following the prescribed standards and steering away many promising candidates from "corrections' door."[20]

Recommendations of the Joint Commission on Correctional Manpower and Training were as follows:

1. A major public information program to change the low image of work in corrections, and a nationwide recruitment program employing such devices as brochures, television, job fairs, and campus recruitment.
2. Summer work-study programs, to attract more younger persons to the correctional field.
3. More intensive efforts to recruit minority-group members and women.
4. Emphasis in recruitment programs on the "feelings of satisfaction and service to society which are possible in correctional work."
5. An end to "overly restrictive supervision" of correctional personnel.
6. More opportunities for advancement, and for lateral entry and promotional mobility within and between jurisdictions.
7. Lowering the entry age for some correctional jobs to 18, and a mandatory uniform retirement age of 70.
8. Replacement of inflexible height and weight requirements with "appropriate physical examinations to assess physical fitness and agility required by particular positions . . . ," and reexamination of hiring policies to maximize employment of the physically handicapped.
9. Elimination of written tests except for those positions for which tests demonstrably measure capacity to do the work required.
10. Elimination of residency requirements and lowering of barriers to hiring ex-offenders in correctional and other government agencies.

---

[20] Ibid., pp. 22, 28.

11. Establishment of career ladders in correctional work, with the undergraduate degree the standard educational requirement for entry-level probation and parole work and comparable positions in institutions. The preferred areas of specialization would be psychology, criminal justice, sociology, social work, criminology-corrections, education, and public administration. Those with high school education or less could enter the field and progress to journeymen positions through work-study programs.[21]

Recruitment of police. The Task Force on the Police of President Lyndon Johnson's Commission on Law Enforcement and Administration of Justice[22] diagnosed poor structuring of the police job as a principal reason for failure to attract better qualified persons to police careers. All patrolmen are required to help the public by providing many "noncrime-related" services which are essential to the community but frequently routine and mechanical in character. At present, according to the Task Force report, a patrolman is equally responsible for the most complex and the most menial of police tasks.

The Task Force recommended that police departments in large and medium-sized cities establish three classes of officer—police agent, police officer, and community service officer (CSO). The classes would represent work of different levels of difficulty and responsibility. Police agents, who would need a college degree, would be assigned to the "most complicated, sensitive, and demanding police tasks," such as serving in high-crime areas and as plainclothesmen to investigate major crimes. Police officers, for whom the requirement would be two years of college, would undertake routine patrol activities, provide emergency services, enforce traffic regulations, investigate crimes that can be solved by immediate follow-up investigations, and serve on police

---

[21] Ibid., pp. 13–20, 28–30.
[22] See Task Force on the Police, The President's Commission on Law Enforcement and Administration of Justice, *Task Force Report: The Police* (Washington, D.C.: Government Printing Office, 1967), p. 122.

teams created to solve crimes and cope with other law enforcement problems. CSOs, visualized as typically between the ages of 17 and 21 and recruited from minority groups, would assist police agents and police officers by performing a variety of services in deprived communities, such as working with juveniles, referring citizen complaints to appropriate agencies, providing emergency aid for the sick, helping families with domestic problems, and investigating minor thefts. They would be recruited from the neighborhoods they serve, and high school education would not be a rigid prerequisite, "priority being given to applicants with promising aspirations, honesty, intelligence, a desire and a tested capacity to advance his education, and an understanding of the neighborhood and its problems."[23] The CSO would be an apprentice police officer who would not have full law-enforcement powers or be permitted to carry arms. Nevertheless, the CSO would not perform clerical duties, as has generally been the case with police cadets.

Noting the poor police image, particularly in the inner city, the Task Force urged police administrators to emphasize the challenge in the police function and avoid making matters worse by publicly citing the adverse conditions under which police work. It found existing mandatory height, weight, vision, and other physical requirements unduly restrictive to recruitment efforts and proposed that these requirements be made more flexible and determinable on an individual basis. The minimum age for patrolman was usually 21; this, combined with the typical high school graduation requirement, explained why those who had failed in other kinds of work often applied for the police force. The Task Force recommended that the 21-year age requirement be waived for persons under that age who demonstrated the "necessary maturity and intelligence to merit special consideration." As to maximum age limits, most departments barred men over 35, and many disqualified those over 30. Since this eliminated many persons with law enforcement experience in other agencies or in the military, the report

---

[23] Ibid., p. 124.

recommended that the maximum be set higher or that police administrators be given wide latitude to grant waivers they consider justified. Many police departments were requiring prior local residence for periods varying from six months to five years, and the Task Force urged prompt elimination of all such requirements.[24]

Very few police departments have restructured police jobs along the lines recommended by the Task Force, but some now require "some" college work for entrance, and a few require a degree. In some jurisdictions, height requirements have been reduced (even eliminated in New York City), and overly restrictive vision and other physical requirements are being altered. The minimum age has been lowered (to 18 in Newark, New Jersey), and maximum limits have been revised upward. More jurisdictions have dropped residency requirements. All of these changes have been part of the growing trend to shed unduly restrictive recruitment practices.

■ POSITIVE RECRUITMENT PROGRAMS

While recruitment practices such as those discussed above persist in many jurisdictions, in many others *positive* recruitment programs were embarked on quite a few years ago, and they have been in the process of being improved. Essentially, positive recruitment means searching out good candidates, rather than sitting back and accepting applications. It reflects the conviction that government deserves the best and can obtain it by offering the proper incentives. The basic strategy is recruiting for careers, capitalizing on the vital and interesting nature of public jobs.

Positive recruitment techniques are numerous, limited only by the imagination. Some were indicated above in the enumeration of recommendations for improving recruitment practices in corrections. In some cases now, applications are received, candidates examined, and appointments made all

---

[24] Ibid., p. 131.

in one visit to a civil service agency. Open, continuous examinations (with no closing dates for filing applications) are very common, and the entire employment process is much faster. Although further improvements are needed, college recruitment is now continuous, rather than sporadic, and work-study and internship programs are far more numerous than in the past. Advances in various fields are being exploited by positive recruitment; as an example, Wide Area Telephone Service is provided in 46 states by the Civil Service Commission so that free calls to Federal Job Information Centers can be made to obtain up-to-date information on federal employment.[25]

An example of the new approaches is the crash program of the District of Columbia Metropolitan Police Force to increase its authorized strength greatly. Advertisements were placed in newspapers all over the country, and recruiting teams traveled to many cities to administer the written examination, arrange for physical examinations, interview candidates, and make background checks. Recruits were also obtained from the military through an extensive worldwide early-release program; the written and physical exams and the interviews were administered at overseas bases with the cooperation of the Defense Department. Recruiters also made numerous visits to D.C. ghetto areas to attract candidates, and, for a brief period, the services of a prominent black militant leader were contracted for to encourage recruitment. College recruitment was also undertaken on a substantial basis for the first time.[26]

Outreach recruitment

The equal employment opportunity (EEO) movement has provided a powerful stimulus through "outreach recruitment," which makes positive efforts to find candidates from minority groups and deprived people. Former President

---

[25] Lawrence T. Lorenz, "Federal Job Information . . . At Your Fingertips," *Civil Service Journal*, 12, No. 4 (April–June, 1972), 16–17.

[26] Executive Management Service, Inc., *A Report on the Recruitment and Selection Process of the District of Columbia Metropolitan Police Department* (Arlington, Va., 1971).

Richard Nixon's 16-point program for the Spanish-speaking is an example of these broad-gauged efforts.[27] This program, initiated in 1970, called for:

1. Appointment of a full-time official in the Civil Service Commission to direct efforts in the federal service to provide equal employment opportunity for the Spanish-speaking.

2. An intensified drive for the agencies to recruit Spanish-surnamed persons for public contact positions in areas with large Spanish-speaking populations (e.g., housing counselor, consumer protection specialist, and social security representative).

3. College recruitment teams with Spanish-speaking members to visit colleges with significant enrollments of Spanish-speaking students.

4. Enhancement of opportunities at all levels for the Spanish-surnamed in federal programs dealing with the Spanish-speaking, to assure that these programs relate effectively to the people served.

5. Acceleration of recruitment for cooperative education programs at colleges with significant numbers of Spanish-speaking students (these programs permit entry from PACE registers without written examination).

6. Appointment of Spanish-speaking persons to positions in which knowledge of Spanish is useful.

7. The convening of a conference of federal officials in the Southwest to promote equal employment opportunity and upward mobility for the Spanish-speaking.

8. Job information and counseling services for high schools in Spanish-speaking areas.

9. Summer employment for high school and college teachers in schools with Spanish-speaking students.

10. Special efforts to inform Spanish-surnamed veterans of availability of noncompetitive appointments through GS–5 for Vietnam veterans.

---

[27] See House Civil Rights Oversight Subcommittee, Committee on the Judiciary, 92nd Cong., 2nd sess., *Federal Employment Problems of the Spanish Speaking* (Washington, D.C.: Government Printing Office, 1972), pp. 6–12, pp. 491–92.

11. Review of agency EEO programs to assure full ap-
plicability to the Spanish-surnamed.
12. Assuring that agencies understand special problems
of the Spanish-speaking.
13. Additional EEO and personnel management training
programs for federal managers in Spanish-speaking
areas.
14. Exploring the feasibility of creating an intergovernmental training facility for upward mobility and skills
training of federal, state, and local employees in the
Southwest.
15. Development of special information on the Spanish-
surnamed in minority employment statistics and
agency reports to provide such information.
16. The inclusion of questions on employment and upward mobility of the Spanish-surnamed in Civil Service Commission agency evaluation checklists.

As a result of these recommendations the full-time Commission official was appointed and the Southwest training
center was established. Some action was taken to implement the other items, but representatives of organizations of
the Spanish-surnamed are critical of the results obtained, and
the Commission itself does not consider agency compliance
adequate. Nevertheless, it is undeniable that programs of
this kind make positive recruitment an obligation of the
public employer, not simply a plan recommended by personnel experts and others.

Employment of those with criminal records

A report by the Georgetown Institute of Criminal Law and
Procedure (Institute Director, Samuel Dash) urges opening
the door to government employment of persons with criminal
records. Funded by the Labor Department's Manpower Administration, this study concentrated on the effect of civil
service requirements in state and local government.[28]

---

[28] Georgetown University Law Center, Institute of Criminal Law and
Procedure, *The Closed Door: The Effect of a Criminal Record on Employment with State and Local Public Agencies* (Washington, D.C., February 1972, distributed by National Technical Information Service, U.S.
Department of Commerce, Springfield, Va. 22151).

Questionnaire data from 337 state, city, and county governments were analyzed, and on-the-site visits were made to six sites — one state, three cities, and two counties.

The findings of the Institute study[29] were as follows:

1. Very few civil service jurisdictions followed a statutory policy of not excluding applicants with criminal records, and even here the statutes provided only "slight amelioration of the effects of a criminal conviction on a job applicant's chances of obtaining civil service employment."

2. Persons with criminal records usually were not hired if there were other qualified applicants.

3. In about one-third of the jurisdictions, any "unfit" person could be rejected, and an incorrect statement on the application form was grounds for rejection.

4. In about one-fifth of the jurisdictions, persons guilty of *infamous* or notoriously *disgraceful* conduct were excluded.

5. In about one-third of the states and a fifth of the cities and counties, the statutes specifically barred individuals for criminal offenses, the terminology varying ("not law-abiding," "having unsatisfactory arrest records," "being found guilty of or convicted of a crime").

6. In approximately 14 percent of the states and 6 percent of the municipalities, the laws expressly provided for discharging employees for criminal conduct, many using the word "conviction" but others "crime" or "violation."

In general, the civil service laws and regulations were so worded as to make it easy to reject arbitrarily any person with a conviction or arrest record.

In the six jurisdictions visited, it was found that the "civil service *process* itself" contributed to excluding persons with criminal records. Employment procedures often dragged on over several months, with much of the delay attributable to time-consuming checks with corrections and police officials. Usually no special efforts were made to reach ex-offenders with civil service job announcements, which often "were

[29] Ibid., pp. 36–44.

written at a level of verbal complexity higher than the job demands," such as a reference to siblings in one for neighborhood aides, a position similar to mother's helper. Minimum experience and education requirements were set too high for the kinds of work involved, thus eliminating most ex-offenders. In one county, the educational requirement for most jobs was a high school diploma, even for manual labor positions.[30]

The Institute has drafted a Model Civil Service Criminal Conviction Statute with an opening statement of principle that the "public is best protected when criminal offenders are rehabilitated and returned to society prepared to take their places as productive citizens." It provides that persons with criminal conviction records be entitled to all rights given other applicants under the civil service rules. In considering such persons, the hiring official would consider the nature of the crime and its relationship to the job being filled, information on the degree of rehabilitation of the person, and the time elapsed since conviction.[31]

■THE PRESTIGE OF GOVERNMENT EMPLOYMENT

The poor image of government employment held by many college students and much of the community has been verified by several research studies, which have found that public jobs are held in lower esteem by those with more education.[32] Nevertheless, college students in fields like forestry, agriculture, and social work for some time have prepared for careers in government, and majors in many other fields have preferred public employment. In the American environment however, the private sector has always been very strong, and for young people aiming at high earnings it obviously has had the advantage over government. Furthermore, government itself has failed to create the

---

[30] Ibid., pp. 110–21.
[31] Ibid., pp. 47–48.
[32] See Franklin K. Kirkpatrick, Milton C. Cummings, Jr., and M. Kent Jennings, *The Image of the Federal Service* (Washington, D.C.: Brookings Institution, 1964).

conditions that would attract many of the able candidates it
has lost to other employers.

Today, many businessmen are concerned with the tendency of college students to reject business values and seek
employment in work they consider more meaningful, as in
the professions, teaching, and government. Certainly the
business community no longer has confidence that it can
snatch the best from the college campuses.[33] At the same
time, there is some reason to believe that "once on the job
public employment is not nearly as unattractive as the
commonly held image," as Glenn W. Miller has noted. In a
recent attitude survey of about 1,140 nonsupervisory, non-
education workers in five small- to moderate-sized cities in
three midwestern states and in one state agency in each of
the states, with roughly 40 percent returning completed
questionnaires, Miller found that a "heavy majority reported
general satisfaction with their jobs. In every one of the 8
employing units surveyed, over 80 percent of the respondents rated their job as important, challenging, and interesting."[34]

Unquestionably, many untrue statements about public
employees circulate in the community without effective
refutation by government. It is not easy to deal with this
situation, particularly since public agencies are suspected,
rightly so in many cases, of employing public relations
gimmicks to create false images. The National Federation of
Federal Employees (NFFE) has conducted a Truth Campaign to demonstrate how an employee organization can
effectively rebut allegations about public employees published in the press or made verbally by spokesmen for different organizations. NFFE now has an established mechanism
for being informed by its members and others of such allegations and sends letters with thorough, well-documented

---

[33] See George Olmsted, "Can Business Meet the Growing Demand for
Managers?" *Personnel Administration,* 32, No. 5 (September–October
1969), 31–32, and Richard E. Dutton, "What Turns Today's College Graduate Off," *Personnel Administration,* 33, No. 6 (November–December 1970),
9–17.

[34] Glenn W. Miller, "Manpower in the Public Sector," *Public Personnel
Review,* 33, No. 1 (January 1972), 51.

comments on the charges to the person who made them. These replies, which are published in the NFFE journal, are a morale booster for the members. No other organization offers a comparable service, although many professional societies, public officials, editorial writers, and community leaders do try to dispel false statements about government workers.

■ THE INFLUENCE OF UNIONS ON HIRING PRACTICES

One of the fears about increased public employee unionization has been that employment would take place through a union hiring hall, in the closed shop arrangement whereby only union members can be considered. Actually, the Taft-Hartley Act prohibits the closed shop, and, although it exists in the building trades and a few other kinds of employment, there never has been any real danger of it in the public sector.

Under a union shop agreement, permitted under Taft-Hartley except where prohibited by state law, the employee need not be a member of the union at the time of employment, but to retain the job he must join the union within a specified period, usually 30 days after appointment. The union cannot obtain an employee's discharge for any reason other than nonpayment of dues, even if it expels him from the union. Under the agency shop, which has been declared legal in the private sector by the U.S. Supreme Court, to retain their jobs nonunion members of the bargaining unit must pay a "fee equal in amount to the union initiation fees, periodic dues, and general assessments" to defray the union's costs in negotiating contracts and otherwise representing them before the employer.[35]

Since both union and agency shops impose an employment requirement unrelated to ability to do the job, they are opposed by many merit system supporters. In the federal

[35] State of California, *Final Report of the Assembly Advisory Council on Public Employee Relations*, March 15, 1973, p. 244.

service, both kinds of shops are prohibited for nonpostal workers by Executive Order 11491 as amended; the Postal Reorganization Act bans the union shop for postal employees. Most state public worker collective bargaining statutes make no express references to union and agency shops, but this does not mean that they are prohibited, and, in fact, they are negotiated in some of these states. A few of these statutes permit or require such shops, with some notable recent additions.[36] In 1973 Rhode Island and Minnesota passed legislation requiring nonunion members in exclusive bargaining units to make payments to the bargaining agent to help meet the costs of representing them. Washington amended both its civil service and higher education personnel laws to permit the certified representative to request the director of personnel to conduct a secret ballot election on the single issue of the union shop, with a majority vote determining the issue.[37]

Although still not common, many agency and union shop agreements now exist in the government, with the prospect of many more being negotiated in the future. With few exceptions, the expected opposition by the civil service employees concerned has not materialized; in Philadelphia, which has a modified union shop (there is an escape clause permitting employees to drop out of the union at specified periods), the director of personnel reports that a few do drop out, and then usually because they think the union has not done enough for them.[38] The theory that the union and agency shops are industrial creations which are offensive to professional workers in government has not been borne out. In truth, some professional groups have a long tradition of strong support for compulsory membership; representatives of the National Education Association and of the American Nurses Association recently both testified in support of a bill for

---

[36] Ibid., pp. 250–56.

[37] See *The Public Employee*, 38, No. 6 (June 1973), p. 6; 38, No. 4 (April 1973), p. 11; and 38, No. 6 (June 1973), p. 11.

[38] See Felix A. Nigro, *Management-Employee Relations in the Public Service* (Chicago: International Personnel Management Association, 1969), p. 96.

federal mandate of collective bargaining in state and local governments with permissive union shop provisions.[39]

Many employee leaders argue that the bigger memberships and financial support made possible by union and agency shops can make them more effective as an aid to management in *strengthening* the merit system. This may seem farfetched, but it is credible in light of the ability of the unions, through collective agreements and court action, to obtain the end of spoils appointments in jobs long filled through party machines, as in Pennsylvania and Illinois.[40] The evidence to date does not indicate that union and agency shops have damaged the merit system. Neither is there any indication that those who are most directly concerned—the general body of civil service workers—are much concerned about this issue.

In their 1972 study of 19 local governments, David Stanley and Carole Cooper found that unions may seek to change qualification requirements when it will benefit their members, as in raising standards of experience so that higher pay can be justified, as was done for building inspectors in Milwaukee and blue-collar craftsmen in San Francisco. Unions also object to changes they believe will debase entrance requirements, as exemplified by the objections of fire and police organizations to reductions in height requirements and the resistance of unions with large memberships of professionally trained workers to any lowering of educational requirements. Some unions either oppose or are lukewarm to special programs for employment of the disadvantaged in which some employment requirements are dropped or modified; others, like District Council No. 37 of the American Federation of State, County, and Municipal Employees in New York City, strongly support such programs.[41]

---

[39] House Special Subcommittee on Labor, *Labor-Management Relations in the Public Sector* (Washington, D.C.: Government Printing Office, 1972), pp. 2, 161, and 416–23.

[40] See David Prosten, "Patronage Takes a Lump in Pa.," *The Public Employee*, 36, No. 11 (November 1971), 16 and "No Firing for Politics, Court Rules," *The Public Employee*, 37, No. 7 (October 1972), 7.

[41] See David T. Stanley, with Carole L. Cooper, *Managing Local Government under Union Pressure* (Washington, D.C.: Brookings Institution, 1972), pp. 32–34.

Unions have concentrated much more on promotions and the grievance procedure than on recruitment; some union leaders have said that civil service commissions should be *limited* to recruitment. Possibly unions will develop their positions on specific phases of recruitment after they have achieved more with respect to other aspects of the personnel program they now deem more urgent.

BIBLIOGRAPHY

Bartholemew, D. J., and B. R. Morris. *Aspects of Manpower Planning*. New York: American Elsevier Publishing Co., 1971.

Brock, Alden L. "Planning the Recruitment Program," in Jerome Donovan (ed.), *Recruitment and Selection in the Public Service*, Chicago: International Personnel Management Association, 1968.

D.C. Government Personnel Office. *Manpower Planning: The State of the Art*, April 1973. Reproduced by National Technical Information Service, U.S. Department of Commerce, Springfield, Va. 22151.

Galloway, Robert W. "The Phoenix Affirmative Action Experience." *Good Government*, 89, No. 3 (Fall 1972).

Georgetown University Law Center. *The Closed Door: The Effect of a Criminal Record on Employment with State and Local Public Agencies*. Washington, D.C., February 1972. Distributed by National Technical Information Service, U.S. Department of Commerce, Springfield, Va. 22151.

Institute for Local Self-Government. *Public Employment and the Disadvantaged*. Berkeley, Calif., January 1970.

International Personnel Management Association. *Employment of the Disadvantaged in the Public Service*. Chicago, 1970.

Joint Commission on Correctional Manpower and Training. *A Time to Act*. Washington, D.C., 1969.

Macy, John W., Jr. *Public Service: The Human Side of Government*. New York: Harper & Row, Publishers, 1971. Chaps. 4–7.

Municipal Manpower Commission. *Governmental Manpower for Tomorrow's Cities*. New York: McGraw-Hill Book Co., 1962.

National Manpower Council. *Government and Manpower*. New York: Columbia University Press, 1964.

Nielson, Gordon L., and Allen R. Young. "Manpower Planning: A Markov Chain Application." *Public Personnel Management*, 2, No. 2 (March–April 1973).

Nigro, Felix A. "Unions and New Careers." *Good Government*, 87, No. 3 (Fall 1970).

"Pacemaker: A Handbook for Civil Service Change, Removing Artificial Barriers to the Poor in Public Employment." *Good Government*, 90, No. 1 (Spring 1973).

Pati, Gopal C. "Ex-Offenders Make Good Employees." *Public Personnel Management*, 2, No. 6 (November–December 1973).

Powell, Norman. *Personnel Administration in Government*. Englewood Cliffs, N.J.: Prentice-Hall, Inc., 1956. Chap. 9.

President's Commission on Law Enforcement and Administration of Justice. *Task Force Report: The Police*. Washington, D.C.: Government Printing Office, 1967.

Watson, Ian C. "Identifying and Reducing Manpower Imbalance in the Public Service of Canada." *Public Personnel Management*, 3, No. 4 (July–August 1974).

White, Leslie R. *New Careers in Local Government*. Berkeley, Calif.: Institute for Local Self-Government, 1969.

Selection

This chapter will first describe traditional civil service selection methods. New requirements for test validity to ensure equal employment opportunities for all potential applicants will then be discussed in detail, and the latest developments in the issues of eligibility, validity, and the merit principle will be briefly evaluated.

■ TRADITIONAL MEASUREMENT DEVICES

In traditional civil service selection procedures there are several measures of capacity which are generally used: (1) minimum qualification requirements, (2) evaluation of training and experience, (3) written tests, (4) performance tests, (5) oral examinations, and (6) background checks. All are not used in filling all jobs, and several are usually combined in a battery of tests and evaluation procedures. Since different kinds of abilities may be needed for satisfactory performance on a job, and since different tests measure different things, efforts are made to include in the battery the best available combination of tests for measuring all the required abilities.

Each test is weighted in accordance with the civil service agency's research or other evidence as to the relative importance of the qualifications it measures. Ideally, the precise weights would be determined only after thorough research on the relationship of given qualities to job success in the particular position. Too often, however, time and funds have not been available for such research, and technicians have had to use their best judgment.[1] In only two of the many possibilities, the written and oral examinations may each be assigned a weight of 5 out of 10, or the written may count for 6 and the oral for 4. The minimum qualifications are not weighted, and neither is the background check; as the latter is generally employed, it is considered qualifying or disqualifying only.

Every selection device should possess *validity*, which means that it should accurately measure what it purports to measure. In civil service selection, what is assessed are the knowledge, skills, abilities, and other worker characteristics deemed necessary or important for performing a particular job. If no careful job analysis is made, or if the analysis is erroneous in significant aspects, tests may be chosen that lack validity for that job, although they may be valid for other kinds of positions.

Selection devices should also possess *reliability*, meaning consistency. Reliability is a measure "of the degree to which chance factors affect . . . scores."[2] A test is reliable if the same persons, taking it on different occasions, make the same relative scores. Many factors affect reliability, such as the physiological or psychological state of the test taker, variations in the conditions under which the test is administered or graded, and the number of items.[3] Obviously, a test cannot be valid unless it is reliable.

[1] See John W. Jackson, "Planning and Constructing Promotion Examinations," in J. J. Donovan (ed.), *Recruitment and Selection in the Public Service* (Chicago: International Personnel Management Association, 1968), p. 326.
[2] Vernon R. Taylor, *Test Validity in Public Personnel Selection* (Chicago: International Personnel Management Association, n.d.), p. 2.
[3] See American Psychological Association, *Standards for Educational and Psychological Tests and Manuals* (Washington, D.C., 1966), p. 26.

Minimum qualifications

Some minimum qualifications for civil service, such as residence and age, may be fixed by law and may reflect social policy. The personnel agency has no discretion in application of these qualifications, beyond determining whether or not to press for changes in the law.

To determine training and experience requirements, personnel technicians depend upon job analysis and consultation with the supervisors in the department in which the positions exist. As part of the position classification survey, classification technicians review statements by supervisors indicating the kinds of work backgrounds they consider essential or desirable for jobs performed under their direction. Those in charge of constructing or selecting available tests should make their own independent job analyses, but often they are principally guided by the minimum-qualification statements in the class specifications.

Generally, validity studies have not been made of minimum-qualification requirements.[4] Demonstrating the validity of any kind of selection device is far from easy, as will be shown later in this chapter, and funds may not be available for such studies. Minimum requirements are often made more flexible by providing for substitution of education for experience up to a certain point, and vice versa, and by including the catch-all phrase "or any equivalent combination of training and experience."

The evaluation of training and experience

For positions beyond the beginning level, a written test, or both a written and an oral test, are often part of the battery, but these tests cannot be assumed to constitute a valid measurement of all the requirements of the position. In these cases some evaluation of training and experience is necessary. Sometimes this evaluation will take the place of

---

[4] See Kenneth A. Millard, "Improving Selection through Research," in Donovan, *Recruitment and Selection*, pp. 370–71.

a written test, because suitable tests are not available or desired candidates will not apply if they have to take them, as may be true of executives and professionals who are already successful in their careers. In such a case, an unassembled examination (candidates do not assemble together in one place to take a written examination) can account for 100 percent of the candidate's examination rating.

The procedure in evaluating training and experience is for a civil service examiner to analyze the information each candidate submits on his background in his application and any supplemental data and then arrive at a numerical grade designating each one's training and experience. The desirable procedure is for the examining staff to prepare beforehand rating schedules showing the relative values to be assigned to various types of training and experience.

One criticism of the evaluation of training and experience is that too much importance is given to length instead of quality of experience. In many cases these criticisms can be substantiated because the evaluation criteria are not sound. The U.S. Civil Service Commission believes that the most promising system is one which provides for evaluating abilities in relation to job elements "defined by a systematic job analysis process."[5] Job elements are knowledges, skills, abilities, and personal characteristics which are determined to constitute significant requirements for workers in the particular jobs. Candidates are rated in accordance with various "evidences" considered acceptable for demonstrating competence in the different job elements. For example, ratings on the job element Knowledge of the Theory of Electronics are based on such evidence as: "verified experience in mathematical analysis requiring electronic theory *or* outstanding record in advanced theory courses *or* score of 85–100 on theory test." This evidence is given the highest point value for the job element; other evidences are assigned lower point values or none at all.[6]

---

[5] Albert P. Maslow, "Evaluating Training and Experience," in Donovan, *Recruitment and Selection*, p. 247.

[6] Ibid., p. 253.

The basic problem with evaluation of training and experience has been lack of research. Validity studies have often not been made.

Written tests

Both achievement and aptitude tests are employed in civil service selection. The purpose of achievement tests is to determine whether the candidate possesses the knowledge necessary to perform the job without additional extended training. Aptitude tests are intended to predict ability to learn the job, not ability to perform the duties immediately. Despite the early emphasis on "practical" tests, civil service agencies have been making substantial use of aptitude testing for some time. Often both achievement and aptitude type questions are combined in the same examination.

All tests have degrees of subjectivity, since the determination of the abilities and knowledges to be sampled, as well as the preparation of scoring keys, is the work of humans who, no matter how expert, are fallible. The form of test most commonly used is multiple choice; since the answers are machine scored, many people refer to them as "objective." Little use is made of essay-type examinations, because time and other constraints make it impossible to include enough essay questions to obtain the broad sample of the candidate's abilities and knowledges required, whereas dozens and hundreds of items can be included in multiple-choice tests. It is also much more time-consuming to grade essay responses, and readers will evaluate the answers differently, which can cause low rater reliability.

Unfortunately, many civil service agencies have not validated the tests their examiners have constructed, or, if the tests were purchased or otherwise obtained from outside sources, they have not exercised sufficient care to assure that they are valid for the positions for which they are used. The reasons include lack of funds, lethargy, and the very low priority given to personnel research. An even more impelling reason, until recently, has been the absence of strong, effective community pressures for test validation. Most private employers also have not validated their tests until pressure is applied.

Performance tests

Practical tests "in which the candidate performs a sample of the actual work that is found on the job"[7] are called performance tests. This type of test has been employed mostly in the selection of typists, stenographers, machine and equipment operators, and candidates for such skilled jobs as cement finisher and tree trimmer. Applicants must demonstrate how efficient they are in the particular skill or equipment use required for the position. Performance tests are eminently practical and are generally favorably viewed both by the candidates and the public. Until recently, little consideration was given, however, to using them for jobs other than those of the types mentioned above.

Oral examinations

The oral examination has generally served to evaluate personality characteristics, but sometimes this type of test is used to ascertain job content knowledges and skills and to assess work background. The greatest use has been for positions at intermediate and higher levels, although an oral examination also is often included in the battery for entrance-level positions. This type of test has an early history of being viewed with great suspicion by candidates and merit system supporters who were anxious to prevent political and other extraneous influences in the examining process. As the importance of personal qualities in determining job success has become clearer, however, the oral examination has become more widely accepted, and attention has shifted to improving it rather than curtailing its use.

The individual interview is the type of oral test usually employed. The candidate appears by himself before an interview panel which questions him, notes his reactions, and rates his behavior. The duration varies, normally from around 20 to 60 minutes. Commonly, the panel members each complete interview rating forms which describe the characteristics to be evaluated, and their ratings then are averaged.

---

[7] Roscoe W. Wisner, "Construction and Use of Performance Tests," in Donovan, *Recruitment and Selection*, p. 190.

In the group oral test candidates are assembled in small groups, and a topic is assigned for discussion. Civil service examiners are seated in the room, but not at the conference table; they function as observers, noting what takes place during the discussion. Advocates of the group oral type of test argue that the candidate's behavior in interacting with others can be evaluated. As listeners only, the examiners have a better opportunity to observe each candidate, and the participants find the process more acceptable since they witness the performance of their competitors.

It is not certain, however, that the candidates would conduct themselves on the job in the same way. Furthermore, the examiners may be so distracted in trying to observe first one candidate and then another that they have less opportunity to size up each person than they would in individual interviews. Raters also may measure each participant against the standard of the particular group instead of in terms of the requirements for the position, in which case the candidate suffers or shines depending upon the verbal skills, maturity, and other characteristics of the persons in the group. Giving both individual and group orals has strong support, and in filling some positions, both kinds are administered.

There has also been a paucity of validity studies and research on the oral examination. It has been demonstrated that the validity of ratings increases with the number of interviewers, but "it does no good to pool ratings [of several interviewers] unless the single judgments are better than a mere guess."[8] Research on the oral is particularly difficult because much depends upon the skill of the individual examiners.

Background investigations

The background investigation may consist of a routine reference check by mail, perhaps supplemented by telephone inquiries, or it may be carried out by investigators who visit with previous employers and others who have direct knowl-

---

[8] Donald R. Morrison, "The Interview in Personnel Selection," in Donovan, *Recruitment and Selection*, pp. 233–34.

edge of the candidate's preparation, work experience, abilities, and personal qualities. Because of financial limitations and time pressures, civil service agencies have generally not made thorough background checks except for positions such as those for police departments, but even in these cases the checking is often far from thorough.

The neglect of this phase of the selection process is regrettable because those who have supervised candidates on previous jobs, have worked with them as colleagues and subordinates, or have known them for substantial periods of time can supply far more information about them than can be obtained in any interview. One of the findings of an intensive New York City–Rand Institute study of the employment histories of the more than 2,000 police officers appointed in 1957 was that "the rating of candidates by Police Department background investigators was a good predictor of later performance. . . . In general, the men they rated 'excellent' turned out to be well above average, and many of those termed 'poor' or 'disapproved' were later found to be departmental discipline problems."[9]

■ ELIGIBLE LISTS AND CERTIFICATION

Selection for civil service in the United States traditionally has meant ranking the successful candidates on eligible lists in the order of their final examination scores and certifying the top three names when filling requests for eligibles. In some merit systems the "rule of one" is substituted; one of the first acts of Mayor Abraham Beame of New York City was to restore the former practice of certifying only one name because of criticisms of favoritism in the previous administration's use of the rule of three.[10] In some jurisdictions, minority groups, convinced that the rule of three is manipulated repeatedly to pass over their members, have urged the rule of one.[11]

---

[9] Bernard Cohen and Jan M. Chaiken, *Police Background Characteristics and Performance* (Lexington, Mass.: D. C. Heath & Co., 1973), p. 83, p. 123.

[10] Murray Schumach, "Beame Says Aides Must Hew to Line on Civil Service," *New York Times*, January 3, 1974.

[11] Ervin Baker, "Rules Tightened for City Civil Service Selections," *Los Angeles Times*, July 17, 1968.

The rule of three has long been criticized, particularly since candidates often are separated on eligible lists by fine differences in numerical grades, sometimes fractions of a point. Even assuming that tests are improved, many appointing officers argue that they should have more discretion in making their selections than is permitted by the rule of three. Frequently, no weighted oral is included in the test battery and the officials, in making their own inquiries about the three persons certified, become convinced that they need more latitude for choice.

The first Hoover Commission on Organization of the Executive Branch of the Government (1949) recommended that "category ratings" be used instead of numerical grades; the categories might be "outstanding," "well qualified," "qualified," and "unqualified." Appointing officers would first consider eligibles certified from the "outstanding" group, but they would not be limited to three names and could ask to see candidates in the lower categories as well.[12] Category ratings have been adopted in very few cases, but in recent years a substantial number of state and local governments has been certifying more than three names, in some cases the entire list.[13] Those who oppose certifying the entire list or supplying quite a few names (such as ten, the new rule in the Minnesota state service for open competitive examinations) believe that this places far too much reliance on the subjective judgments of the appointing officers who interview the candidates. During much of the post–World War II period, personnel shortages in many kinds of work have made the rule of three less restrictive than previously; with few names on the registers, most eligibles in these shortage areas received job offers fairly quickly.

Under *selective certification*, an eligible with specialized qualifications may be certified no matter what his standing on the register. However, the appointing officer must first con-

---

[12] See Commission on Organization of the Executive Branch of the Government, *Task Force Report on Federal Personnel* (Washington, D.C.: Government Printing Office, 1949), pp. 24–25.

[13] See Jacob J. Rutstein, "Survey of Current Personnel Systems in State and Local Government," *Good Government*, 88, No. 1 (Spring 1971), 15; and Citizens League Report, *Strengthening Leadership in the Career Public Service* (Minneapolis, 1973), pp. 16, 23.

vince the central personnel agency that such specialization is required and that the desired candidate possesses these qualifications. Selective certification has long been permitted in civil service systems, although on a limited basis, the fear being that it might be abused to the detriment of the merit principle.

■ NEW REQUIREMENTS FOR TEST VALIDITY

In *Griggs* v. *Duke Power Company*,[14] the U.S. Supreme Court ruled that if a test has an adverse effect in terms of race, color, sex, religion, or national origin, and if its validity has not been demonstrated, its use constitutes unlawful discrimination under Title VII of the Civil Rights Act of 1964. Since the Equal Employment Opportunity Act of 1972 amended this legislation to extend coverage to "governments," "governmental agencies," and "political subdivisions,"[15] this ruling now applies to both public and private sectors.

If no adverse effect can be shown in court, evidence of validity is not required. In court cases, the plaintiffs have used four methods[16] to show adverse effect:

1. Comparison of the rejection rates of one subgroup with those of another subgroup (e.g., blacks compared to whites, women to men).
2. Comparison of the percentage of the employer's work force represented by the number of employees in a subgroup with that subgroup's percentage of the total population in the jurisdiction.
3. Comparison between percentage of a subgroup's employment with that percentage for similar employers.
4. Proof that the hiring policy excluded or restricted employment of a subgroup's members.

---

[14] 401 U.S. 424 (1971). See National Civil Service League, *Judicial Mandates for Affirmative Action* (Washington, D.C., 1973), pp. 5–19. Includes entire text of decision.

[15] Public Law 92–261, 92nd Congress, H.R. 1746, March 24, 1972, Sec. 2 (1).

[16] Richard E. Biddle, *Discrimination: What Does It Mean?* (Chicago: International Personnel Management Association, 1973), pp. 8–13.

The courts have not fixed a certain percentage which automatically proves adverse effect, but an Equal Employment Opportunity Commission (EEOC) attorney has said, "My guess is that if the court can't 'eyeball' the figures and determine the disparity—plaintiff will be in big trouble."[17]

In the *Griggs* case, the Supreme Court stated: "Under the Act, practices, procedures, or tests neutral on their face, and even neutral in terms of intent, cannot be maintained if they operate to 'freeze' the status quo of prior discriminatory practices."[18] Thus the validity of *any* employment practice must be demonstrated, or the court will rule it illegal; lack of intent to discriminate is not an allowable defense.

Before passage of the 1972 amendments, the EEOC had issued "Guidelines on Employer Selection Procedures," which sets forth requirements for establishing validity of selection instruments.[19] In the summer of 1973, to provide a coordinated approach by the various federal agencies with civil rights responsibilities, the Equal Employment Opportunity Coordinating Council (created by the Civil Rights Act of 1964 and consisting of the EEOC, the Commission on Civil Rights, the Civil Service Commission, the Department of Justice, and the Department of Labor) issued a draft of proposed uniform guidelines to be applied by each Council member.[20] As this is written, these proposals were still under consideration. The salient features are:

1. Systematic and comprehensive job analyses are required before any test is used for *any* employment decision, not just original appointment.

2. Selection devices intended to predict performance on a higher level job than the one for which the employee is initially selected are permissible only when it is probable that the appointee will progress to such a job within a reasonable period of time.

---

[17] Ibid., p. 11.

[18] National Civil Service League, *Judicial Mandates for Affirmative Action*, p. 17.

[19] See *Federal Register*, 35, 12333, August 1, 1970.

[20] Equal Employment Opportunity Coordinating Council, *Uniform Guidelines on Employee Selection Procedures, Discussion Draft* (Washington, D.C., August 23, 1973).

3. If a test has an adverse effect on a subgroup, its validity must be demonstrated, relying on one or more of the following methods: criterion-related validation, content validation, or construct validation.[21]

In *criterion-related validity,* test scores are compared with criteria of job performance. In one method, after individuals have been on the job for some time the scores they made on their entrance examinations are compared with job performance measures. In another method, a proposed new test is tried out on existing employees, and their scores on this test are compared with job success criteria[22] especially developed as part of the experiment. An example of this second method is presented later in this chapter.

In *content validity,* the test is constructed to constitute a representative sample of the duties or abilities, skills, and knowledges necessary or desirable for successful job performance. Examples are written job-knowledge tests appropriate for the kind of work and level of responsibility and performance tests in which the actual duties are performed, as in typing and in welding.

In *construct validity,* the test is intended to measure a theoretical construct or trait which is less directly observable than in content validity (e.g., intelligence, mechanical comprehension, verbal fluency). It must be demonstrated that the test does measure the trait and that the trait is related to successful job performance.

A test for a legal position provides an example of the difference between content and construct validity. Such a test has content validity if it asks questions about specific provisions of law with which the incumbent must be familiar. It has construct validity if it accurately measures "ability to read and interpret material of the same complexity as that in which the laws are written. It is hypothesized that it would test ability to read and understand the laws."[23]

If performed correctly, each of the three methods of de-

---

[21] See APA, *Standards for Educational and Psychological Tests,* pp. 12–24.

[22] See Ohio Department of State Personnel, *Handbook of Job Proficiency Criteria,* GLAC Report, July 1973, p. 8.

[23] Taylor, *Validity in Public Personnel Selection,* p. 5.

termining validity requires considerable work and presents certain difficulties.

Difficulties with criterion-related validity

In small jurisdictions, usually not enough people are tested or hired in single job classifications to give a statistical sample sufficiently large for criterion-related studies comparing applicants' scores with measures of their performance after some time on the job. Even in large jurisdictions, the sample is big enough only in "relatively few classifications."[24] Since those who failed the test were not tried out on the job, such prior tryout not being feasible in civil service selection, it is possible that some or even many of them would have performed satisfactorily on the job. On the other hand, when tests are tried out on present employees, "it is not known whether the experimental subjects performed on the tests as they would have in a competitive situation."[25] Nor is it known to what extent their test scores were affected by the experience they had gained on the job.[26]

The development of valid job performance criteria is no easy task. Often the criterion used is ratings by supervisors. For more valid ratings, several persons — both supervisors and colleagues — may be asked to rate an employee, but (as discussed in Chapter 8) the subjective element in supervisory ratings is formidable. Other criterion measures are: actual job performance data (e.g., production records); such personnel data as absenteeism and turnover rates; job knowledge tests; and simulated performance measures (e.g., work samples). Several criterion measures should be employed rather than just one, for all have strengths and weaknesses.[27]

Procedures in content validity studies

In explaining the procedures followed in making content validity studies, we will rely on a special report prepared by

---

[24] Ibid., p. 10.
[25] Ibid., p. 11.
[26] Millard, "Improving Selection through Research," p. 370.
[27] Ohio Department of State Personnel, *Handbook of Job Proficiency Criteria*, pp. 7–9.

the Great Lakes Assessment Council, with funding under the Intergovernmental Personnel Act.[28] The Council, which consists of representatives from state and municipal agencies in Illinois, Indiana, Michigan, Minnesota, Wisconsin, and Ohio, is primarily concerned with the improvement of validation procedures in the selection process.

The position of housing inspector is given as an example. In the first step, the test construction technicians review all materials already prepared which provide information about the position, such as job descriptions and functional statements in inspection department handbooks, and they also observe some housing inspectors carrying out their work. The technicians then prepare a tentative goal statement (relationship of the position to the goals of the organization), as well as detailed statements of position tasks. These materials serve as the basis for meetings with the inspection department head, division and field supervisors, and experienced housing inspectors, in which the participants are asked to review critically the tentative task statements.

Once agreement is reached on these statements, each participant is asked to list the knowledges, skills, and personal characteristics required for satisfactory performance of each task, justifying each requirement by describing an actual case where its presence or absence resulted in effective or ineffective job behavior. The technicians review all material so obtained and then prepare a tentative list of required knowledges, skills, and personal characteristics for further discussion with the participants and final review and alteration as necessary. For each task in the tentative list, general categories of knowledges and skills are listed, as well as subcategories; for example, the general category "familiarity with general construction and environmental factors relating to the housing code" is subdivided into (a) structure; (b) electrical; (c) plumbing; (d) heating; (e) ventilation: (f) fire protection; (g) health; and (h) safety.

---

[28] Stephen J. Mussio and Mary K. Smith, *Content Validity: A Procedural Manual* (Chicago: International Personnel Management Association, 1973).

After the final list is prepared, it is sent to the participants who are asked to weigh both the general categories in terms of their importance for the job as a whole and the subcategories within each general category. The average weights for categories and subcategories are then computed and converted into percentages. Thus, in the example above, the percentage for the general category might be 20, with 10 percent for each subcategory except health and safety, both of which might be 20 percent. The sum of all general categories is, of course, 100 points, as it is for all subcategories in each general category.

The test technicians then develop examination content, which is as similar as possible to the job tasks. The preferred format is job task replica or simulation, but, if this is not feasible, others can be used. For example, in testing "knowledge of general construction principles" it would be difficult in a replicated or simulated work sample to measure comprehensively the needed representative sample of content knowledge, so a written multiple-choice test can be given. To assess "ability to translate observations into written form," if there are too many applicants for an on-site test the candidates are asked to observe and comment in writing on slides showing unsafe or unsanitary housing (simulation). A similar use of slides is appropriate for measuring "ability to explain purpose of code and hazardous consequences of noncompliance"; the task cannot be replicated because knowledge of the code is not a prerequisite for employment.

After the test technicians have prepared all the test items, a panel of three or more experts in the "specific content area under consideration" is asked to review all "examination content selections" as to job relevancy, accuracy, and fairness. The panel members do this independently by placing the item cards into three categories: unacceptable, acceptable, and acceptable with minor revisions. If they disagree on the acceptability of an item, it is placed in the unacceptable category; items initially classified as acceptable with minor revisions become acceptable only by unanimous agreement of the experts.

The experts are also asked to fill out a relevancy scale to

record their judgments on each item with respect to whether the knowledges and skills represented by the item reflect minimum, better than average, or superior performance. The average score for each item is used to determine which items are *basic* (required of any employee) and which are *advanced* (discriminate between average and superior employees). The division into these two components is the basis for setting the examination cutoff (passing) score, which is the number of basic components. For example, if 30 components were identified, 15 basic and 15 advanced, a total score of 15 would be passing. The score of 15 could be made up of any combination of basic and advanced components.

Content validity is preferred by many personnel agencies because it avoids the technical and other difficulties of criterion-related studies. Supervisory ratings, which are considered by many test experts to be the largest source of errors in criterion-related studies, are not required for content validity. Yet since the judgments of the expert panel are not infallible, some subjectivity remains.

Test expert Thelma Hunt believes that

> content validity is a completely satisfactory validation procedure only in those cases of testing for coverage of a defined knowledge or other content. . . . In the case of police officer applicants, for example, there may be fairly well defined content for aspects of police academy training. However, there is no defined content for police work generally upon which selection tests for applicants can rest.[29]

Other experts believe that content validity tests can be developed for any job and that content validity should therefore be the primary strategy for public employment tests.[30] Vernon R. Taylor states that "content validity is particularly

---

[29] Thelma Hunt, "Various Approaches to Validity in Employee Selection," paper presented at International Conference on Public Personnel Administration, November 25–30, 1973, Miami Beach, Fla.

[30] Comment by William Gorham, Director of the U.S. Civil Service Commission's Personnel Research and Development Center.

applicable to achievement tests" and construct validity to aptitude tests.[31]

Construct validity

The constructs hypothesized in tests for public employees most often are intelligence, aptitudes of different kinds, and learning ability. Written tests, whether of the achievement or aptitude variety, require knowledge of certain vocabulary and familiarity with certain cultural concepts, and general intelligence tests are viewed by many (test experts and others) as particularly unfair to minority groups. It is argued that often the constructs hypothesized, such as verbal ability, numerical ability, and abstract reasoning, have no demonstrable relationship to successful job performance. In this case, general intelligence tests are invalid selection devices for applicants of any ethnic background.

William Enneis has pointed out that "all our educational and employment tests are *ability* tests, that all ability tests are achievement tests which tap the product of learning and biographical structure, and that the only real difference between an achievement test and an aptitude test is the *purpose* for which it is given." The use of aptitude tests is based on "the assumption that all applicants have been exposed to the same general opportunities for learning, since, on the basis of the 'equal exposure concept,' those persons who have the greater capacities for learning will have achieved more, as measured by tests, and would be the more likely persons to learn, for example, job skills."[32] Persons from deprived backgrounds have not had equal opportunities for learning the verbal skills and other achievements in the dominant white, middle-class culture which are measured by aptitude tests. This does not mean that they cannot learn the skills required in the jobs concerned or,

---

[31] Taylor, *Validity in Public Personnel Selection*, p. 19.

[32] William H. Enneis, "Misuses of Tests," in *Personnel Testing and Equal Employment Opportunity* (Washington, D.C.: Government Printing Office, 1971), p. 33.

for that matter, cannot perform them well immediately upon appointment.

Mean scores for blacks on most paper-and-pencil tests of general ability, intelligence, aptitude, and learning ability are lower than those for whites because of the background of poverty of many blacks. As children, their ability to con-ceptualize is limited by the paucity of objects in their home environment. They lack curiosity and self-confidence, and "have had little experience in receiving approval for success in learning a task, an assumption on which the school culture is organized." They also have a "cognitive style which responds more to visual and kinesthetic signals than to oral or written stimuli," and they learn better by inductive rather than deductive approaches and by "moving from the part to the whole rather than from the whole to the part."[33] Deprived persons of other ethnic backgrounds, such as the Spanish-speaking, experience similar difficulties with gen-eral ability tests.

A major study. In 1972, the U.S. Civil Service Commission and the Educational Testing Service, with funding from the Ford Foundation, completed a six-year study[34] undertaken to determine whether aptitude tests accurately predicted job performance, whether they had equal validity for both minority and nonminority group members, and whether they unfairly discriminated against members of any group. The subjects in the study, the largest of its kind reported to date, numbered 1,409, including 423 blacks, 174 Mexican-Americans, and 812 Caucasians employed in three occupa-tions: medical technician, cartographic technician, and in-ventory manager. These occupations were selected because they included sizable groups of non-Caucasian individuals who were employed under common supervision in similar

[33] Phyllis Wallace, Beverly Kissinger, and Betty Reynolds, "Testing of Minority Group Applicants for Employment," in *Personnel Testing and Equal Employment Opportunity*, p. 3.

[34] Educational Testing Service, *An Investigation of Sources of Bias in the Prediction of Job Performance, A Six-Year Study*, proceedings of Inter-national Conference, New York, June 22, 1972 (Princeton, N.J., 1972).

jobs and with generally comparable backgrounds and who had not been selected through aptitude tests.

Based on intensive job analysis, tests were carefully selected to measure the "aptitude and ability factors considered critical to job performance," different sets of tests being used for each occupation. Test scores were then compared with at least two kinds of performance measures (1) in every case, supervisory rating scales specially constructed for each occupation, and (2) either job knowledge tests or work samples, or both. In the work samples, for example, cartographic technicians were given partial information about the characteristics of a certain terrain and then asked to construct a full map of the area. Statistical analyses were made of the correlations between test scores and the performance measurement criteria, and the results showed that the tests were positively related to the performance measures and were about as valid for one ethnic group as for the others.

The educational preparation of the blacks and Mexican-Americans in the study was good, mostly high school graduation or better, with a substantial percentage having some college work. They did not score as high as the Caucasians on either the aptitude tests or the objective criterion measures (job knowledge tests or work samples), which is why a test expert from the Institute of Afro-American Affairs emphasized that the "study does not vindicate tests as a 'color-blind' technique" and that it merely means that "with our present state of knowledge we do not find any measurable differences in prediction."[35] If the tests are color blind, the differences in raw scores must be satisfactorily explained. This expert believes that the lower scores of minority group members on both the tests and the objective criterion measures are attributable to the cumulative effect of variables resulting from the societal context "which are not usually measured and possibly, at the present time, cannot be measured in a reliable fashion." As an example of such variables, he offered his opinion that minority group mem-

[35] Ibid., p. 101.

bers who have not had peer relationships with whites often are "less aggressive, less competitive, and less innovative in searching out various solutions to practical on-the-job problems."[36]

The Institute test expert stated his opinion that

> It really is unreasonable to hire people with differential performance or aptitude scores at the time of recruitment, put them on the job, give them practically no training and then expect them to perform at identically the same level of people who came in with somewhat higher levels of aptitude. This is, in fact, what we have in the present study.[37]

His recommendation was to set relatively low cutoff scores for entry-level selection; two or three tests which measure the very basic skills required in a job would be administered, thus making possible the appointment of minimally qualified persons whose potential could then be developed through on-the-job training. In this way, minority group members who otherwise would fail the tests or not do as well on them as other applicants would be given the chance to show what they could do—a chance usually denied them because "society has provided neither adequate education nor social support for programs to improve the skills of minorities."[38] Those disagreeing believe that such a procedure cannot be reconciled with the merit principle of selection from among the best qualified.

Another expert reviewing the results of the study commented, "I can think of few, if any, real-life situations providing the time, facilities, and technical personnel to permit the kind of test validation represented by this study."[39] The Associate Director of the Civil Service Commission's Personnel Research and Development Center, noting the "great expense, considerable time, and . . . numerous technical problems," believed it questionable that the federal government or other employers will "want to conduct many

---

[36] Ibid., p. 102.
[37] Ibid., p. 103.
[38] Ibid., p. 104.
[39] Ibid., p. 87.

more research studies on this problem."[40] The Director of the Commission's Bureau of Policies and Standards thought that most public employers "will not be able to follow the path of doing criterion-related validation, particularly differential validation, for various subgroups."[41]

Implications of court decisions and guidelines on validity

The proposed uniform guidelines on employee selection procedures referred to earlier have been resisted by many state and local government officials, not on principle but because of the expected great cost of conducting so many validity studies and the lack of qualified personnel to conduct them. Much depends on how the guidelines are administered and the standards the judges apply in deciding court cases. No one expects public employers to be able to validate all phases of the selection procedure in a short time.

It is clear that employment standards and tests will become much more job related and that this is an important aspect of the new public personnel administration. For the foreseeable future, the courts will be making many technical personnel judgments, but hopefully they eventually will be able to reduce their role as public employers improve their validity capability.

■ ELIGIBILITY, VALIDITY, AND THE MERIT PRINCIPLE

A recent disagreement between the City of Sacramento, California, and the U.S. Civil Service Commission illustrates the conflicting opinions with respect to the effect on merit principles of proposed new rules for certifying names from eligible lists.[42] The Sacramento Civil Service Commission

---

[40] William A. Gorham, "Is Testing Fair For All? New Answers on Employment Tests," *Civil Service Journal*, 13, No. 2 (October–December 1972), 11.

[41] Educational Testing Service, *Investigation of Sources of Bias*, p. 91.

[42] See William F. Danielson, "Affirmative Action in the Public Sector: Where Do We Stand Today?" in Lloyd G. Nigro (ed.), "A Mini-Symposium, Affirmative Action in Public Employment," *Public Administration Review*, 34, No. 3 (May–June 1974), 241–42.

adopted a rule permitting selection certification on the basis of race, the objective being to make faster progress in achieving affirmative action goals for the employment of blacks in the fire department. The number of blacks already employed as firefighters was so small that the personnel director and the commission were convinced it would take many years to increase it substantially. They saw no violation of merit principles because, as the personnel director argued, the firefighter position did not require previous experience, and eligible list rankings did not really distinguish between the eligibles in terms of ability to do the job. The U.S. Civil Service Commission disagreed and recommended suspension of federal grant-in-aid funds for civil defense activities in the city, since the new certification rule covered all civil service appointments.

The personnel director for Phoenix, Arizona, which has adopted the "rule of the entire list," believes that if affirmative action is to be realizable, there must be "some preference to redress past injustices. This does not mean hiring minorities just because they are minorities but hiring qualified minorities where they have been previously excluded, and where the factor of relative ability is either negligible or not verifiable."[43] In its model law, the National Civil Service League provides that the

> ... Director of Personnel, using objective criteria, shall categorize those persons eligible for a position as qualified. The appointing officers shall then make their selection from among such persons. If the list of qualified persons is excessively long, the jurisdiction may consider only certifying a workable number of persons to the appointing authority.[44]

The League has advocated using selective certification "when there is a job-related factor that will improve delivery of services" (e.g., empathy with a client group, as in welfare

---

[43] Robert Galloway, "Are Goals or Quotas Essential for Affirmative Action?" in *Advance*, 1, No. 2 (Summer 1973), p. 8. Studies in Public Manpower Modernization from the National Civil Service League's National Program Center for Public Personnel Management.

[44] National Civil Service League, *A Model Public Personnel Administration Law* (Washington, D.C., 1970), p. 7.

programs). It also has suggested selective certification where
the selection process has not been validated and "where
there is a clear racial or sex disparity in the appointment
process," as is frequently the case in police and fire services.[45]

Evaluation of developments

There are many new concepts of what merit means in public
service selection besides those reflected in the challenge
to the rule of three mentioned above. "Hire first and train
later" has many supporters, but this conflicts with the
traditional civil service requirement that the applicant be
qualified on appointment to perform the duties of the job.
Preexamination tutoring sessions, while not unknown under
civil service, have generally not been considered an obligation of the public employer. Examination passing scores
have been made flexible, but not with the objective of assuring employment of the minimally qualified. If it is demonstrated that the same range of test scores predicts job performance differently for minority group members than for
others, eligible list rankings should not be based on the
same raw scores. Frequent retesting of applicants who have
increased their training and experience is also emphasized
in equal employment opportunity programs. Although the
proposed guidelines state that this requirement is met if
the employer gives examinations periodically, in the past
many examinations have not been given frequently enough
to be considered periodical.[46]

Many public officials and members of the public reject the
idea that adjustments should be made in existing civil
service requirements to compensate for society's neglect of
the disadvantaged. They maintain that this inevitably will
destroy the merit system and that the remedies for social
injustice should be sought elsewhere. Some even see a new
spoils system developing, to provide jobs for blacks and

---

[45] "The National Civil Service League's Policy Statement on Equal
Employment Opportunity," in *Advance*, 1, No. 2 (Summer 1973), 29.

[46] EEO Coordinating Council, *Uniform Guidelines.*

other minorities. Nevertheless, traditional selection practices have had many weaknesses, and many of the recent changes —above all making test validity a legal obligation of the employer—represent solid improvement. Despite some dangers, therefore, the new developments are viewed by many as generally desirable.

BIBLIOGRAPHY

American Psychological Association. *Standards for Educational and Psychological Tests and Manuals.* Washington, D.C., 1966.

APA Task Force on Employment Testing of Minority Groups. "Job Testing and the Disadvantaged," *American Psychologist,* 24, No. 7 (July 1969).

Berger, Bernard, James McCormack, Harry Reiner, and Charles J. Setzer. *The Essay Test in Public Personnel Selection.* Chicago: International Personnel Management Association.

Biddle, Richard E. *Discrimination: What Does It Mean?* Chicago: International Personnel Management Association, 1973.

Dicks, Robert H. "Public Employment and the Disadvantaged: A Close, Hard Look at Testing." *Good Government,* 86, No. 4 (Winter 1969).

Donovan, Jerome J. (ed.). *Recruitment and Selection in the Public Service.* Chicago: International Personnel Management Association, 1968.

Educational Testing Service, *An Investigation of Sources of Bias in the Prediction of Job Performance, A Six-Year Study.* Proceedings of International Conference. New York, June 22, 1972. Princeton, N.J., 1972.

Educational Testing Service, *Selected References in Educational Measurement.* 3rd ed. Princeton, N.J., 1970.

Great Lakes Assessment Council. *Legal Aspects of Personnel Selection in the Public Service.* Chicago: International Personnel Management Association, 1973.

Lopez, Felix M., Jr. *Personnel Interviewing: Theory and Practice.* New York: McGraw-Hill Book Co., 1965.

Mandell, Milton M. *The Selection Process: Choosing the Right Man for the Job.* New York: American Management Association, 1964.

Mussio, Stephen J., and Mary K. Smith. *Content Validity: A Procedural Manual.* Chicago: International Personnel Management Association, 1973.

National Civil Service League. *Performance Testing.* Washington, D.C.

Office of Equal Employment Opportunity. *Personnel Testing and Equal Employment Opportunity.* Washington, D.C.: Government Printing Office, 1971.

Ohio Department of State Personnel. *Handbook of Job Proficiency Criteria.* GLAC Research Report, July 1973.

Sasso, Carmen D., and Earl P. Tanis. *Selection and Certification of Eligibles.* Chicago: International Personnel Management Association, 1974.

Taylor, Vernon R., *Essentials of Effective Personnel Selection,* Chicago: International Personnel Management Association.

U.S. Civil Service Commission. *How to Prepare and Conduct Job-Element Examinations.* Washington, D.C.: Personnel Research and Development Center, 1974.

Career
Management

8

Career management is a positive concept which stresses management's responsibility to help employees develop their potential at every stage in their employment with the organization and also with regard to continuation of their careers with other employers. It is an integrating concept because it considers the entire personnel program and how its various parts can be developed and interrelated so it will meet each employee's needs.

Career management, therefore, embraces all of the in-service personnel program—the management policies and status changes of individuals after appointment. In this chapter, we will describe the elements in an ongoing career management program and then examine the following aspects of the in-service personnel program: the probationary period, performance evaluation, promotion, transfer and mobility, reductions in force, and discipline. Training is dealt with in detail in Chapter 9, and grievances and appeals are considered in Chapter 10. Pay and classification systems were discussed in Chapter 5. Thus many parts of the career management process are treated in a single chapter, but other phases are covered in separate chapters.

■ ELEMENTS OF CAREER MANAGEMENT PLANNING

The results of an unprecedented effort to improve the management of the State Department which utilized 13 task forces of foreign service professionals from within the Department, the Foreign Service, and other federal agencies with international programs were published in 1970.[1] The summary report of all the task forces urged increased commitment to the principle of functional specialization in the recruitment, assignment, and promotion of Foreign Service Officers (FSOs). This principle, which had been strongly advanced by previous study groups, had guided FSO personnel policies since 1954, in recognition of the "wide range of special aptitudes, skills and knowledge which the new diplomacy requires" in such activities as agriculture, labor, commerce, finance, development economics, science, and information.[2]

The responsibility for recommending career management and assignment policies was given to Task Force I, which began its report[3] by reviewing the FSO career pattern agreed upon by all the task forces under a program of functional specialization. Before appointment, FSOs would choose a field of specialization (cone) from one of the following: political, economic/commercial, administrative, or consular. They would serve a probationary period of two to four years, during which time they would be given at least one overseas assignment in their tentative cones. The number of probationary FSO appointments each year would depend upon the estimated needs in each cone. (The entrance grade is FSO–7 or FSO–8.) Formal training during probation would

---

[1] U.S. Department of State, *Diplomacy for the 70's, A Program of Management Reform for the Department of State* (Washington, D.C.: Government Printing Office, December 1970).

[2] Ibid., p. 5.

[3] Ibid., p. 32.

consist of a brief orientation course and instruction in the required foreign languages. Taking into account those selected out and other "fallouts" during probation, an estimated two-thirds of the original group would receive commissions as FSO–6s.

By agreement with the Office of Personnel, the new FSO–6s would either continue in their tentative field of specialization or change it. As a transitional assignment from probation, they would undergo extended basic training. Between FSO–6 and FSO–3, they would receive assignments mostly in their specialties but also to broaden their backgrounds in the other cones. They would also get some assignments that had broader scope than a single cone, as in program direction or managerial work, and they would receive language instruction and training in the problems of certain geographic areas. Officers demonstrating managerial ability would be identified and given special training at the FSO–3 level. Many FSOs would retire as FSO–3s after 20 years of service.

At the FSO–2 and FSO–1 levels, assignments would be mostly "interfunctional," such as program direction and executive work, but a few assignments would be made to high-level specialist positions. There would be some additional training for the FSO–2s and for a very few FSO–1s in "broad policy problem exercises."

Up to FSO–3, promotions would be semiautomatic. As explained in the report of another task force, the great majority of officers progressing from Classes 6 to 3 have reached Class 3 at about the same time. Thus, the time and effort spent on selection board review of the files of officers at each class interval were not justified; "with much less effort, the majority could pass through the middle grades on a planned, orderly, and less hectic basis."[4] Semiautomatic promotion would mean that the officers would be advanced on the basis of seniority, as vacancies in the next higher rank occurred. Those rated particularly outstanding on their performance evaluations would be eligible for

---

[4] Ibid., p. 81.

faster promotion than those rated satisfactory; promotions for those judged weak would be delayed and, if they did not improve, they would be considered for possible selection out. After FSO–3, promotions would be by selection board and would be fully competitive. Class 3 officers would also be subject to selection out "as necessary."

Task Force I stressed the need to develop a system for placing the right persons in the right jobs at the right time (this is also an objective of the proposed Federal Executive Service, described in Chapter 4). While this is difficult to achieve in any organization, systematic planning with this precise objective had not characterized the Foreign Service assignment process in the past. Accordingly, it was suggested, all positions in the Department should be carefully reviewed and periodically reexamined to determine in which cone they belonged and the proper grade level, as well as to assure that the correct category of FSO was assigned to each position.

The personnel structure should assure challenging jobs for officers in the early stages of their careers. The report noted that this structure had become top-heavy, with too many officers in the senior grades and too few in the lower ones, thus causing serious underutilization of the abilities of the younger FSOs. It suggested that this should be corrected by "systematic reclassification of job levels to move more responsibility back down the ladder."[5] Promotion opportunities should be "approximately equal for all officers of equal competence without regard to cone," officers would remain in their cones from entry to retirement, with broadening assignments outside their cones, and the identification and training of those with managerial capacities would be carried out systematically.[6]

Adoption and implementation of these recommendations by the State Department have been only partial, but the proposals do illustrate what is meant by career management. The recommendation for semiautomatic promotion has not

[5] Ibid., p. 18.
[6] Ibid., p. 39.

been implemented, and selection boards still pass upon the promotion of all FSOs. While foreign service activities may be more predictable than many domestic programs, the same elements in career management planning are applicable in any public agency. Other policies in such areas as promotion in the middle ranks may be preferred, however.

The Internal Revenue Service (IRS) has a management careers program for the selection and development of all managerial personnel,[7] with management careers boards and subboards (the latter for each functional field such as audit-appellate) in each IRS region. Training officers help both applicants to and members of the managerial corps prepare individual development plans, which are then reviewed by training advisory committees and training advisory councils. The councils annually evaluate the effectiveness of the training and development aspects of the management careers program. The candidates themselves have an important role, submitting reports of their previous accomplishments and proposing their individual development plans, which include both work assignments and training courses. The General Accounting Office (GAO) has career counseling committees in each major organization unit which annually prepare a mutually agreeable development plan of the same kind for each auditor in Grades GS–7 to GS–13.[8]

■ THE PROBATIONARY PERIOD

The probationary or working test period is important for several reasons. From the selection standpoint, it is the last stage in the sifting process; no matter how much effort is put into making preemployment tests valid, they may not screen

---

[7] U.S. Department of the Treasury, Internal Revenue Service, *Southeast Region Management Careers Handbook,* and *1974 Executive Selection and Development Program,* April 2, 1973.

[8] William Kushnick and Leo Herbert, "Career and Professional Development in the U.S. General Accounting Office," *Public Personnel Review,* 32, No. 2 (April 1971), 87–90.

out some candidates who lack the ability to perform satisfactorily in the specific jobs. Since performance depends so
much on motivation, interest, and response to factors in the
work environment, probation gives supervisory officers the
opportunity to evaluate new employees in daily work situations over a period of time and to approve for permanent
status only those whose services have been satisfactory.
Probationary employees usually do not have appeal rights.
If they are not separated at this stage, it generally is much
more difficult to remove unsatisfactory employees later.

From the standpoint of career management, probation
marks the beginning of management's opportunity to benefit
from its investment in recruiting the new employee. This
entails increasing that investment with appropriate work
assignments and training. To the recruits, probation is a
test not just of themselves but also of the employer: if the
employer fails to offer them effective guidance and stimulus,
they may quit or, if they remain, work without enthusiasm.

In practice, only a tiny percentage of appointees—sometimes less than 1 percent—is weeded out as unsatisfactory
during or at the end of probation. This has always been the
case, despite such schemes to prod supervision as requiring
the appointing officer, ten days before the end of the trial
period, to certify in writing to the personnel office that the
employee's services have been satisfactory, or all salary
payments to the employee will be suspended. The appointing officer perfunctorily complies by rating the employee
satisfactory. Supervisors do not relish making decisions
which require the termination of a subordinate's employment, and they will not make effective use of the probationary period when they know the other supervisors are
not doing so. The personnel office cannot step in and make
this kind of determination because this would usurp the
functions of the program managers.

If the probationary period is not allowed to become a dead
issue, the question of its length is important. Usually the
duration is the same for all positions, but in some jurisdictions it is variable, depending upon the kind of position.
The reasoning is that for some kinds of work it takes longer

to decide whether the individual meets the job requirements. In any case, the length of the probationary period
usually does not exceed one year.

Normally, decisions as to the retention of probationers are
based on supervisory ratings, but sometimes a special procedure is followed. In the District of Columbia Metropolitan Police Department, a Board of Evaluation and Review, consisting of three sergeants selected by the chief of
police, was instituted in 1970 to review supervisory ratings
and all other information relating to the performance of all
probationary patrolmen, including their original appointment papers, police academy training scores, and medical
histories. The board interviewed the officers during their
9th, or no later than their 11th, month on the force, and
made this total review at that time. The final decision on
retention or separation of an officer was made by the chief
of police after he received the board's recommendation in
the case. The board mechanism was adopted because of the
rapid buildup in the force and the consequent possibility
of errors in recruitment due to haste. The composition of
the board has changed, but it continues with essentially the
same functions.[9]

The State Department task forces discussed above recommended that foreign service officers not only serve a longer
probationary period but also be passed upon by a Career
Review Panel before being approved for permanent status.
The Department accepted this recommendation, instituting
the review before promotion into Class 5. From the time of
admission, all junior officers remain in "career review"
status for a minimum period of three years, after which they
are eligible for "threshold review" and selection into
Class 5. Eligible officers are interviewed by a Threshold
Review Panel made up of three FSOs which considers the
officer's performance file. A Threshold Review Board, consisting of officers of the Department, with representatives
from other agencies and a public member as well, reviews

[9] Executive Management Service, Inc., *A Report on the Recruitment and
Selection Process of the District of Columbia Metropolitan Police Department* (Arlington, Va. April 1971), pp. 39–40.

the panel's findings and the officer's performance file and decides whether to make a recommendation for promotion to Class 5.[10]

Field research in 1969 in 15 cities and four counties reported by David Stanley and Carole Cooper indicated that union negotiators have been successful in some cases in reducing the length of the probationary period.[11] They cite Dade County, Florida, where the duration was reduced from six to four months for positions not requiring an examination, and Hartford, Connecticut, where it was cut from six months to 90 days for clerical workers. In Hartford management has the right to extend probation for 60 additional days, unless the union objects; management considered this "helpful in hiring members of minority groups since it gives them more time to show that they can do the work." The unions argued that the trial periods should be shortened because management could make quicker decisions as to the acceptability of the probationers' performance. Stanley and Cooper comment that this union pressure might have the beneficial effect of inducing management to make "far more prompt and incisive evaluation of employee performance." The danger is that, as collective bargaining is extended to middle and upper level positions, unions may be successful in obtaining unduly brief trial periods for such employees as well, but to date there are no research findings which show that this has happened.

■ PERFORMANCE EVALUATION

As employees pursue their career goals, they must have some concrete idea of how well they are performing on their current jobs, as well as their potential for higher level positions and how they can improve it. It is management's responsibility, in consultation with the employees, to de-

---

[10] U.S. Department of State, *Promotion Reform: Threshold Review and Mid-Career Tenure*, Management Reform Bulletin No. 27, July 6, 1971.

[11] David T. Stanley with Carole L. Cooper, *Managing Local Government under Union Pressure* (Washington, D.C.: Brookings Institution, 1972), p. 35.

velop a performance evaluation system which will help employees meet their developmental needs and will also provide management with an informed, equitable basis for determinations about the salary advancement, training, promotion, transfer, dismissal, and other treatment of employees.

In general, the history of performance evaluation in the public service has been dismal. Probably more derisive statements have been made by employees about service ratings than about any other phase of personnel administration. Confidence in the rating process is so low that supervisors discharge this responsibility perfunctorily, frequently giving mostly high ratings—sometimes to a ridiculous extent.

The Hoover Commission proposals

A task force of the first Hoover Commission on Organization of the Executive Branch (1949)[12] reported that one agency had rated 55 percent of its employees "excellent," 41.5 percent "very good," and 3.5 percent "good." While this is one of the worst examples, it was by no means an isolated case, and at all levels of government, ratings still show such unbelievable distributions. The task force believed the system of "public rewards or penalties" explained why supervisors were giving such liberal evaluations; ratings were tied in with various personnel decisions affecting the employee's career, such as salary increments, promotions, and dismissals. At that time employees could not be promoted or given a within-grade increase unless their efficiency ratings were "good" or better; they had to be dismissed if it was less than "good." Supervisors were unwilling to mete out these public penalties, particularly since there was no assurance that other supervisors would do the same with their subordinates.

Both Hoover Commissions recommended that summary adjective ratings be eliminated and that the tie-in of ratings

---

[12] Commission on Organization of the Executive Branch of the Government, *Task Force Report on Federal Personnel* (Washington, D.C.: Government Printing Office, 1949), pp. 60–62, 71–72.

with personnel actions be ended. Supervisors would be required to rate each subordinate at least annually on improvement in work performance, and on their growth potential. They would then have a confidential chat with each employee to discuss strengths and weaknesses and work out a concrete program for correcting deficiencies and speeding future development. Supervisors would be required to report to management periodically on the progress of subordinates, identifying those with promise for advancement, those *not* deserving within-grade increases, and those who should be transferred because they were not fitted to their present assignments. The reasoning was that elimination of the system of "public rewards or penalties" and addition of confidential evaluation conversations between superiors and subordinates would put supervisors in a better position to do a serious job of evaluation. Thus the rating process, for the first time, would really be of help to employees in improving their performance.[13]

McGregor on performance appraisal

In the private sector, supervisors had also resisted conventional appraisal systems because, as Douglas McGregor said, they did not enjoy playing the role of judge or God and making judgments which could have a damaging effect on subordinates' careers.[14] In these conventional systems, the supervisor functioned like an inspector, treating human beings like physical objects on an assembly line and accepting or rejecting them. McGregor recommended that subordinates be given a prominent, positive role in the evaluation process. The first step would be for subordinates themselves to take the initiative and develop clear statements of the major features of their jobs; they would discuss

---

[13] Commission on Organization of the Executive Branch of the Government, *Personnel Management* (Washington, D.C.: Government Printing Office, 1949) pp. 33, 40; and Commission on Organization of the Executive Branch of the Government, *Personnel and Civil Service* (Washington, D.C.: Government Printing Office, 1955), pp. 63–65.

[14] See Douglas McGregor, "An Uneasy Look at Performance Appraisal," *Harvard Business Review*, 35, No. 1 (May–June, 1957), 89–94.

this statement with their superiors and come to an agreement. After six months, they would appraise their own performance and then meet again with their immediate supervisors to discuss their self-appraisals and to reset their work
targets. At every step the supervisors would have veto power,
but McGregor believed they would rarely have to exercise it
because most subordinates underestimate their accomplishments and potentialities. The basic assumption in the
procedure is that subordinates are in the best position to
analyze their needs and plan their own development, and
the contribution of the supervisor should be to help subordinates relate their career planning to the needs of the
organization.

While McGregor's plan differs from that of the Hoover
Commissions by making the subordinate the active agent,
the basic thinking is the same. Both point out the inconsistency of having the supervisor play the judge role and yet
expecting the evaluation process to be helpful to the employee. The validity of the supervisors' criticisms is questioned by many employees, even though they usually do
not say so. In fact, many rating officials have not had an
opportunity to become familiar with all aspects of the performance of all the subordinates they are required to evaluate.

Critical or even "judgmental" remarks made by supervisors during the evaluation interview often do not have the
desired beneficial effect. In one research study, only 20 of
the 84 subjects mentioned as goals for their improvement
those aspects of their performance which the supervisor
during previous appraisal interviews had criticized the
most.[15] Yet McGregor and the Hoover Commissions would
not change the conventional role of supervision in making
decisions on the salary advancement, promotion, and other
treatment of employees. McGregor admitted that he had
"deliberately slighted the many problems of judgment
involved in administering promotions and salaries" but he
believed that, once the "fundamental problem inherent in

[15] Herbert H. Meyer, Emanuel Kay, and John R. P. French, Jr., "Split
Roles in Performance Appraisal," *Harvard Business Review*, 43, No. 1
(May–June 1957), 89–94.

the conventional approach was understood," administrative methods could be "tempered."[16]

Review of the literature and response to proposals

Reviewing the entire literature on evaluations, Ronald Burke and Linda Kemball concluded that the "goal setting and review approach" is the most congruent with behavioral science research factors associated with success or failure in reaching the goal of employee development.[17] However, all subordinates are not capable of self-analysis, and all managers are not employee centered or nondirective. They cite one study in which the "best predictor of whether or not the subordinate took constructive action" based on the evaluation was how the manager handled the appraisal feedback discussion. In the public service, training programs for supervisors in how to rate subordinates and how to conduct the appraisal interview have been inadequate.

Except for a few state and local jurisdictions, ratings are still tied in with personnel actions, and the inconsistency in the "judge" and "helper" roles is sometimes not even perceived. Although the Civil Service Commission strongly endorsed the Hoover Commission recommendations, Congress has not acted, and the only change has been to make within-grade increases dependent on a determination by the department head, not the employee's last rating.[18] Department heads rarely withhold the raises, so this partial reform has not worked. Employee organizations are wary of increases in management discretion in pay and other areas, and Congress apparently has seen no great advantages in making major changes in the present system. The Civil Service Commission has been making an extended study of the problem, however, and there may soon be new proposals.

Commonly used rating plans

Both in government and private enterprise, the typical procedure has been to evaluate employees by using a

---

[16] McGregor, "Uneasy Look at Performance Appraisal," 93.
[17] Ronald J. Burke and Linda J. Kemball, "Performance Appraisal: Some Issues in the Process," *Canadian Personnel and Industrial Relations Journal*, 18, No. 6 (November 1971), 26, 32.
[18] Section 701(a) (B) Public Law 87–973, 87th Congress.

graphic scale to rate both quality and quantity of work.[19] These scales mostly provide for assessment of personal characteristics such as cooperativeness, initiative, enthusiasm, tact, resourcefulness, judgment, adaptability, and attitude toward the job. Some also include some performance factors, such as productivity and accuracy. In completing the form, the rater is asked to indicate the degree to which the employee can be said to possess each characteristic. The big advantage in using graphic scales is that the supervisor can quickly rate dozens of subordinates simply by making check marks.

While ease of administration is a great advantage, the system should be sound. There are many drawbacks to trait ratings. Raters should all have the same understanding of what a trait means, but this is a virtual impossibility because performance that to one rater is evidence of initiative, for example, may to another simply signify the satisfaction of minimum job requirements. When are employees resourceful? When do they show good judgment? Sometimes brief definitions of each trait are given on the rating form, but usually they consist of descriptive phrases and adjectives which also do not have the same meaning to all raters. Even if there is agreement on what the trait means, it is very difficult to make judgments as to the *extent* to which each employee possesses the characteristic. The gradations may be in the form of adjectives such as "fair amount of courage," "marked courage," and "unusual courage," and what is "marked courage" to one fire chief, for example, may represent only a "fair amount of courage" to another. The graphic scale diverts attention from the important considerations — the job itself and the employee's performance in it. While it is true that certain qualities may be important for job success, the tendency is for the supervisor to react to the subordinates' personalities and rate them positively or negatively in all matters in accordance with the impression they make. Trait ratings also have the disadvantage that, because in the evaluation interview supervisors must attempt to justify their

---

[19] See Winston Oberg, "Make Performance Appraisal Relevant," *Harvard Business Review*, 50, No. 1 (January–February 1972), 61–67.

appraisals of frequently nebulous personality traits, they often appear vague and unconvincing to the employee.

Expert opinion, as illustrated by the Hoover Commission recommendations, has favored ratings based on performance standards or requirements, rather than personal traits, for some time. In one version, the supervisor, in consultation with the subordinate, prepares performance standards for *each* significant task in the position. These standards are both quantitative (e.g., number of cards filed per hour) and qualitative (deals tactfully with visitors). The supervisor rates the subordinate on each task and then arrives at an adjective rating for performance on the job as a whole. There are problems in developing the standards, particularly the qualitative ones, but the big drawback with this plan is that it is very time-consuming. Most positions have at least a half dozen important component parts, supervisors may have more than a few subordinates, and the agency may have thousands of positions to be analyzed in this way. Even if the performance standards are prepared for classes of positions rather than every position, the work volume is great, except in small organizations.

As long as the rater is instructed to concentrate on the work requirements and to evaluate the subordinate on performance rather than general personality characteristics, the desired objective in performance evaluation can be obtained. There may not be any need for a rating form as such; the supervisor can make the evaluation in a narrative report. Of course, supervisor and subordinate must have the same conception of what the position requires and what constitutes satisfactory performance in each task. Emphasis on individual task analysis can be counterproductive, however, because the employee's efforts should be assessed in terms of how well they meet work goals assigned as part of the total objectives of the organization. Management by objectives and goal setting for individual positions as a cooperative enterprise of supervisor and subordinate go hand in hand.[20]

---

[20] See Robert G. Pajer, "A Systems Approach to Results Oriented Performance Evaluation," *Personnel Administration and Public Personnel Review*, 1, No. 3 (November–December 1972), 42–47.

Employees' participation and rights

While rating plans in government usually do not allow subordinates to be the type of active agent proposed by McGregor, public service employees do frequently participate in setting work targets. All rating officers cannot be trusted to discuss the ratings with the employees, so there may be a space on the form for the latter to certify that they have seen the rating, and the rater did discuss it with them. Under one plan, the employees first rate themselves and then discuss these self-appraisals with the immediate supervisors, who are supposed to compare them with their own views and then make their final evaluations. The standard procedure has been for the immediate supervisor to be the rating officer and the department head the reviewing officer. While the department head usually accepts the rating officer's evaluation, review is an indispensable step because then raters know their decisions are subject to higher level approval. A State Department working group recommended that FSOs be allowed to request that, besides being rated by their immediate supervisors, they be rated by another officer familiar with their work,[21] but this proposal was not implemented. The same group flatly rejected peer group evaluations, saying they "would be more open to questions of motivation than the traditional supervisor-subordinate evaluations" and would lead to "charges of backstabbing, revenge, or deceit."[22] Peer evaluations are generally not used in the public service, but one exception is in faculty promotions in higher education.

At one time numerous levels of appeal were provided, setting in motion what sometimes became prolonged battles between supervisors and subordinates. In the federal service, the Performance Rating Act of 1950 requires agencies to provide "one impartial review" if the ratee requests it; those rated unsatisfactory can also appeal to an agency board of review, which makes the final decision. These boards consist of one member named by the agency head, another

---

[21] U.S. Department of State, *Diplomacy for the 70's,* p. 75.
[22] Ibid., pp. 77–78.

selected by the Civil Service Commission, and a third designated by the employees.

One of the fears about unions is that they might make individual ratings subject to binding arbitration. This has not been a real threat in the federal service because it would conflict with the above-cited law, but it could happen in state and local jurisdictions, where changes in civil service laws to accommodate contract provisions can be made more easily. The unions have not been pressing for such binding arbitration, concentrating instead on questions of procedure and rating standards. The U.S. Civil Service Commission, in its review of the *Federal Personnel Manual* (see Chapter 1), decided that certain aspects of service rating procedures could be opened to negotiation without endangering the merit principle. There are many desirable features of service rating procedures which are often not included in the laws and regulations, such as requiring supervisors to furnish employees with copies of any appraisals made of the employees' supervisory potential.

■ PROMOTIONS

In state and local merit systems, the procedures for evaluating candidates for promotion are generally the same as in competitions for entrance. Minimum qualifications are determined, a battery of tests is given, and names are certified from the resultant promotional registers, according to the same rules as for initial appointments. Additional points are sometimes given for length of service, but usually not very many, and often the candidate's last service rating is given some weight.

The objective has been to protect the merit principle by providing formal procedures which will not permit appointing officers to promote on the basis of favoritism or other extraneous considerations. In the process, however, excessive rigidity has been built into these promotion systems, and employee groups often will exert pressure for maintenance of the status quo. Seniority has been a very important factor in promotion because the area of competition has been narrowly defined; eligibility for consideration may be limited to employees in the organization unit or department in which the vacancy occurs. Recently, promotional tests have been attacked as unfair, and the courts have been enjoining the use of promotional as well as original entrance tests, applying the standards described in Chapter 7.

In the federal service, more informal promotion policies existed until 1959. Appointing officers were supposed to propose persons for promotion on the basis of merit, but the only requirement was that the individuals meet the Commission's minimum qualification requirements of training and experience for the kinds of positions concerned. Instead of critically evaluating those with the minimum qualifications and choosing the best qualified, appointing officers tended to promote on the basis of length of service. Since 1959, the Commission has required the agencies to establish formal promotion plans which must meet certain standards: the area of consideration must be as broad as possible, to assure real competition; ranking procedures must be based on job-related criteria; and length of service or experience may be a ranking factor only when clearly and positively related to job performance. Written tests may only be used when approved by the Commission in advance or when it deems them necessary in in-service placement.

An example — The IRS promotion plan

In the Internal Revenue Service promotion plan,[23] the minimum area of consideration is one in which it is reasonable to expect to locate enough highly qualified candidates for the positions covered. The precise boundaries in terms of organization units and positions are attached to the plan as exhibits. These areas have been determined by such factors as the presence of a significant supply of eligible candidates to produce enough highly qualified candidates, the desirability of affording employees broad promotional opportunities, and the necessity of keeping the area of search within the limits of administrative efficiency. Generally, promo-

---

[23] Internal Revenue Service, manual, *Promotion.*

tions are filled from within the IRS, especially to lower level jobs. The decision whether to consider employees within the IRS and outside candidates concurrently is based on the kind of job being filled and the number of highly qualified candidates available. For positions at GS-14 and above, consideration is given to outside applicants who are eligible for transfer, reemployment, or reinstatement and who are within reach on appropriate registers.

In determining basic eligibility, Civil Service Commission minimum qualification standards, plus any selective placement factors which are essential for successful performance and cannot be readily attained after promotion, are employed. All employees found eligible are evaluated in accordance with already established job-related criteria, and all those meeting these criteria are designated as "highly qualified." If the number of highly qualified candidates exceeds five, when compared together the three to five top-ranking ones become the "best qualified." While three to five best qualified candidates are certified for each vacancy, up to ten may be certified "if meaningful distinctions cannot be made among a smaller number of highly qualified candidates."

The methods for evaluating candidates are agreed upon by selecting officials and the personnel office. These methods should be appropriate for the positions concerned and should measure the candidates' total qualifications. Ratings by supervisors are required in all cases, and the other methods include: review of personnel folders, applications, and resumés; interviews; evaluation of candidates' training, self-development, and relevant outside activities; and evaluation of experience, with length of service or experience a ranking factor only when, after all other evaluation factors have been considered, the candidates have achieved equal rankings. Use of evaluation panels is strongly recommended, but a ranking official from within the activity where the vacancy exists may serve instead. Panels should consist of at least three voting members, including an official directly concerned with the position being filled and a personnel office representative, the latter usually a nonvoting member.

Records of each promotion made must be kept for two years and, at the employees' request, the supervisors must show them any supervisory evaluations of past performance used in considering them for promotion, as well as any report of potential used in considering them for nonsupervisory positions. The promotion plan must be reviewed at least annually, at which time unions with exclusive recognition are given the opportunity to express their views. When proper promotion procedures are followed, failure to be selected for promotion is not a basis for a grievance or for review under any other procedure.

Review of basic policy issues in promotions

The basic policy issues in promotions are designation of the area of competition and determination of the criteria and methods for ranking candidates. In some state and local governments, competition has been widened by such methods as permitting all employees in the jurisdiction who meet the minimum qualifications to take promotional examinations. In general, however, the area of consideration remains too restricted at the state and local level. In the federal government, the Civil Service Commission's standard is flexible, the agencies being free to use whatever area for consideration assures sufficient competition in the particular case.

There is a long-standing debate about the pros and cons of "promotion from within" and "promotion from without." It is necessary to define what the "within" and "without" refer to: a division or section, a larger subdivision of the agency, the entire agency, or the entire jurisdiction? Too much promotion from within is often criticized as inbreeding, but if the reference is to an entity as huge as the Department of Defense the criticism has far less validity than if it is to a small organization unit in a municipal agency. It has been suggested that there should be a balance between promotion from within and without, but this is a vague guideline, since there are differing opinions as to when such a balance has been reached. Employee morale suffers greatly when superiors pass up subordinates for promotion, seeming to prefer outside candidates they think glitter by comparison. Selecting officials, like everyone else, can suffer from the illusion that the grass is greener on the other side of the street; they know their subordinates' faults, and familiarity may breed contempt. If candidates from the outside are to be considered, they should rank with the best qualified internal candidates.

As in original entrance, thorough job analysis is the indispensable first step in determining the skill and qualification requirements of promotional positions, and the measurement devices selected should be validated. William Enneis believes that

> It is unethical to use tests to determine suitability for promotion of present employees, unless the nature of the test is such that it can clearly demonstrate that some workers would be a danger to either themselves or those around them or that they would be definitely incapable of performing the job to which they might be promoted. An employee's work history is a more reasonable indicator of probable success in a higher job.[24]

Enneis's verdict also is negative as to the validity of general intelligence tests, but, as noted in Chapter 7, other experts disagree. Present research has not shown conclusively that written tests have no value as part of the assessment process for promotions. Since their use is exceptional in federal government promotions, it is in state and local governments that this matter will be resolved. Present indications are that attempts will be made to improve written tests, rather than stop using them.

Since supervisory ratings of both past performance and potential can greatly influence promotion decisions, as in the State Department, improving these appraisals is particularly important. The composition and functioning of promotion panels which weigh the evidence relating to each candidate are also very important; the ranking process is difficult and must be approached with great care. Minority-group repre-

---

[24] William H. Enneis, "Statement Before the House Post Office and Civil Service Subcommittee," in *Personnel Testing and Equal Employment Opportunity* (Washington, D.C.: Government Printing Office, 1971), pp. 16–20.

sentation on promotion panels contributes to the validity and acceptability of their determinations.

The union role in promotions

Some unions press for seniority as the principal basis for promotions. The International Personnel Management Association states that "If the jurisdiction has one or more strong unions (and a strong labor relations law), seniority is almost certain to be demanded as an important consideration in promotion."[25] In the Stanley and Cooper study cited above, it was found that while most union contracts with local governments did not contain provisions for seniority in promotions and the civil service laws were the controlling factor, employee pressures, both nonunion and union, had succeeded in "narrowing areas of competition for promotion, increasing the weight of seniority in promotion examinations, and placing more reliance on written tests than on oral examinations and performance appraisals."[26] Written tests were preferred by unions that believed them to be more objective and thus a better control over management discretion. The civil service associations and the police and fire unions supported competitive promotion procedures, while the American Federation of State, County, and Municipal Employees and the Teamsters favored writing the seniority principle into the agreements. The union agreements in Detroit were unusual because they prescribed lines of promotion in detail, providing for advancement to higher rated, nonsupervisory jobs on the basis of seniority.[27]

Stanley and Cooper reason that promotion of the most senior qualified employees in jobs like truck loader does no real damage to the merit principle and is also beneficial for morale, but the same principle applied to supervisory positions would "seriously weaken the fabric of urban govern-

---

[25] International Personnel Management Association, *Guidelines for Drafting a Public Personnel Administration Law* (Chicago, Ill.), pp. 18, 38.

[26] Stanley and Cooper, *Managing Local Government Under Union Pressure*, p. 44.

[27] Ibid., pp. 41–43.

ment." They view the unions as generally trying to "narrow and inhibit management's freedom of choice in making promotions—a freedom that is already limited by civil service provisions."[28] In another Brookings Institution study, Jack Steiber and two assistants conducted approximately 300 interviews in 53 cities and 23 states and found that "some police and firefighter leaders prefer merit to seniority as a criterion for promotion because it would advance the course of professionalization."[29] The Assembly of Government Employees, a loose federation of state associations with a total membership of about a million, is strongly opposed to having promotions and other aspects of the merit system subject to collective bargaining. In the absence of comprehensive nationwide research on contract provisions, it cannot be demonstrated with hard data whether or not the unions have been responsible for restricting or further restricting management discretion in promotions through collective bargaining.

Public employee associations generally reject the principle of promotion for the most senior qualified man, and employee organizations as a whole seem to believe that there is enough seniority built into civil service, at least for the time being, and they can therefore concentrate on more pressing issues. The belief, as in Germany, that "seniority is the only safe guide for ensuring that the best men are chosen" and that "those with the longest service are likely, all things being equal, to have wider experience and greater administrative culture" has never taken hold in the United States, nor is it likely to do so. Nor are we likely to adopt the system of some European countries of filling a certain quota of higher positions by seniority and a smaller quota by competition.[30]

One approach to accommodation of collective bargaining with the merit principle (see Chapter 3) is to exclude promo-

---

[28] Ibid., pp. 44–45.

[29] Jack Steiber, *Public Employee Unionism, Structure, Growth. Policy* (Washington, D.C.: Brookings Institution, 1973), p. 122.

[30] Brian Chapman, *The Profession of Government* (London: Allen & Unwin, 1959), pp. 167, 170.

tions as well as original appointments from the bargaining process. This is the approach taken in the Connecticut statute, which is unusual because it permits negotiation of contract provisions which conflict with civil service laws and regulations. If there is a conflict with existing law, the conflicting provisions do not go into effect, unless the legislative body approves the entire contract.[31] Some state collective bargaining laws define bargaining scope broadly and do not attempt to solve the problem of possible conflicts of contract provisions with merit system laws. This has been the case in Michigan, where some circuit courts have ruled that where a conflict exists the contract provisions, including the promotion clause, prevail.[32] The Michigan example has often been cited, justifiably in our opinion, as opening the way to possible complete destruction of the merit principle.

In the federal service, Executive Order 11491, as amended and as interpreted by the Federal Labor Relations Council (FLRC), permits negotiation of promotion procedures, provided management retains the right to decide *who* will be promoted. This is illustrated in the FLRC's decision in a negotiability case involving the Veterans Administration Independent Service Employees Union and the VA Research Hospital in Chicago. The union and the hospital negotiated a contract provision enabling the union steward to request review of a promotion decision by the "next highest level supervisor who has not participated in the proposed selection under review" before the promotion could be made effective. When the contract proposals were reviewed at VA headquarters, the agency head ruled this provision nonnegotiable under the Executive Order, but when the case was appealed to the FLRC it disagreed. The FLRC concluded that the agency head had misinterpreted the proposal when he said that the union was asking to participate in the promotion selection and was seeking to

---

[31] See State of California, *Final Report of the Assembly Advisory Council on Public Employee Relations*, March 15, 1973, pp. 166–67.

[32] Fred Hustad, "Legal Conflict between Civil Service and Collective Bargaining in Michigan," *Public Personnel Review*, 31 (October 1970), 269–72.

substitute the steward's judgment for that of the selecting official. Rather, the proposal would merely permit the union "to obtain review of a first-line official's promotion selection by a higher level supervisor whose decision would be final." The FLRC's reasoning in this and similar cases has been that nothing in the order bars "negotiations of procedures, to the extent consonant with law and regulations, which management will observe in reaching or taking the action involved, provided that such procedures do not have the effect of negating the authority reserved."[33]

Since cases come to the FLRC only on appeal, it is only through the Civil Service Commission's periodic evaluations of agency personnel systems that the effect of contract provisions on merit promotion policies can be ascertained. Review of the labor relations program is a part of these evaluations, so it becomes a question of the frequency, thoroughness, and accuracy of these evaluations.[34]

■ TRANSFERS AND MOBILITY

Transfer may refer only to horizontal movements—that is, movement between positions in job classes neither higher nor lower in the salary plan—or it may include promotions as well. We will be concerned here with all movements of administrative, professional, and technical (APT) personnel to achieve the advantages of *mobility*, a concept much emphasized in career management. Transfers also can be permanent or temporary, which contributes to administrative flexibility.

There has been concern for some time that in the American public service, movement of APT personnel has been much too restricted—between agencies in the same jurisdiction, between jurisdictions, and between the public and private sectors. John Macy says that "We have encouraged in-

---

[33] U.S. Federal Labor Relations Council, *Report of Case Decisions,* FLRC No. 71 A–31. Washington, D.C., November 27, 1972.

[34] See U.S. General Accounting Office, *Agencies' Personnel Management Can Be Enhanced by Improving the Evaluation Process* (Washington, D.C., September 17, 1974).

dividuals through supervisory advice and incentives to identify with narrowly defined professional goals, and have thereby complicated the enormously important process of gaining acceptance and response to much larger national goals."[35] More than three-fifths of all federal executives (full-time employees of the executive branch whose base salary equals or exceeds the beginning salary of GS–16) are "nonmobile," having remained in the same agency since reaching GS–13 or its equivalent. Only 17 percent are classified as mobile because they have held positions of substantial responsibility in three or more federal agencies.[36]

The limitation of careers by restricting movement to within a single agency has also been a characteristic of state and local governments. Little interchange has taken place between the federal government and state and local jurisdictions, and, while many government workers have a background of some private employment, there has been little planned interchange of executives. The business community is generally reluctant to encourage junior executives to accept tours of duty in government.

The rationale of mobility

As illustrated in the Federal Executive Service proposal discussed in Chapter 4, the more mobile the APT work force is, the more flexibly can management deploy talent to achieve program objectives. The individual development plans discussed in this chapter often provide for exposure to new experiences through planned assignments in different parts of the agency, as in headquarters or field offices, and line or staff functions. A fresh flow of capable individuals with different backgrounds and new ideas contributes to the vitality of any office. In the case of intergovernmental transfers, because so many important functions of government are now shared by all levels of government, interchange makes

---

[35] John W. Macy, Jr., "Merit System Revisited," *Looking Ahead*, 9, No. 6 (September 1961), p. 1 (monthly report of National Planning Association).

[36] U.S. Civil Service Commission, Bureau of Executive Manpower, *Executive Manpower in the Federal Service* (Washington, D.C., January 1972), p. 20.

for better understanding of the points of view of counterpart personnel, as in welfare, public health, agricultural, and law enforcement programs. The line between government and business management practices is now virtually nonexistent, but there still are diverse ways of thinking which can be reconciled if personnel of one sector are allowed to experience the problems confronting the other.

The obstacles to employee mobility have been numerous. Once they have achieved certain status, employees will weigh transfers carefully; in addition to possible disruption of family life, there may be other real or perceived risks in making the change. Some are overcautious and others lack drive, but management has the responsibility to do everything possible to remove obstacles that can deter even the most enterprising. As one example, there frequently is reluctance to accept transfers to field offices for fear that headquarters, seeing less of the employee, will overlook them for future good assignments and promotion; in Washington, D.C., great importance is placed on being near the "throne." This fear can be counteracted by an agency promotion plan and a governmentwide Executive Assignment System, as in the federal service, which would assure that all qualified persons will be considered in filling promotional positions.

Since 1967 the U.S. Civil Service Commission as part of the Executive Assignment System just mentioned has maintained an Executive Inventory file on some 35,000 current employees in Grades GS–15 or equivalent and GS–16–18. The data are taken from an 11-page record completed by each person appointed or promoted to a position in Grade 15 or above or at an equivalent salary level under another pay system. Status changes of each employee are entered into the inventory monthly, and employees are given the opportunity to update their records annually. In filling vacancies in Grades GS–16–18, the agencies are required to request an inventory search. The Commission screens the inventory by computer to identify potential candidates and refers the names of those it deems best qualified. The agency then considers these candidates, together with those who have been identified through the agency promotion program or by the Executive Assignment Board, an instrumentality of the Commission which exists in each major agency. In this way, the best candidates, both from within the agency and outside it, are considered. The inventory search is not required in all cases; it may be waived by the Commission in cases where the agency "employs a preponderance of potential candidates in the occupational area," has "a well-established executive development plan in a given career field," or has "for a significant period of time been grooming the candidate for the executive position being filled."[37] Significantly, Commission Chairman Robert E. Hampton, in urging the adoption of the Federal Executive Service, told a Congressional subcommittee, "In actual practice, the person moving into a supergrade vacancy quite often is selected principally because he happens to be in the agency in the specific program at the right time. Rarely are his qualifications compared with those of other individuals from outside the organization."[38]

Interchange of personnel under the IPA

Until passage of the Intergovernmental Personnel Act (IPA) in 1970, with very few exceptions employees could not transfer between the federal government and state or local jurisdictions without losing retirement, leave, and other fringe benefit rights, not to mention the salary loss often involved if the move was from the generally higher paying federal agencies to a state or local government. Title IV of the IPA provides for temporary assignments (up to two years) of federal employees to state and local governments (including institutions of higher education) and vice versa, to perform "work of mutual concern" to the participating agencies. The transferees are either detailed from their home agencies or given leave without pay.[39]

---

[37] U.S. Civil Service Commission, Bureau of Executive Manpower, *Executive Manpower in the Federal Service* (Washington, D.C., March 1973), pp. 11–12.

[38] House Subcommittee on Post Office and Civil Service, 92nd Cong., 2nd sess., *The Federal Executive Service* (Washington, D.C.: Government Printing Office, 1972), p. 17.

[39] Public Law 91–648, 91st Cong., S. 11, January 5, 1971, pp. 12–17.

In the case of federal employees, their salary, annual and sick leave, life insurance, health benefit, and unemployment compensation rights remain the same as if they had continued in their usual assignments with their agencies. The federal, state, or local agencies concerned negotiate arrangements for payment of salary and travel and transportation expenses to or from the place of assignment; one of the participating agencies can pay all salary and travel costs, or these costs can be shared. When state or local government employees are assigned to federal agencies, the latter may reimburse the state or local entity for all or part of the transferees' salaries; the same applies to travel expenses. The federal agencies can pay employer contributions for retirement, life insurance, and health benefits if the state or local government fails to continue these contributions. This legislation is administered by the Bureau of Intergovernmental Relations of the U.S. Civil Service Commission, and in negotiations over payment of salary or travel expenses, the principle is that the jurisdiction benefiting the most from the transfer should generally pay the larger share. Hundreds of transfers have already been made under Title IV, and the program has been well received.[40]

Transfers between government and the private sector

An executive interchange program between the federal government and the private sector has been functioning since 1970, based upon an executive order issued by President Lyndon Johnson. The purpose is to promote better understanding between the sectors. Assignments are for periods up to two years, and the participants are men and women in midcareer. The program has been small, but is slowly being expanded.[41]

The second Hoover Commission made a strong recommendation for more vigorous efforts to attract business

---

[40] See Joseph M. Robertson, "Talent Sharing for Better Government Performance," *News and Views*, 23, No. 10 (October 1973), 7–9 (published by the American Society for Public Administration).

[41] See Len Famiglietti, "Executive Interchange Plan Seen as Full Grown Project," *Federal Times*, March 15, 1972.

executives to such posts as agency or assistant agency head. It also recognized the difficulties with such a program, particularly the fear of private managers on the rise that they might lose promotional opportunities by being away on assignment to government. As the Task Force on Personnel and Civil Service commented, "It is not fun to return from Washington and go to work for a former subordinate—as sometimes happens." The Task Force argued that "corporations which pride themselves on their progressive personnel policies and which try to skim the cream from the colleges, the scientific institutes, and the law schools have an obligation to make that talent available for leadership in public affairs."[42]

Employee organization views on transfers

As revealed in the committee hearings on the FES proposal, employee organizations do not contest the need for mobility, but they want to be sure that employees' rights are fully protected. Although they offered amendments to certain provisions during the legislative history of the IPA, employee organization leaders supported the principles of the legislation, including the desirability of intergovernmental transfers.[43]

The framework of reference in most collective bargaining agreements on transfers is the entire work force, and the concern is with protection of employees' rights in voluntary and involuntary transfers. Some contracts simply state that management will establish a system whereby employees may indicate their preferences for transfers to appropriate vacancies, and others provide that in filling vacancies by transfer, seniority shall govern. Unions are concerned that employees on temporary detail to work in higher classifications should receive the pay of the higher class, and this is

---

[42] Commission on Organization of the Executive Branch, *Personnel and Civil Service*, pp. 42–47.

[43] Senate Subcommittee on Intergovernmental Relations, *Intergovernmental Personnel Act of 1967, Intergovernmental Manpower Act of 1967* (Washington, D.C.: Government Printing Office, 1967), pp. 231–43.

frequently provided for, to take effect immediately upon re-assignment or after a certain number of days.

As to involuntary transfers, the contract may require management to give notice in advance and to explain to the employee the reasons for the action. It may also specify that employees with the least seniority are to be transferred first. In some school teacher contracts, all involuntary transfers to a different school are prohibited. Transfers for disciplinary reasons may be barred, and grievances over transfers may be subject to binding arbitration. Management rights clauses usually include the right to transfer personnel; while this means that transfers are not a mandatory subject for negotiation, management may, in its discretion, negotiate aspects of transfer policy and procedures to the extent legally possible.

■ REDUCTIONS IN FORCE

Management policies and actions are severely tested when reductions in force are necessary because of budgetary cuts, program changes, or reorganization. Programs may peak and then decline or even be phased out; such instability is characteristic of government. While reductions in force occur with greater frequency and impact in the federal government, they also constitute a serious problem in state and local governments, where they are accentuated by the financial pinch resulting from limited, inflexible revenue sources.

The basic policy questions are: Who should be laid off, in what order, and according to what criteria? Should order of layoff be based on seniority or some plan that considers both seniority and merit? What weight should be given to veterans' preference? What consideration, if any, should be given to the agency's future needs for certain kinds of workers? What should the role of employee organizations be in the formulation and implementation of reduction-in-force policies?

In the federal service, as provided in Civil Service Commission regulations, the agencies decide which jobs to eliminate; this is a management determination which is not reviewable by the Commission. The agencies fix the competitive area, which usually is a single office or installation in the field service or a bureau or similar organization at headquarters, and then group positions by competitive level, that is, by the type and grade of work. In each competitive area, employees with similar jobs compete for retention—GS–3 stenographers with GS–3 stenographers, GS–11 accountants with GS–11 accountants. Retention registers are prepared for each competitive level.

Ranking within retention registers is on the basis of a formula which combines four factors: type of appointment (tenure); veterans' preference; length of service; and performance rating. Specifically, three tenure categories are established: Group I, consisting of career employees not serving probation; Group II, career employees still serving probation and career-conditional employees, who have not completed a three-year service requirement; and Group III, indefinite employees and those serving on temporary appointments pending establishment of registers. Employees with temporary appointments for less than a year and those with unsatisfactory performance ratings are not placed in any of these categories. They do not compete for retention and must be released from the level before any person in Groups I, II, or III is released.

Within each tenure category, employees are divided into two subgroups: A for veterans and B for nonveterans. Within these subgroups, they are ranked by service dates which reflect their total federal service, both civilian and military. An employee with an outstanding service rating receives four additional years of service credit.

Selection of those to be released from the competitive level starts with the lowest tenure category and with the employee in subgroup B who has the latest service date, which means that nonveterans are released before veterans. Employees in Group III can be separated because they have no right to another job; employees in Groups II or I must be offered reassignments if the agency has suitable positions from which the incumbents can be bumped. Suitable position is one in the same or a lower grade in the competitive area for which the individual is fully qualified and which is occupied by someone in a lower subgroup. The bumped person is entitled to displace someone in a lower subgroup. Thus many individuals may be bumped simply to lay off one employee. Names of those laid off are placed on reemployment priority lists, for two years in the case of those in Group I and for one year for those in Group II. During this time, the agency must consider those on these lists for any vacancies in the commuting area for which they can qualify. In addition, those in Groups I and II can apply through their agencies for placement assistance under the Civil Service Commission's Displaced Employee Program.[44]

This system gives great weight to veterans' preference because in each subgroup nonveterans with long years of service are displaced before veterans with *any* service. Consequently, some nonveterans have been wary of federal employment. Besides the dislocations, bumping creates much paperwork; some years ago a Senate subcommittee estimated that one reduction in which 30 employees were finally laid off cost almost $450,000.[45]

In state and local governments reductions in force and later reemployment are based on previous work performance and/or seniority, with the latter usually the predominant or the more important consideration. The criterion of future worth to the agency, based on a special evaluation at the time of reduction in force, has not been established as an important factor at any level of government although it was strongly recommended by the personnel task force of the second Hoover Commission.[46]

The employee organization role in reductions

In the federal government, union contracts may provide policies and procedures that supplement but do not conflict

[44] U.S. Civil Service Commission, *Fed Facts 13*, February 1973, and Part 351, *Federal Personnel Manual*.

[45] Senate Subcommittee on Federal Manpower Policies, 82nd Cong., 2nd sess., *Reduction-in-Force System in the Federal Government* (Washington, D.C.: Government Printing Office, 1953), p. 2.

[46] Commission on Organization of the Executive Branch, *Task Force Report on Personnel*, pp. 104–5.

with law and Civil Service Commission regulations. The agreements often provide for advance notice to the union of impending layoffs and of the reasons for such action, and the union is given the opportunity to present its views on the implementation of the reductions. The employer may agree to furnish the union with the names and classifications of the affected employees, but the agency is not obligated to provide this information.[47] In some contracts the employer commits itself to filling existing vacancies as far as possible with employees who otherwise would be separated. The employer may also agree to make the competitive areas as broad as possible. The union may agree to help explain to the employees the reasons for the reductions. As in state and local government, unions exert political pressures to prevent layoffs, and sometimes they are successful. The no-layoff agreement in the contract with the postal workers is an exception; the Postal Service is under the NLRB, as provided in the Postal Reorganization Act of 1970.

There are some cases of no-layoff clauses, in state and local governments, but generally "arbitrators have upheld the right of the employer to abolish jobs or reduce the work force for economic reasons."[48] Contracts in these jurisdictions sometimes provide for layoff and reemployment in order of seniority and for bumping rights, and advance notice to the union is commonly required. In the 1970 survey by the Bureau of Labor Statistics of municipal agreements in large cities, references to layoffs were relatively infrequent because the subject was already well covered in most of these cities by civil service commission regulations.[49]

At all levels, the union role is significant in protecting employee rights under existing laws, regulations, and contract provisions. Policy on order of layoff is frequently well

---

[47] U.S. Civil Service Commission, Office of Labor Management Relations, *The Federal Labor-Management Consultant*, May 11, 1973.

[48] June Weisberger, *Job Security and Public Employees* (Ithaca, N.Y.: Institute of Public Employment, New York State School of Industrial and Labor Relations, Cornell University, March 1973), p. 54.

[49] U.S. Department of Labor, Bureau of Labor Statistics, *Municipal Bargaining Agreements in Large Cities*, Bulletin 1759 (Washington, D.C.: Government Printing Office, 1972), p. 18.

established, and it is this protective role which often is
most important.

■ DISCIPLINE

Our brief discussion of discipline in this chapter will omit
the grievance procedure, appeals, and employees' legal
rights. These are the topics of Chapters 10 and 11.

Much has been written about how discipline should be
viewed positively, as a means of correcting and stimulating
employee performance rather than as a punitive weapon.
The Los Angeles County Civil Service Commission stresses
that there should be a clear-cut written statement of disciplinary policy "which is known to all employees and is
uniformly and impartially carried out. Such a policy statement may include the agency's definition of 'discipline,'
under what conditions corrective actions will be taken, what
they consist of, and the agency's position regarding fairness,
consistency, and adequate investigation and review." It
should also specify the responsibilities of all concerned with
disciplinary matters — supervisors, agency heads, personnel
officers, the central personnel agency, employee organizations, and employees themselves. All legal requirements,
contract provisions, and procedural steps should be set forth
unambiguously in the administrative manuals and instructions. The responsibilities and authority of first-line supervisors should be given particular attention, since skillful
supervision removes the causes of many grievances and,
when formal disciplinary action is necessary, permits dealing
effectively with the problem rather than exacerbating it.[50]

In their survey of 132 U.S. and Canadian state, provincial,
and local governments, Saso and Tanis found that 106 had
written disciplinary policies and the remainder had at least
well-known informal rules and traditional practices. Only 15
of the respondents had penalty schedules showing the
penalty for each kind of infraction of the rules. Many per-

---

[50] Carmen D. Saso and Earl Tanis, *Disciplinary Policies and Practices*,
Public Employee Relations Library, No. 40 (Chicago: International Personnel Management Association, 1973), pp. 5–6.

sonnel experts believe these schedules are too inflexible and do not take into account the circumstances of particular cases and the employee's previous record. In the jurisdictions studied disciplinary policy guidelines were formulated by the central personnel agency or by the personnel director, pursuant to legal requirements. In the majority of cases, the union role was limited to representing employees in grievance proceedings and formal hearings.[51]

In the federal service, Civil Service Commission regulations govern disciplinary policies and procedures in accordance with the law. Union contract provisions may further define disciplinary policies or provide additional protection for employees. The following are examples:

> The Employer agrees that no personnel shall be assigned to perform the work of a collection agency for debts allegedly due by an employee to a private individual or firm. It is recognized that all employees are expected to pay promptly all just financial obligations.[52]

> A meeting between an employee and his supervisor and/or other line management officials during which the principal topic of discussion is discipline or potential discipline will entitle the employee involved to request to be accompanied by his Union representative during such meeting. If such a request is made, the supervisor or other line management official will honor the request.[53]

Such provisions illustrate what one of the authors has dubbed "personnel administration by handshake."[54] Contract provisions help unions and agency managements fill in gaps in existing laws and regulations. While there will be disagreement about the advisability of some of these provisions, they illustrate both the faith of the employee in collective bargaining and the enhanced role of the unions.

---

[51] Ibid., pp. 4–5, 7–11.

[52] Unit Agreement between Tampa Insuring Office and Orlando Service Office, HUD, and American Federation of Government Employees, Local No. 2508.

[53] Multi-District Agreement between Internal Revenue Service and National Association of Internal Revenue Service Employees, Internal Revenue Service, Document 6165 (6–72), pp. 14–15.

[54] Felix A. Nigro, "Personnel Administration by Handshake," *Civil Service Journal*, 12, No. 4 (April–June 1972), 28–30.

BIBLIOGRAPHY

Atwood, Jay F. *Interchange of Public Personnel: Progress, Problems, and Prospects.* Chicago: International Personnel Management Association.

Bacchus, William I. "Diplomacy for the 70's: An Afterview and Appraisal." *American Political Science Review*, 58, No. 2 (June 1974).

Burke, Ronald J., and Linda J. Kemball. "Performance Appraisal: Some Issues in the Process." *Canadian Personnel and Industrial Relations Journal*, 18, No. 6 (November 1971).

Chapman, Brian. *The Profession of Government.* London: Allen & Unwin, 1959.

Chartrand, P. J., and K. L. Pond. *A Study of Executive Career Paths in the Public Service of Canada.* Chicago: International Personnel Management Association, n.d.

The Civil Service, vol. 2, *Report of a Management Consulting Group*, 1966–68. London: Her Majesty's Stationery Office, 1968.

Coffey, Matthew B. "A Death at the White House: The Short Life of the New Patronage." *Public Administration Review*, 34, No. 5 (September–October 1974).

Corson, John J., and R. S. Paul. *Men Near the Top: Filling Key Posts in the Federal Service*, Supplementary Paper No. 20 of Committee for Economic Development. Baltimore: Johns Hopkins Press, 1966.

Drumm, Robert H. "Peer Ratings as Predictors of White Collar Performance." *Personnel*, 49, No. 3 (May–June 1972).

Field, Hubert S. and William H. Holley. "Performance Appraisals —An Analysis of State-Wide Practices." *Public Personnel Management*, 4, No. 3 (May–June 1975).

International Personnel Management Association, *Guidelines for Drafting a Public Personnel Administration Law*, Chicago.

Iverson, Robert W. *Executive Manpower Management: A Conceptual Scheme, Identifying Problem Areas and Suggesting Research Needs.* Syracuse, N.Y.: Maxwell School, 1968.

Lopez, Felix, Jr. *Evaluating Employee Performance.* Chicago: International Personnel Management Association, 1968.

McGregor, Douglas. "An Uneasy Look at Performance Appraisal." *Harvard Business Review*, 35, No. 3 (May–June 1957).

Mustafa, Husain. "Performance Rating Revisited." *Civil Service Journal*, 9, No. 4 (April–June 1969).

Nigro, Felix A. *Public Personnel Administration.* New York: Holt, Rinehart, & Winston, 1959. Chaps. 9 and 10.

Powell, Norman. *Personnel Administration in Government.* Engle-wood Cliffs, N.J.: Prentice-Hall, 1956. Chap. 16.

Robertson, Joseph P. "Personnel Administration and the New Federalism." *Civil Service Journal,* 13, No. 3 (January–March 1973).

Saso, Carmen, and Earl Tanis. *Disciplinary Policies and Practices.* Chicago: International Personnel Management Association, 1973.

Stanley, David T., with Carole L. Cooper. *Managing Local Government under Union Pressure.* Washington, D.C.: Brookings Institution, 1972.

Steiber, Jack. *Public Employee Unionism, Structure, Growth, Policy.* Washington, D.C.: Brookings Institution, 1973.

U.S. Department of State, *Diplomacy for the 70's, A Program of Management Reform for the Department of State.* Washington, D.C.: Government Printing Office, 1970.

Weisberger, June. *Job Security and Public Employees.* Ithaca, N.Y.: Institute of Public Employment, New York State School of In-dustrial and Labor Relations, Cornell University, 1973.

Training

9

Today's organizations rely on successful role performances in a large number of different, highly specialized functional areas. Training is a primary instrument for sustaining and improving the capacities of employees to contribute to organizational efforts.

Because of the complexity of their programs, most public agencies try to recruit persons who already possess the necessary intellectual, social, and other skills; in other words, they look for *pretrained* candidates for employment. Of course, complete control over the talents and values of entering employees is seldom, if ever, achieved. Further, the existing skills and knowledge of even the best prepared personnel must be added to as the agency is called on to cope with new situations. For these reasons, postentry training programs are essential. Regrettably, however, it has only been during the past 20 years or so that formal training for government employees has become an accepted practice, and even now training is generally not a highly developed function in most public personnel programs.[1]

---

[1] See Arthur D. Kallen, "Training in the Federal Service – 170 Years to Accept," *Public Administration Review*, 19, No. 1 (Winter 1959), 36–46.

■ A DEFINITION OF TRAINING

Although training is difficult to define with great precision, it is most often considered to be a "learning" experience or series of experiences which prepare the individual to carry out job-related tasks. General education, on the other hand, need not relate directly to vocational activities, as noted in this statement:

> With particular reference to the public service, education is understood to be the general cultural preparation which a young person receives before entering public employment, while training is understood to be the specific preparation received just before entering public employment or at a later point in the career and directed towards the performance of the duties assigned to the individual.[2]

Since in modern societies it is almost impossible to separate the lives of individuals from the organizations within which they are employed, the line between training and education is blurred. In an "organizational culture," it is inevitable that general preparation will include a large share of preparation for work in organizations.

■ THE ORGANIZATIONAL FUNCTIONS OF TRAINING

Formal organizations are held together by a "glue" of formal and informal rules defining how members should think and behave. Jobs are performed according to accepted procedures, and relationships between employees and work units are controlled by a web of laws, policies, traditions, and group norms. Complex organizations are characterized by numerous detailed regulations covering the technical side of work. Such processes as formulating a budget, designing a bridge, or programming a computer are controlled by complicated decision rules that must be followed. There is virtually no aspect of organizational life that escapes the influence of rules. Many of these rules are fairly straight-

---

[2] United Nations, *Handbook of Training in the Public Service* (New York: Department of Economic and Social Affairs, Public Administration Branch, 1966), p. 15.

forward, such as everybody shall report for work at 9 A.M. Others which concern interpersonal behavior and authority relations are much subtler and harder to detect.

It is important to recognize that preentry and postentry training play an essential part in making organizations manageable. Without a membership that is for the most part "programmed" to make organizationally appropriate (rational) decisions, organizations would have to control employees much more closely. Herbert A. Simon has written that

> . . . training influences decisions 'from the inside out.' That is, training prepares the organization member to reach satisfactory decisions himself, without the need for the constant exercise of authority or advice. In this sense, training procedures are alternatives to the exercise of authority or advice as means of control over the subordinate's decisions.[3]

Training is a key variable in the design of administrative systems. Highly trained personnel mean savings in supervisory costs and time.[4] In contrast, an untrained or undertrained work force forces management to limit opportunities for employee discretion and to control behavior directly through very close supervision of all phases of the work process. Any initial savings in salary expense or training budgets are quickly lost in increased managerial costs.

Insofar as it effectively supplies employees with the facts, frames of reference, and values involved in making acceptable decisions, training is an invaluable resource. It is critically important in contemporary organizations, which achieve control through instilling habits of coordination and cooperation rather than through the exercise of command or the imposition of hierarchical authority.[5] Where technical or professional specialization is involved, administrators do not have the expertise to tell subordinates how to do specialized jobs. Under these conditions, controls must be in-

---

[3] Herbert A. Simon, *Administrative Behavior: A Study of Decision-Making Processes in Administrative Organization*, 2d ed. (New York: Free Press, 1957), p. 15.

[4] Ibid., pp. 15–16.

[5] See Harlan Cleveland, *The Future Organization: A Guide for Tomorrow's Managers* (New York: Harper & Row, Publishers, 1972), pp. 65–88.

ternalized so that employees are self-controlling. The task of training, therefore, is not only to help build and maintain a technically competent staff. It also must serve as a central process through which influence can be exerted throughout the organization and a powerful source of control over individuals' behavior.[6]

The self-development value

Contemporary training concepts and techniques concurrently emphasize employee self-development and organizational requirements, as Bertram Gross has noted.[7] This self-development value has historically been associated with training in the United States. The organization focuses on the intellectual, social, and psychological growth of the individual, with the rationale that mature, creative, innovative employees will contribute greatly to organizational effectiveness over the long run.

The mutuality of training as a benefit to both the organization and the individual is a dominant theme of modern views of training which see it as a process aimed at changing behavior. The desired "new" behavior must be considered valuable both to the organization and the individual.[8] This was the opinion of the "founder" of scientific management, Frederick W. Taylor. Although he is very much identified with such developments as standardizing work and training workers to conform to organizational demands, he also stressed development of the individual worker:

> After we have studied the workman, so that we know his possibilities, we then proceed, as one friend to another, to try to develop every workman in our employ, so as to bring out his best facilities and to train him to do a higher, more interesting and more profitable class of work than he has done in the past.[9]

---

[6] Simon, *Administrative Behavior*, p. 227.

[7] Bertram M. Gross, *The Managing of Organizations* (New York: Free Press, 1964), p. 789.

[8] William G. Scott, *Organization Theory, A Behavioral Analysis for Management* (Homewood, Ill.: Richard D. Irwin, Inc., 1967), p. 326.

[9] Frederick W. Taylor, "The Principles of Scientific Management," in Harwood F. Merrill (ed.), *Classics in Management* (New York: American Management Association, 1960), p. 93.

Taylor's words are as appropriate now as they were in his times. Executed well, training can serve the best interests of both the organization and the individual.

■ THE PSYCHOLOGY OF TRAINING

If the psychological dimensions of training are not understood and taken into account, even technically well-conceived programs may fail. A training program can be a significant change experience for the participants, who may perceive it as threatening, especially if it poses a challenge to beliefs they hold deeply or questions the ways they have been doing their jobs. Administrators and trainers must be prepared to deal with these psychological responses. Effective training programs anticipate such variables as (1) motivation, (2) perceived relevance, (3) psychological climate, and (4) feedback, and are designed with them in mind.

Motivation

Trainees learn best when they are positively motivated to participate and feel the need for training on a personal level. Change is far easier to accomplish when trainees are psychologically "ready" for training and believe that it will help them function better. Douglas McGregor maintained that many employers follow a "manufacturing model" of training that is entirely organization centered: "The requirements of the organization are paramount. Individuals are selected, oriented, appraised, rotated, promoted, sent to school—all within an administrative framework which leaves them relatively little voice in their own career development."[10]

From a psychological standpoint, voluntary training is probably the most likely to be accepted and profited from. Failing this, training methods should be geared to individual differences in readiness and motivation.

---

[10] Douglas McGregor, *The Human Side of Enterprise* (New York: McGraw-Hill Book Co., 1960), p. 19.

Perceived relevance

A major problem encountered by trainers is resistance by trainees who do not believe that what they are undergoing is relevant to *their* work. Organizational psychologist Harold Leavitt states that "learning cannot be exclusive of the needs of the learner. And what is learned best is what is relevant to the current needs of the learner, not what may be relevant to his future needs."[11]

Unfortunately, too often administrators and trainers decide on training needs without bothering to consult with employees. Management assumes that what it believes is logical and relevant will be so perceived by the trainees. A sound approach is to carefully study the perceptions of the employees and to involve them in the process of planning and executing the training experience.

Supportive climate

Training is most likely to succeed when it is conducted in an atmosphere of trust and support. The supervisor frequently functions as trainer, giving on-the-job instructions to subordinates, and a threatening supervisor can severely hamper the learning process. Subordinates are very much aware that the supervisor will later make evaluations of how they are performing on the job. They are hesitant to risk errors during the learning process and may not report their own training needs because they believe it would "look bad" on their records.

Rensis Likert has observed a general "unwillingness of subordinates to bring their problems to the man who has the major control over their destiny in the organization. His influence upon their promotions and their future in the company is so great that they cannot afford to let him see their weaknesses."[12] Likert points to research findings that when the training and performance evaluation roles are separated, the employee is more willing to report problems and to solicit help from the supervisor-trainer.[13] It is apparent

---

[11] Harold J. Leavitt, *Managerial Psychology*, 2d ed. (Chicago: University of Chicago Press, 1964), p. 307.
[12] Rensis Likert, *New Patterns of Management* (New York: McGraw-Hill Book Co., 1961), pp. 53–54.
[13] Ibid., p. 54.

that supportive managerial and group settings reduce psychological tensions and create conditions under which employees find it easier to accept the challenge of trying to learn new skills and improve their ability to perform assigned responsibilities.[14]

Feedback

Quick, specific feedback about performance helps trainees learn with a minimum of wasted time and effort. They should not have to wait any longer than necessary to find out how well they are doing. Accurate feedback given at the proper time provides useful information and guides their efforts at improvement.

James Mosel sees the training process as consisting of three phases: input, output, and feedback.[15] *Input* is the content or substance of the training exercise, such as learning how to prepare a budget statement; *output* is the behavior produced, in this case the trainees' efforts to apply what they have learned about preparing such statements; and *feedback* is the information given them about how well they are preparing the statements. *"As knowledge of performance increases, learning increases both in rate and level."*[16]

Mosel stresses that feedback is most effective when (1) it adds meaningfully to the receivers' knowledge about their output, (2) it tells them "what to do, as well as what not to do," (3) it informs them when they are performing correctly, and (4) it is specific rather than general.[17] Likert stresses the value of short feedback cycles:

> Short feedback cycles can give each individual continuous information about his successes and failures. He can then concentrate on correcting his weaknesses and need not waste time learning what he already knows. This is a much more efficient training process than company-wide programs which assume that all individuals need the same training.[18]

---

[14] Ibid., pp. 166–69.

[15] James N. Mosel, "How to Feed Back Performance Results to Trainees," in Robert T. Golembiewski and Michael Cohen (eds.), *People in Public Service* (Itasca, Ill.: F. E. Peacock Publishers, Inc., 1970), p. 388.

[16] Ibid., p. 389. Italics in original.

[17] Ibid., pp. 391–93.

[18] Likert, *New Patterns of Management*, pp. 204–5.

Professional trainers anticipate and are prepared to deal with blockages in the feedback loop. It is always possible that those undergoing training will reject or misinterpret feedback information for emotional reasons or because they do not understand it. Special care should be taken to see that feedback is presented in clear, unambiguous terms, and whenever possible in ways that do not threaten the trainee's self-concept.[19]

The four dimensions of training psychology discussed above hardly exhaust the subject. Public personnel administrators should be aware of the contributions learning theory and psychology can make to improving the efficacy of public service training.

■ ACADEMIC TRAINING FOR PUBLIC SECTOR ADMINISTRATION

Public employers use various strategies to establish relationships with suppliers of trained manpower (see Chapter 2). Government draws its pretrained personnel from both internal sources and outside agencies such as universities, professional associations, and consulting organizations. Of particular interest are college and university training programs for public-sector administration. Although such training dates back to the 1930s, its present widespread availability is a recent phenomenon. This development is significant because it is an institutional reflection of the belief that people can be meaningfully prepared for roles as public administrators.

Administrative, supervisory, and management-related technical skills are now taught regularly in a growing number of public and private colleges and universities. Degree offerings in public administration have been solidly established in their curricula, and courses are offered in such sub-

---

[19] Mosel, "How to Feed Back Performance Results," p. 396. See also B. F. Skinner, *Beyond Freedom and Dignity* (New York: Bantam–Vintage Books, 1971), pp. 56–59, and Earle R. Gomersall and M. Scott Myers, "Breakthrough in On-the-Job Training," *Harvard Business Review*, 44, No. 4 (July–August 1966), 62–72.

jects as organization theory, administrative behavior, finance, management science, and planning. In addition to general programs of study in public administration, special curricula for persons seeking administrative careers in such functional fields as public health, criminal justice, pollution control, welfare, and public works can be found in all sections of the country today.

Public administration training and education should provide students with both the necessary skills and a clear understanding of the problems and responsibilities they will face. The scope and complexity of governmental responsibilities in contemporary society demand administrators who are broadly educated, capable of integrating their knowledge, and adept at applying it to the solution of practical problems.[20] The National Association of Schools of Public Affairs and Administration (NASPAA) has urged that educational processes should clearly communicate the realities of public service to students by exposing them as directly as possible to the wide range of challenges they will face. NASPAA recommends that classroom studies be balanced with practical experiences such as internships and that training be designed to help students develop intellectual and behavioral abilities which will be useful to them throughout their careers.[21]

Internships

As NASPAA emphasizes, academic training for those who expect to become practicing public administrators should not be considered a substitute for experience. The experience needed to gain a personal understanding of the administrative process can be developed only through actual

[20] See Rufus E. Miles, Jr., "The Search for Identity of Graduate Schools of Public Affairs," *Public Administration Review*, 27, No. 4 (November 1967), 347–51, and John C. Honey, "A Report: Higher Education for Public Service," *Public Administration Review*, 27, No. 4 (November 1967), 294–321.

[21] National Association of Schools of Public Affairs and Administration, "Education for Public Administrators: Action Proposals," unpublished report, Washington, D.C., October 12, 1973, pp. 3–4. See also James A. Medeiros, "The Professional Study of Public Administration," *Public Administration Review*, 34, No. 3 (May–June 1974), 254–60.

immersion in the day-to-day problems of administration. Cooperative relationships between schools and public agencies make it possible to provide preentry students with first-hand knowledge of substantive problems and administrative operations. The prime vehicle for such co-operation usually is the student internship.

Public service interns spend a specified period (usually from six months to a year) working in a public agency as an integral part of their educational program and professional training. Qualified representatives from the school and the agency supervise and guide their activities; although procedures vary from school to school, interns often take classes concurrently. They are sometimes paid for their work by the agency, and summer internships are a convenient arrangement.[22]

The fundamental purpose of the internship experience is to place students in an environment where they can begin to form *personal comprehension* of the administrative process.[23] The internship is a way of bringing students face to face with the fact that administration involves real people, real choices, and real consequences. Working in a real-world organization allows interns to test the concepts and techniques they have learned in the classroom and to see how they are applied in practice. Perhaps even more important, they can acquire and internalize a "feel" for problems and managerial styles. Active participation and observation are the keys. As Mary Parker Follett, one of the founders of modern organizational psychology, put it: "Concepts can never be presented to me merely, they must be knitted into the structure of my being, and this can be done only through my own activity."[24]

---

[22] See A. B. Villanueva, "Public Affairs Internship Programs in Illinois," *Public Personnel Management*, 3, No. 3 (May–June 1974), 185–92, and Richard W. Gable, "A New Internship Program for the State of California," *Public Personnel Review*, 31, No. 4 (October 1970), 250–53.

[23] Michael Polanyi, *The Study of Man* (Chicago: University of Chicago Press, 1959), pp. 11–39.

[24] Mary Parker Follett, *Creative Experience* (Gloucester, Mass.: Peter Smith, 1951), p. 151. See also Charles H. Levine, "Maximizing the Benefits of Summer Work Programs for Graduate Students," *Public Personnel Review*, 29, No. 4 (October 1968), 231–33.

An effective internship program is built on continuous efforts at cooperation between public agencies and schools. Bilateral planning and execution are required. Both sides should clearly understand the roles interns will play, the commitments and responsibilities of all parties, and the overall rationale of the internship in the agency's view as well as in educational terms. So that everybody concerned will know what is going to happen and why, joint committees of administrators, teachers, and students are of value in the planning and evaluation of internship programs. Someone in the agency, perhaps the personnel director or an aide, should supervise and monitor the on-the-job performance of interns, and a representative of the school should be formally designated as responsible for the academic phase of the program.[25]

Working interns should not be isolated from their academic home bases. Too often, the internship stage is compartmentalized, and little effort is made to integrate it into the mainstream of the students' education in public administration. This is unfortunate, because the basic purpose of an internship is to help the student integrate concepts and experiences into a meaningful whole. Guidance and feedback from faculty and other students should be readily available, perhaps through seminar meetings in which students, faculty, and practicing administrators can meet on a regular basis to discuss and analyze each intern's experiences and perceptions.

Internships can also be of substantial benefit to the host organization. Interns contribute skills and viewpoints which can be profitably tapped if the organization's regular personnel make the effort to do so. Understaffed and underfinanced departments can deploy interns to meet manpower needs and to help develop more effective technical and administrative procedures.[26] The first step is to locate and place interns where they are most likely to help. In-

---

[25] United Nations, *Handbook of Training in Public Service*, pp. 255–58.
[26] Douglas C. Montgomery, "Target of the Educational Revolution: Students and the Public Service," *Public Administration Review*, 32, No. 5 (September–October 1972), 522.

discriminate use of interns as "labor" destroys the purpose of internship, besides alienating the interns involved. Work that is relevant to each intern's interests and career goals is far more likely to stimulate a meaningful contribution. It is essential that agency personnel make interns feel welcome and valued, rather than treating them as a burden that must be tolerated. This tends to become a self-fulfilling prophecy, in that neglect by the host agency leads to apathy and disinterest in the intern. Concern and support for the intern, in contrast, provide fertile ground for the growth of motivation and commitment.[27]

■ POSTENTRY TRAINING: INTERNAL AND EXTERNAL

Postentry training can be divided into two categories: internal and external. *Internal training* is provided by the agency itself, utilizing its own premises and resources. *External training* takes place at facilities outside the agency, either elsewhere within government or outside it, as in public or private institutions of learning; foundations; industrial or commercial organizations; and trade, labor, agricultural, and scientific organizations. Examples of external training *within* government are the U.S. Civil Service Commission's training centers for middle-level managers and its Federal Executive Institute, mentioned in Chapter 2.

Although internal training can be closely controlled by the agency management, it does have several drawbacks. For one thing, many agencies are unable to support an in-house training staff of the size, diversity, and specialized skills required to meet all training needs that might arise. Besides personnel costs, it is very expensive to buy and maintain the equipment, libraries, and other facilities that are necessary for a comprehensive intraorganizational training program. Internal training also tends to be parochial, frequently serving as a vehicle for teaching standard procedures and inculcating organizational viewpoints and values. In this case it is largely limited to functioning as a mechanism for organizational maintenance. Change-oriented or "broad-

---

[27] Ibid., 524–25.

ening" training for employees is difficult to execute successfully within the constraining atmosphere of long-established
agency attitudes. Testing new ideas or experimenting with
alternative behavioral patterns usually produces best results
in a challenging as well as supportive social-psychological
environment. Edgar H. Schein describes the limitations of
internal training as follows:

> The essential elements to unfreezing are the removal of
> supports for the old attitudes, the saturation of the environ-
> ment with the new attitudes to be acquired, a minimizing of
> threat, and a maximizing of support for any change in the right
> direction. . . . it becomes immediately apparent that training
> programs or other activities which are conducted in the organi-
> zation at the place of work for a certain number of hours per
> day or week are far less likely to unfreeze and subsequently
> influence the participant than those programs which remove
> him for varying lengths of time from his regular work situa-
> tion and normal social relationships.[28]

Although external training takes employees away from
their normal work environment, it too has problems. One is
the difficulty trainees may experience when they return to
their agencies and try to use what they have learned. It
cannot be assumed that the knowledges, skills, and viewpoints acquired will fit easily into established organizational routines. If agency management does not encourage
use on the job of what has been learned, some trainees will
be frustrated in attempts to do so and others will not try to
apply the new methods and ideas.[29] Management should
actively participate in the planning phase of external training
and be prepared to make organization changes to accommodate the expected impact of the training. There should be
a clear understanding throughout the agency of the relationships between the training and the needs of the organization.

---

[28] Edgar H. Schein, "Management Development as a Process of Influence," in David R. Hampton (ed.), *Behavioral Concepts in Management*
(Belmont, Calif.: Dickenson Publishing Co., Inc., 1968), pp. 114–15. See
also Yoram Zeira, "Is External Training Effective for Organizational
Change?" *Public Personnel Management*, 2, No. 6 (November–December
1973), 400–407.

[29] Robert J. House, "Leadership Training: Some Dysfunctional Consequences," *Administrative Science Quarterly*, 12, No. 4 (March 1968),
556–71.

Most important, management should provide psychological support for trainees when they return; otherwise, the consequences for both the trainees and the organization could be highly dysfunctional.[30]

■ TRAINING METHODS

Successful training depends on the appropriateness of the instructional methods chosen and the skill with which they are employed. The relative efficacy of the available techniques depends on many situational factors, such as the substance of what is being imparted or taught and the age, experience, and other characteristics of the participants. Training specialists sometimes become overenthusiastic in extolling the virtues of one method over all others. In practice, several different training devices are usually employed in any one program, because no one method is invariably the most effective. Some of the instructional methods commonly used are discussed below.

On-the-job training

In on-the-job training, workers are instructed while they carry out their regularly assigned duties and responsibilities. An excellent example is the apprenticeship training given beginners by journeymen in the skilled trades. Journeyman carpenters or plumbers, for example, assign tasks to an apprentice and then monitor his or her performance. They may demonstrate how a tool should be used or a particular work operation executed. During the training process both journeymen and apprentices are working and meeting production schedules. The apprentices may not turn out much work, but they do produce something while *learning* the job.

On-the-job training is not limited to the skilled trades; there are apprentices and beginners in many other kinds of work. As one example, the "rookie" FBI agent may be assigned to accompany an experienced investigator who is responsible both for carrying out his regular work and for

---

[30] Ibid.

training the recruit. The senior agent may have to question suspected lawbreakers or witnesses to crimes, for example. The junior officer notes the methods used, participating very little in the actual work, but is there to help if needed and is constantly absorbing important details.

As the above examples indicate, "coaching" is an integral aspect of on-the-job training. Gross describes coaching as follows:

> In coaching, the supervisor does more than merely help a subordinate perform his job with ever-increasing competence. The coach's aim is to help someone else exploit his potentialities as a self-developing individual. He gives his subordinate increasing opportunities to perform difficult tasks on his own. This usually involves tasks that are not far enough beyond the subordinate's capacity to break him down. It also involves enough counselling to help the subordinate keep afloat but not enough to save him the painful effort of self-propulsion and self-instruction.[31]

Coaching is exemplified by apprenticeship systems for managerial personnel, in which the training takes place within the context of a one-to-one relationship between the trainee and an experienced executive. In the assistantship model, trainees are assigned to executives as aides or deputies and are given a series of developmental assignments to familiarize them with the activities and problems of the particular work activity. The administrator-coach not only provides information and guidance but also serves as a role model for trainees. As trainees note how the coach perceives problems, copes with different situations, and deals with superiors and subordinates, they learn and internalize organizationally appropriate behaviors. The coach must be prepared to devote the necessary time and energy to work closely with the trainee, carefully select problems to be worked on, and provide feedback at the most telling points in the learning process. The coach cannot regard the trainee as a competitor or a convenient handler of menial tasks. A trusting relationship must be developed in which the trainee

---

[31] Gross, *Managing of Organizations*, p. 884. See also Gilbert B. Siegel, "Management Development and the Instability of Skills," *Public Personnel Review*, 30, No. 1 (January 1969), 15–20.

feels able to rely on the executive's judgment and feedback.

Most on-the-job training is carried out by supervisors, and coaching—formal or informal—is basically a supervisory responsibility. Supervisors should be trained in coaching skills and evaluated on how they perform in this respect. Ultimately, an organization's on-the-job training capacity will depend on the coaching skills of all levels of supervision.

Rotation

In job rotation plans employees' work assignments are varied on a planned basis in order to expose them to a succession of valuable learning experiences. Trainees may be rotated from one part of an activity to another until they have obtained experience in all parts, as when personnel interns are assigned in turn to each division of the personnel office. Rotation may be between organization units without change in the kind of work, the purpose being to provide the trainee with the stimulus of a new work environment, or it may be between different functions, such as from line to staff activities. The transfers may be for limited periods of time or on an indefinite basis, but the purpose is always the same: to help each man or woman develop his or her potential.

Individualized planning and coaching are integral elements of sophisticated rotation systems. Job transfers should be geared to each employee's needs and capabilities, so that the employee is kept on each job long enough to be able to profit from it. Excessive rotation is a real danger, particularly if the assumption is that the change in and of itself will benefit the employee. Without attention from management, rotation can become a formalistic and largely purposeless ritual. If this happens, the "rotated employee is in danger of learning superficially, like a tourist in a foreign land."[32]

Lectures

The lecture is an economical method of delivering factual knowledge to large groups of people, but, as many teachers and students know, there is no guarantee that learning will

---

[32] Leavitt, *Managerial Psychology*, p. 306.

take place. A major problem is the passivity of the targets. In the lecture format, communication flows in only one direction—from the lecturer to the listeners. Trainees do not have much opportunity to practice what they have "learned" and receive comparatively little feedback. Since the lecture technique is geared to groups, not individuals, everybody gets the same treatment at the same pace, and individual abilities, interests, and motives are not recognized.

It is generally agreed that lectures can transmit factual and conceptual materials if the lecturer is skilled and well organized. However, there is little evidence that lectures significantly change attitudes or behavior.[33]

Discussions

Guided by a leader who is competent in group dynamics, problem-centered discussion groups can be an effective learning device. The group should have a predefined purpose or goal and should not be allowed to drift from the subject or become a forum for individual opinions. When properly structured, discussion groups permit two-way communication, an opportunity to clarify and amplify information and points of view, and an atmosphere conducive to effective feedback and positive reinforcement. The key to effectiveness here is the ability of the trainer or leader to act as a *facilitator*.

In effectively conducted discussions, the participants think for themselves; they are not presented with ready-made solutions or statements of principles, as in lectures. If they are allowed to contribute to the discussion, they are more likely to apply on the job what they have learned.

The case method

Both in academic classes and in government training programs, cases are frequently used as a basis for discussion. The case is a description, usually in written form, of a real-life situation which has occurred in some phase of administration. In human relations training, cases are selected to

---

[33] United Nations, *Handbook of Training in Public Service*, pp. 235–41.

illustrate problems arising in the relationships among people within an organization, at the same level and different levels, as well as situations involving relations with people outside the organization. The facts in the case are described in detail, and the solution which was actually reached to the particular problem may either be stated or omitted. In the latter case, those participating in the discussion are asked to suggest a solution. Cases vary in length, and no set format is used in preparing them; different ways of presenting the material are used.

The participants' interaction with one another in analyzing the case constitutes an important part of the learning experience. There are no predetermined "right" answers. Well-planned discussions can refine and test each participant's observations and conclusions, facilitate feedback, and generate social-psychological support.[34]

Role-playing

Role-playing is a form of practice experience which is based on case situations. In the procedure usually followed, a conference leader prepares the case beforehand, in writing, and as the session opens distributes copies to each person present. The case typically presents a problem in human relations which involves two or more persons, such as an employee having done something for which he should be disciplined.

One person in the group plays the role of the supervisor and another acts out the part of the subordinate. On the basis of the facts presented in the case, the supervisor calls in the subordinate and administers discipline as he would in real life. The other members of the group, who form the audience, critically watch the performance of each principal in the act. Once the drama is concluded, the conference leader asks the audience for comments. The act may be repeated with two other persons in the group playing the roles of

---

[34] See Norman R. Smith, "Employee Development Methods," in Kenneth T. Byers, (ed.), *Employee Training and Development in the Public Service* (Chicago: International Personnel Management Association, 1970), pp. 164–68.

supervisor and subordinate, perhaps until everyone present has enacted one or more of the roles.

Role-playing is an inexpensive training method which deeply involves the role-players and usually maintains high interest on the part of the observers. Human relations skills are practiced under conditions permitting a wide margin of experimental trial and error, and, since the mistakes made are fictional only, they do not cost the enterprise anything.[35]

Simulation and management games

Simulations have been used widely in training for technical and physical skills and are now popular in management training as well. In a simulation, trainees are placed in carefully contrived situations and asked to perform certain operations or accomplish specified objectives. Participants are given roles to play, and each is given a "data" package with information on the situation, roles, and rules of the game. Trainees face a series of tasks relating to managing relationships, organizing to accomplish objectives, and designing and acting out problem-solving strategies. During the simulation, participants and groups are asked to make decisions and solve problems as they occur. Actions taken at one stage will affect the course of the simulation as it moves through succeeding phases. Some of the more sophisticated simulations use computers to generate information and feedback on decision outcomes.

Because feedback on all of these activities is given rapidly and at appropriate points in the simulation, the actors can apply it within the context of the simulation and learn more effective behaviors as they proceed. After the simulation is finished, a debriefing or group critique of what happened takes place in which the entire sequence of events is examined in the light of relevant concepts and practices.

The primary value of simulations and games is their capacity to motivate and actively involve trainees in bridging the gap between theory and practice. Situational thinking is required, and real-world issues must be dealt with under

---

[35] Ibid., pp. 160–64.

conditions of uncertainty and risk. Participants get a feel for the importance of teamwork and communication. A well-designed simulation can be generalized and related to similar processes and problems in many different organizations. If this goal is achieved, the simulation is far more than an entertaining game; it is a powerful learning experience.[36]

Laboratory training or T-groups

One of the most controversial and misunderstood training methods is laboratory training, or the use of T-groups. Many administrators are apprehensive about it; they may have read articles in newspapers and magazines about the activities of "fringe" groups which practice what is loosely called laboratory training. Nonetheless, professionally conducted laboratory training is an established and potentially effective way of changing behavior in organizations. It begins with the individual but its ultimate success depends on organizational change. Robert Golembiewski notes, "It initially emphasizes *behavioral* changes in the attitudes, feelings, and beliefs of organization members, and subsequently *formal* restructuring which is facilitated and reinforced by behavioral changes."[37]

There are several types of T-groups in general use. The "basic" sensitivity group focuses on personal learning and self-awareness. Trainees meet under the supervision and guidance of a professional trainer to explore the impact of their behavior and attitudes on others and to try to develop more effective interpersonal styles.[38] Team training moves the process into the organization, where established functional groups concentrate on improving the instrumental as

---

[36] Eugene B. McGregor and Richard F. Baker, "GREMEX—A Management Game for the New Public Administration," *Public Administration Review*, 32, No. 1 (January–February 1972), 24–32. See also Gilbert B. Siegel and Donald Sullivan, "Building an Environmental Training Model," *Training and Development Journal*, 21 (May 1967), 41–42, 44–48, 50.

[37] Robert T. Golembiewski, "The 'Laboratory Approach' to Organization Change: Schema of a Method," *Public Administration Review*, 37 (September 1967), 211.

[38] Carl R. Rogers, "The Process of the Basic Encounter Group," in James F. T. Bugental (ed.), *Challenges of Humanistic Psychology* (New York: McGraw-Hill Book Co., 1967), pp. 261–76.

well as social effectiveness of the team. In organization development efforts, team training is systematically related to the organization's mission.[39]

In organizational terms, the training-group approach is strongly linked to the adoption of participative managerial styles, supportive group processes, and open or authentic interpersonal relationships. Changes at both the individual and organizational levels are considered to be interrelated and interdependent. For example, when participants develop increased insight and self-knowledge, this converts into open and honest communication throughout the organization.[40]

■ DETERMINING TRAINING NEEDS

One of the most important aspects of training is determining the training needs of the organization. This is often a responsibility of the personnel specialist, but he or she should not be asked to assume it alone. Management at all levels should participate in the process, and the views of potential trainees should also be sought.

A useful approach to analyzing fundamental training needs is in terms of goals and cause-effect relations. Assuming that inadequacies in worker performance are found to exist, what can the training be expected to accomplish? What will its operational goals be? Opinions on these matters run from virtual unanimity to almost complete disagreement.

Inadequate performance by lathe operators, for example, would suggest such highly specific training objectives as satisfactory output and acceptable quality. However, the objectives in a situation where groups of workers or organizational units are unable to cooperate or coordinate are less easily specified. Several can be suggested: (1) improved interpersonal relationships, (2) increased administrative capability in coordination and control, or (3) a greater

---

[39] Richard Beckhard, *Organization Development: Strategies and Models* (Reading, Mass.: Addison-Wesley Publishing Co., 1969), pp. 21–22.

[40] Golembiewski, " 'Laboratory Approach' to Organization Change," 217.

understanding of the technical and social dimensions of the other unit's functions. The root causes of the problem must be fully understood before training goals can be selected.

Without some form of agreement on these goals, it is impossible to move to the next step: selecting the most effective training methods. Here again, certainty may run from very high to very low. Even with relative certainty about *what* should be accomplished, there are usually real questions to be answered about *how* to attain the desired ends. These are problems in cause-effect relations. There are no universal remedies for any and all organizational problems, although at one time or another many executives and trainers have acted as if scientific management and T-groups were the answers to all difficulties. Program objectives and training methods should be integrated in a training plan which top management is willing to support and promote.

The strategic behavior of the personnel specialist throughout this decision process is an important variable.[41] Depending on the degree of certainty about goals and cause-effect relations (means), certain strategies will have to be utilized. In one situation there is high certainty about both goals and means, so the logical behavior is to implement the indicated training program. In a second situation, there is agreement on means but not on goals. The likely reason for this is a tendency to have "faith" in a training technique if it has worked once before. The appropriate strategy is for the personnel specialist to challenge this assumption and to ask that a rationale for a particular training method be given before it is implemented. In a third situation, agreement on both goals and means is low, which obviously suggests the need to initiate a diagnostic process and search for agreement on both goals and means. In a fourth situation, goals are specific and agreed on, so a controlled search for methods should begin.

---

[41] Felix A. Nigro and Lloyd G. Nigro, "The Trainer as a Strategist," *Public Personnel Management*, 3, No. 3 (May–June 1974), 193–98. See also James D. Thompson, *Organizations in Action* (New York: McGraw-Hill Book Co., 1967), pp. 84–95.

Trainers who make this kind of analysis are contextual strategists who are guiding a process of change and development in the direction of the highest possible certainty along both dimensions—goals and cause-effect relations. This process may not seem to be directly related to the organization's immediate problems, but it represents a conscious effort to create conditions under which it will be possible to attack and eliminate these problems at the lowest cost to the organization.

■ EVALUATION OF TRAINING PROGRAMS

Recent increased interest in productivity in government as personnel service budgets (and consequently taxes) have risen increases the need for evaluation of training programs. In most cases, the results of training programs are much less visible to legislators, taxpayers, and others than work-load data for other phases of the personnel program, such as recruitment and examinations. While numbers of recruits and examinations do not tell anything about the quality of either the persons hired or the tests, it is recognized that recruitment must take place and the candidates must be examined. Community attitudes toward education and training have become more favorable in recent years, but in times of severe budgetary limitations there is appreciable skepticism about expenditures for training of government employees.

Evaluation is easiest when quantitative measurements of worker performance can justifiably be used. The output of such employees as machine operators and clerks can be examined to determine whether or not it is satisfactory, and their production can be measured before and after training. In some kinds of training for nonproduction workers, such as reading improvement, physical counts of performance can also be made before and after the instruction given (in this case number of comprehended words per minute), but there are only a few such programs.

For the bulk of government employees, quantitative measurements of performance are unavailable or, where available, are unreliable because they do not indicate how

well the employee is doing the job. The services of re-
searchers cannot be evaluated on the basis of how many
reports they write or how many requests for data they
answer, any more than a medical doctor's worth can be
measured by the number of patients served. In a great many
government jobs, such as those of executives, the personal
qualities required are intangible, and agreement may even
be lacking as to what the critical duties and responsibilities
of the job are.

The real problem in government has not been these difficulties in evaluating the results of training efforts but inatten-
tion to the need for such evaluation, a deficiency which is
being corrected in many jurisdictions. For example, within
the personnel profession, institutes and panel sessions on
methods of evaluating training results have been held more
frequently.

The trainees themselves should be asked for their reactions as to how relevant the program was to their needs
and the effectiveness of both the instructional methods and
the instructors. Justifiably, however, there is some cynicism
about the common practice of requesting the participants
at the end of a training course to complete questionnaires
requesting their reactions. Often they have been the guests
of a sponsoring organization, even being housed at its facilities, and consequently are reluctant to criticize the host.
There also is a tendency to fill in the questionnaires quickly
in order to make airline connections or otherwise return to
work. However, if the questionnaires are well designed and
seek answers to specific questions rather than general reactions, and if the participants are given sufficient time to
complete the form and are urged to do so carefully, the replies should provide significant feedback about at least some
aspects of the training program.

Another possibility is to devote the final session of the
course to a meeting with all the participants to obtain their
frank reactions, face to face. A representative of the sponsoring organization other than one of the instructors should
preside over this meeting, although the instructors can be
present. This permits more thorough probing of the par-

ticipant's reactions, but it need not preclude the use of questionnaires, which provide for the expression of opinions participants may prefer to submit in writing (questionnaires usually do not have to be signed).

The real test of the effectiveness of the training is in the employees' performance after they return to their jobs. They may fail to apply on the job what they have learned, or it may develop when they return that they have not learned as much as they thought. As discussed earlier in this chapter, the supervisory "climate" may discourage employees from trying to apply the new beliefs or techniques they have learned. Sometimes, however, the employees may believe themselves to be different after their training experience but may fail to demonstrate this in their actual work behavior. This is often the case when a new attitude or philosophy is involved: it is generally easier to verbalize a principle than to act in accordance with it.

While the employees' opinions about their job performance after training should be sought and analyzed, more objective information will be obtained from their supervisors, colleagues, subordinates, and others with whom they are frequently in contact. In-depth interviewing is the best way to obtain information from these persons, but time and money usually restrict the extent of such interviewing.

The posttraining evaluation should not be attempted until some time after the participant's reincorporation into the job, because it takes time for new behaviors to surface and to be discerned. Even if the evidences of improved job performance are clear, they may be attributable at least in part to influences other than the training program.[42]

■ TRAINING: AN INVESTMENT IN PERSONAL AND ORGANIZATIONAL RENEWAL

Before closing this chapter, we want to reemphasize that training can be a vehicle for organizational and personal development. The rapid pace of social and technological

[42] See Herbert M. Engel, "Evaluating Employee Development," in Byers, *Employee Training and Development*, pp. 253–76.

change has made adaptation a virtual necessity for both organizations and people. The days when a high school or college graduate could reasonably assume he or she had been "prepared" for a lifelong career or vocation are gone. People must now face the prospect of a relatively continuous educational process. The same applies to organizations — their survival and effectiveness depend on the willingness of management to promote the development of every employee.

The concept of training as a lifetime process gives it a different definition than the one many in the public sector are prepared to accept. As Clark Kerr points out,

> There is a case for some degree of generality in the educational system because of the rapidity of change and growth of knowledge during the course of a career. A technically trained work force needs to be able to follow and adapt to changes in its specialties and to learn to shift to new fields. Generality is also required for those coordinating and leading the specialists.[43]

To say, as some do, that training is a luxury or something that cannot be afforded is to say that we are willing to accept the gradual erosion of our human and organizational capabilities. The question to be asked of managers, personnel administrators, and the public is: Can we afford not to train and educate our public employees?

BIBLIOGRAPHY

Andrews, Kenneth R. *The Case Method of Teaching Human Relations.* Cambridge, Mass.: Harvard University Press, 1953.

Bass, Bernard M., and James A. Vaughn. *The Psychology of Learning for Managers.* New York: American Foundation for Management Research, Inc., 1966.

Buersmeyer, Daniel C., and Joe A. Reinhart. *Organizing and Administering an Employee Training Program.* Washington, D.C.: International Personnel Management Association, 1971.

Byers, Kenneth T. (ed.). *Employee Training and Development in the Public Sector.* Chicago: International Personnel Management Association, 1970.

---

[43] Clark Kerr et al., *Industrialism and Industrial Man* (New York: Oxford University Press, 1964), p. 20.

Heisel, W. D., E. R. Padgett, and C. A. Harrell. *Line-Staff Relationships in Employee Training.* Washington, D.C.: International City Management Association, 1962.

International City Management Association. *Post-Entry Training in the Local Public Service.* Washington, D.C., 1963.

Investment for Tomorrow: A Report of the Presidential Task Force on Career Advancement. Washington, D.C.: Government Printing Office, 1967.

Marrow, A. J., D. G. Bowers, and S. E. Seashore (eds.). *Strategies of Organizational Change.* New York: Harper & Row, Publishers, 1967.

Maslow, A. H. *Eupsychian Management.* Homewood, Ill.: Richard D. Irwin, 1965.

Murphy, Thomas P. (ed.). *Government Management Internships and Executive Development.* Lexington, Mass.: D. C. Heath & Co., 1973.

National Academy of Public Administration. *The Federal Executive Institute, U.S. Civil Service Commission, An Evaluation.* Washington, D.C., 1971.

Rosen, Bernard. "The Developing Role of Career Managers." *Civil Service Journal,* 13, No. 3 (January–March 1973).

Sackman, Morris. "Make Your Own Simulations To Train Public Managers in Collective Bargaining." *Public Personnel Management,* 4, No. 4 (July–August 1975).

Salinger, Ruth. *Disincentives to Effective Employee Training and Development.* Washington, D.C.: Bureau of Training, U.S. Civil Service Commission, 1973.

Schaffer, Bernard (ed.). *Administrative Training and Development: A Comparative Study of East Africa, Zambia, Pakistan, and India.* New York: Frederick A. Praeger, 1974.

Schein, Edgar H., and Warren A. Bennis. *Personal and Organizational Change through Group Methods.* New York: John Wiley & Sons, 1965.

Tickner, Fred J. *Modern Staff Training.* London: University of London Press, 1952.

United Nations. *Handbook of Training in the Public Service.* New York: Department of Economic and Social Affairs, Public Administration Branch, 1966.

U.S. Civil Service Commission. *Self and Service Enrichment through Federal Training: An Annex to the Report of the Presidential Task Force on Career Advancement.* Washington, D.C., 1967.

Grievances and Appeals

 10

Historically, merit systems were first concerned with providing appeal rights for employees against whom adverse actions were taken, particularly disciplinary action. A paramount consideration was to protect the employee from discriminatory treatment for partisan political or other non-merit reasons. As modern personnel administration became prevalent, more attention was given to trying to understand *all* causes of employee dissatisfactions, including those with their source in poor supervisory practices, and formal procedures were developed for hearing grievances, whether or not they originated from adverse actions. In large jurisdictions, agency grievance procedures were sometimes established, in conformance with guidelines of the civil service commission. While in some jurisdictions the appeals jurisdiction of the civil service commission extended to any grievance, typically it was limited to adverse actions, and all other complaints were channeled through these agency grievance procedures.

Since collective bargaining was very rare in government, the above-mentioned civil service commission appeals systems and the agency grievance procedures were not negotiated with the unions. Thus we refer to these arrangements as management-adopted.

Today, in civil service jurisdictions without collective bargaining programs, these same management-adopted procedures continue. In such jurisdictions, most appeals heard by civil service commissions deal with adverse actions, specifically "disciplinary measures imposed by . . . appointing authorities."[1] Apart from the civil service commission appeals system, agency grievance procedures often also exist, but not universally.

In civil service jurisdictions which now also have collective bargaining programs, the unions negotiate grievance procedures, so that the process is a bilateral one. These negotiated procedures sometimes completely replace existing agency grievance procedures, but usually adverse action appeals still remain within the jurisdiction of the civil service commissions. Sometimes the agency procedures are not replaced but their scope is reduced by the negotiated grievance procedures. In the latter case, employees often can choose under which grievance procedure to file their grievances but cannot file them under both.

Ideally, the unions would like to see eliminated *all* management-adopted grievance systems, and for discharges and all other kinds of grievances to come under the negotiated procedures. The unions view a grievance filed under the collective agreement as roughly analogous to a citizen's lodging a complaint against his government for alleged denial of a legal or constitutional right. In their interpretations of contract clauses and past practices, arbitrators apply concepts of fairness, just as judges do in reviewing the actions of administrative agencies. This is why the contract provisions concluded at the bargaining table are so important; the scope of these provisions determines what matters

---

[1] Carmen D. Saso and Earl Tanis, *Disciplinary Policies and Practices,* Public Employee Relations Library, No. 40 (Chicago: International Personnel Management Association, 1973), p. 14. See also Winston S. Crouch, *Guide for Modern Personnel Commissions* (Chicago: International Personnel Management Association, 1973).

can be grieved. This scope may be broad or narrow, depending upon the viewpoints and strength of the parties at the bargaining table.

■ MANAGEMENT-ADOPTED PROCEDURES

It is difficult to generalize about the detailed features of management-adopted grievance procedures, but some observations can be made.[2] In the early versions of these plans, employees were represented by persons of their choosing who occasionally were union officials, but management frequently was not enthusiastic about union representation. Now that in some public agencies both union-negotiated and management-adopted grievance procedures exist, grievants invoking the agency procedure are represented by union officials more often; in the changed climate, union representation raises no eyebrows.

Much emphasis is placed on the ability of supervisors to informally resolve complaints to the mutual satisfaction of management and employees. Accordingly, it is sometimes provided that the employee should initially present his grievance to his immediate superior orally, not in writing. If the grievance cannot be resolved in this way, the employee then submits it in writing to the immediate supervisor. If the supervisor denies the grievance, the employee can appeal to higher levels, up to the agency head.

Since multiplication of appeal rights proves cumbersome, efforts are made to keep them to a minimum. One of the intermediate steps in some procedures is for fact-finding committees to investigate and make recommendations. The grievant and management might each designate one member for such a committee, with a third chosen by mutual agreement. One formal hearing may be guaranteed the employee at a specific step in the procedure, and sometimes several hearings are allowed, which draws out the total process.

---

[2] See *Handling Employee Grievances*, Public Employee Relations Library, No. 2 (Chicago: International Personnel Management Association, 1968), pp. 14, 22.

Even with civil service guidelines, agency procedures can vary greatly, with some agencies permitting endless hearings and others failing to provide adequate safeguards for the employee's rights. Review by the personnel director may be one of the steps in the procedure, but many personnel experts argue against this. They believe the personnel office can only function effectively in grievance matters if it provides advisory services to supervisors and employees and if it is not required to grant or deny individual employee grievances.

■ THE NEGOTIATED GRIEVANCE PROCEDURE

Since it is drafted by mutual agreement of management and the union, like any other contract provision, the negotiated grievance procedure has an entirely different aspect for unions and many employees than a management-devised system has. Particularly when final-step binding arbitration is provided, it becomes a key element in bilateralism, whereby the employer and the union agree to bargain until they reach agreement on matters subject to negotiation, as opposed to unilateral rulings by management (see Chapter 1).

Bargaining scope and grievability

That the agreement contains a grievance procedure is significant, but by itself this does not reveal how important the role of the union is and how extensive the rights of the workers are. Contracts vary greatly in the range and specific nature of the rights and benefits granted the employees, the pledges made by the union in such matters as productivity, and the arrangements for management-labor cooperation. The bargaining scope, as determined by law, sets the outer limits, but within these limits what is negotiated may be extensive or restricted, depending upon what the parties decide. In the federal service, executive orders have prohibited the negotiation of conditions of employment that are covered by existing statutes, such as compensation and fringe benefits. Many of the agreements recently concluded, however, cover quite a few aspects of personnel policy which were not encompassed in the first contracts under Executive Order 10988.[3]

This is why simply examining the grievance procedure cannot provide the answer to the impact of the agreement on the merit principle. Other clauses may deal with such vital questions as criteria for promotion; their inclusion makes these matters grievable, whereas otherwise they would not be. Breadth of contract provisions may indicate gains for management, for unions, or for both. Through contract provision, for example, management may be able to devolve certain responsibilities on the union, as in the maintenance of safety at the work site or in the area of productivity. Both benefit from the joint planning of training and other programs which is provided in some contracts.

The grievance definition

The contract's grievance definition can limit grievances to the interpretation, application, and enforcement of the provisions of the agreement, or it can extend them to complaints concerning the application to employees of any existing laws, rules, procedures, regulations, administrative orders, or work rules (including "past practices") involving employment conditions. It can even apply to any wrong *felt* by the employee. This is how the grievance procedure and the grievance definition can be made the basis for stipulating many management actions as grievable, other than those covered by the specific contract provisions. It explains why the union generally tries to make the grievance definition very broad, and management tries to restrict it.

The agreements do make clear that grievances cannot be filed over the substance of the contract (what it should provide), but unions may try to obtain through the grievance procedure what they failed to gain at the bargaining table. This is particularly true when some contract provisions are unclear, as often is the case. One reason why arbitrators'

---

[3] See U.S. Federal Labor Relations Council, *Labor-Management Relations in the Federal Service, Amendments to Executive Order 11491 with Accompanying Report and Recommendations* (Washington, D.C., 1975).

decisions are so important is that the contract may authorize them to decide whether a grievance is arbitrable, subject in some cases to appeal to the courts. Successful appeals of this type are rare, however, in view of court precedents to rule in favor of arbitrability "unless it can be said with positive assurance that the parties excluded the issue from the scope of their arbitration clauses."[4] In some jurisdictions grievance arbitrability is determined by the public employment relations agency, as in New York City, where it is decided by the Board of Collective Bargaining.[5] Under the federal program, the parties may submit the matter either to arbitration or to the Assistant Secretary of Labor for Labor-Management Relations for decision.[6]

If grievances are limited to differences over interpretation, application, and enforcement of the contract, the union may still be able to negotiate contract clauses incorporating provisions of existing laws and regulations, even in their entirety. If so, the "narrow" grievance definition turns out in practice to be quite broad. In the federal service the nature and scope of the negotiated procedure are to be negotiated by the parties, subject only to the explicit limitation that matters already covered by statutory appeals procedures, such as adverse actions, may *not* be negotiated.[7] In some state and local governments, adverse actions are both grievable and arbitrable; in most they are not.

The union's responsibilities

One of the often-heard criticisms of unions is that they either coerce some workers or fail to act in the interests of all workers. Under collective bargaining, the union that commands majority support in the bargaining unit is re-

---

[4] Robert Coulson, *Labor Arbitration—What You Need to Know* (New York: American Arbitration Association, 1973), p. 75. See also Tim Bornstein, *Arbitration: Last Stop on the Grievance Route* (Washington, D.C.: Labor Management Relations Service, 1973), pp. 10–11.

[5] See Arvid Anderson, "The Structure of Public Sector Bargaining," in Sam Zagoria (ed.), *Public Workers and Public Unions* (Englewood Cliffs, N.J.: Prentice-Hall, Inc., 1972), pp. 47–48.

[6] Executive Order 11491, as amended, Section 13 (a).

[7] *Report of Case Decisions*, FLRC No. 73A–21, U.S. Federal Labor Relations Council (Washington, D.C., January 31, 1974).

sponsible for representing all employees of the unit who desire representation in grievance cases, whether or not they are members of that majority union. If employees do not desire representation by the majority union, they can themselves present their grievances to management and have "such grievance adjusted, without the intervention of the bargaining representative, as long as the adjustment is not inconsistent with the terms" of the agreement, and provided that "the bargaining representative has been given the opportunity to be present at such adjustment."[8] The quotation is from the Labor Management Relations Act of 1947 (Taft-Hartley); and much the same language appears in many public worker bargaining statutes.

The purpose of such provisions is to protect the interests of both individual workers and the bargaining representative. The union cannot force itself on the employee, but the employee cannot obtain special treatment from management. How vigorously the union represents employees in grievances is another matter, but the criticism is also heard that a union official, to maintain voting support within the union, will support a nonmeritorious grievance simply to placate the complainant. Both kinds of criticisms can be verified in some cases, but nevertheless employees overwhelmingly depend upon the unions for help in grievance cases, and many of them would feel insecure about submitting grievances if they had to deal with management without such help. The thesis can be defended that, in any organization lacking a negotiated grievance procedure, upward communication will be deficient.

The union steward is the key figure in providing help to the employee in grievance processing. Union agreements frequently specify the number of stewards and state that they will be allowed a "reasonable" amount of time "on the clock" to investigate grievances. The word "reasonable" is used because the time stewards need is very difficult to

---

[8] *Text of Labor Management Relations Act, 1947, as Amended by Public Law 86–257, 1959, Public Law 101–80th Congress* (Washington, D.C.: Government Printing Office), p. 10.

predict; some managements want to restrict it, and some unions to stretch it. Management sometimes charges that stewards are abusing this privilege. At one federal military installation, the commanding officer, convinced that a union official was guilty of such abuse, set a ceiling on the percentage of time to be allowed him in the future — this was upheld by the arbitrator who, after reviewing the facts in the case, concluded that excessive time had been taken.[9] Many supervisors, however, believe they profit from the presence of conscientious, hardworking stewards who bring legitimate complaints to their attention and discourage union members from filing ill-founded grievances.

Steps in the grievance procedure

As in the case of management-adopted grievance systems, there is no single pattern in negotiated procedures. Some effort is usually made to keep the number of steps to a minimum and to establish reasonable deadlines at each step. In some contracts it is stipulated that the grievance is first to be submitted to the immediate supervisor orally; in others (but not many) it is first submitted in writing. Hearings may be provided at one or more of the stages in the procedure. It sometimes is provided that group, as well as individual, grievances can be filed by union representatives. The procedure may specify when and how either the union or the employer may submit a grievance charging alleged failure to respect or interpret properly the contract terms.

Arbitration

Although binding grievance arbitration is not found nearly so much in government as in the private sector (where it is provided for some or all grievances in nearly 95 percent of collective agreements), it is increasingly being adopted in government. The resistance to binding determinations by private individuals as an illegal delegation of governmental sovereignty has diminished as court challenges have failed.

---

[9] See Felix A. Nigro, "Field Operation of Federal Labor-Management Relations," in *Managing Governments' Labor Relations* (Washington, D.C.: Manpower Press, 1972), p. 46.

(Arbitrators usually are not public employees, although they may be.)

The objective of any dispute settlement procedure is to provide "finality"—a final step at which the conflict is resolved. If this finality is a unilateral decision by a management official or body, the unions have no use for the entire procedure. Before binding grievance arbitration took firm hold in industry, unresolved grievances caused many strikes. Strikes are still generally illegal in the public service but they do occur, sometimes over grievances in the absence of arbitration. The argument for binding grievance arbitration is basically the same for both industry and government: the fairness of settling the dispute by submitting it to a neutral who carefully studies the facts and contentions. Judicial review of arbitrators' decisions is available, the main grounds being whether the arbitrator exceeded his powers under the contract, whether in making his decision he decided incorrectly a question of federal or state law, and whether he "has been guilty of fraud, corruption, conflict-of-interest or some other breach of his obligation to decide the case before him with scrupulous fairness." Arbitration decisions are rarely appealed to the courts, and "it is even rarer for courts to upset arbitration decisions."[10]

There are various arrangements for the final step in the grievance procedure. A study by the Public Employment Relations Board of 104 contracts negotiated in cities in New York State reported that in 72 of these arrangements the final step was binding arbitration; in 3, it was advisory arbitration; in 19, grievance boards, which make nonbinding recommendations; in 6, mediation; in 3, decision by the legislative body; and in 1, decision by the chief executive.[11] During the first stage of the federal program (EO 10988), only advisory grievance arbitration was permitted; under EO 11491 as amended, binding arbitration clauses may be negotiated. As evidence of the reservations of public management about

---

[10] Bornstein, *Arbitration*, pp. 9–10.

[11] New York State Public Employment Relations Board, *Report on Grievance Procedures in City Contracts with Public Employee Organizations, New York State* (Albany, N.Y., January 1970), pp. 11–12.

binding arbitration, in one of its two suggested state public labor–management relations acts – the meet and confer version – the Advisory Commission on Intergovernmental Relations recommends advisory arbitration only, whereas the collective negotiations version authorizes the binding variety.[12]

If the grievance definition is broader than the contract provisions and binding arbitration is not limited to grievances interpreting the agreement, many more items are subject to binding arbitration. The New York State Public Employment Relations Board studied 106 Nassau and Suffolk County employee organization–school district agreements that had arbitration as the final step in the grievance procedure. In 42 of them arbitration was advisory for all issues; in 10, advisory for contract items only; in 34, binding for *all* issues; in 14, binding on contract, advisory on other issues; in 6, binding on contract, with the board of education deciding other issues. In one district the district principal had the final say.[13]

The arbitrators. Arbitration may be by single individuals or by a board of three or more. Recently the trend has been to use single arbitrators. The parties themselves may select the arbitrators, or they may avail themselves of legal provisions for the labor relations agency or other public agency to provide lists of arbitrators. It is common to provide in state legislation for the labor relations agency to establish panels of qualified persons available to serve as arbitrators, mediators, or members of fact-finding boards. In the federal government, the Federal Mediation and Conciliation Service (FMCS) may be requested to supply names of arbitrators. Procedures for permitting the parties to select or veto names vary; sometimes a list is supplied of several names, perhaps

[12] State Public Labor-Management Relations Act, Suggested Legislation, Advisory Commission on Intergovernmental Relations, Washington, D.C.

[13] New York State Public Employment Relations Board, *Report on Grievance Procedures in Public Employee Organization – School District Contracts in Nassau and Suffolk Counties, New York State* (Albany, N.Y., March 1970), pp. 14–15.

five or seven, and if the parties cannot agree on the arbitrator, each party in turn strikes one name from the list until only one remains, and that person becomes the arbitrator. The toss of a coin may determine which party starts the process of striking off names. Some agreements provide for the FMCS and others for the American Arbitration Association (AAA) to refer names of arbitrators from a national panel. In some jurisdictions a permanent umpire is employed, in the interests of consistency in awards and on the basis that he will have better knowledge of the kinds of grievances that recur. The ad hoc approach—picking different arbitrators on a case-by-case basis—is more widespread, largely because in most situations the volume of cases is small, and the parties may prefer not to be "locked in" by one individual who might decide too many cases against them.[14]

The background of arbitrators varies; many are attorneys by background, but others are professors or have had careers in business or government. Since the supply is limited, the FMCS, the AAA, and other organizations and universities have been developing training programs to prepare a greater number of qualified persons. As a service, arbitration extends to many other conflict situations besides employee grievances and interest disputes. It is increasingly being employed for settlement of tenant-landlord disputes, consumer complaints, and community conflicts of various kinds.

The arbitrators' fees, usually ranging from $150 to $250 per day of hearing and per day of study time required for preparation of the award, are usually split between the parties,[15] as are other costs such as those for preparation of a stenographic record if required. If arbitration were provided free to the parties, they might request it unnecessarily, and costs do discourage overuse.

Arbitrators hold hearings at which the parties submit

---

[14] Frank P. Zeidler, *Grievance Arbitration in the Public Sector*, Public Employee Relations Library, No. 38 (Chicago: International Personnel Management Association, 1972), pp. 6–7. See also Bornstein, *Arbitration*, pp. 6–7.

[15] Coulson, *Labor Arbitration*, pp. 22–25.

written statements and offer testimony and witnesses to support their side of the case. As Frank Zeidler, permanent umpire for Milwaukee County, states, the "proceedings should be neither too formal nor too informal"; strict rules of evidence like those in court proceedings are not followed, which puts the burden on the arbitrator to exercise good judgment in allowing testimony and admitting documents for the record.[16] As explained by the AAA, the customary order of the proceedings is:

> (1) opening statement by the initiating party, followed by similar statement by the other side; (2) presentation of witnesses by the initiating party, with cross-examination by the responding party; (3) presentation of witnesses by the responding party, with cross-examination by the initiating party; and (4) summation by both parties, usually following the same order as in the opening statements.[17]

In disciplinary cases, the employer usually goes first.

The arbitrator may ask questions during the proceedings to clarify the facts and the issues. Where testimony is contradictory, as it frequently is in disciplinary cases, he must decide whom and what to believe. After reciting the checklist of 11 criteria from the *California Evidence Code* for determining the credibility of witnesses, a participant at an annual meeting of the National Academy of Arbitrators commented:

> anyone driven by the necessity of a decision to fret about credibility, who has listened over a number of years to sworn testimony, knows that as much truth must have been uttered by shifty-eyed, perspiring, lip-licking, nail-biting, guilty-looking, ill at ease, fidgety witnesses as have lies issued from calm, collected, imperturbable, urbane, straight-in-the-eye perjurers.[18]

The common law of the shop. The only thorough way of finding out how arbitrators decide cases is to read a good

---

[16] Zeidler, *Grievance Arbitration in Public Sector*, p. 14. See Bornstein, pp. 7–9.

[17] Coulson, *Labor Arbitration*, p. 45.

[18] U.S. Civil Service Commission, Office of Labor Management Relations, *The Federal Labor-Management Consultant*, May 26, 1972.

sample of their decisions. Zeidler has listed 16 points based on past arbitration in private industry which constitute a kind of "common law of the shop." Not all arbitrators accept these principles, and private-sector precedents are not binding in government. Nevertheless, there are common threads to be noted in all arbitration decisions.

1. Management must make sure it gives orders which are clear and unmistakable.
2. Rules and regulations should be uniformly applied and no laxness shown toward one employee, when severity is shown to another.
3. Management should be consistent in its rules and orders.
4. Management should try to impose discipline progressively where possible: a verbal warning, a written warning, then penalties in gradual steps.
5. Management should impose penalties which are reasonable and consistent with the degree of offense.
6. Management should not try to discipline persons who use the grievance procedure.
7. Management should not try to invade the work which is understood to belong to a bargaining unit. (This is not, of course, the same as changes in the organization of work determined by management and where such a "management right" is reinforced in a written agreement.)
8. Usage, custom, past practice will prevail when both sides have acquiesced, in absence of clear language in a contract.
9. The language of the contract or agreement prevails over oral claims of modification.
10. The tendency of an employee to commit a certain kind of infraction in the past is not conclusive evidence that he has committed a specific claimed infraction.
11. Employees, if they are protesting an order to work, should do the work unless it is hazardous, and grieve later; otherwise they are insubordinate.
12. Management is responsible for its agents (or supervisors).
13. Unless modified by agreement, management determines objectives, methods, tools, work force, and scheduling.
14. Management is expected to be more tempered in its response to infractions than the employee is to threatened discipline or to discipline—the theory being that management ought to be more inclined to correct an erring employee than to punish him.

15. Specific language in agreements, rules or regulations is more important than general language if a conflict appears.
16. Reasonableness as a principle is applied to contract language meaning, interpretations of rules and regulations, orders and directives in case of ambiguity.[19]

■ADVERSE ACTIONS IN THE FEDERAL SERVICE

Some changes were recently made in the adverse-action appeal system in the federal service which point up fundamental issues in the controversy over this system. In the federal service, the technical definition of adverse action is any personnel action in which the employee is removed, reduced in rank, suspended for more than 30 days, or furloughed without pay. The governing legal provisions have been the Lloyd-LaFollette Act of 1912, the Veterans Preference Act of 1944, and Executive Orders 10987 and 10988, issued by President Kennedy in 1962, supplemented by Civil Service Commission regulations. EO 10987 was revoked by President Richard Nixon's EO 11787, effective September 9, 1974.

Employees against whom agencies file adverse actions are not guaranteed a trial-type hearing by law, but under Civil Service Commission regulations, the agencies are required to provide one such hearing, either before or after the decision to decree the action. Most agencies provide the hearing after the action is taken. Prior to Executive Order 11787, employees could appeal, either within the agency or to the Commission. If they decided to appeal directly to the Commission, they could not appeal within the agency. In a few agencies, two levels of appeals were allowed; if the second appeal was requested, this precluded appeal to the Commission.

If the appeals were within the agency, the hearing officers submitted their findings and recommendations in writing to the agency officials, who decided the cases. These officials had to occupy positions above those of the persons who

---

[19] Zeidler, *Grievance Arbitration in Public Sector*, pp. 22–23.

originated the adverse actions. If they believed less severe penalties than those recommended by the hearing officers were justified, they could impose such lesser penalties; if they found the hearing officers' recommendations too lenient, they could refer the appeal files with their comments to a higher level in the agency for decision. The employee could appeal the agency's decisions to the Commission regional office, where another hearing was held unless the employee notified the Commission in writing that another hearing was not desired. The hearing officers made their recommendations to the regional director, who could sustain or reverse the agency decisions but had no authority to modify the penalties.

The agency or the employee could appeal this decision to the Commission's Board of Appeals and Review in Washington. The board reviewed the entire case file and made its decision on that basis; it did not hold hearings or hear oral arguments. Its decision was final except that the Civil Service Commissioners could reopen the case upon a showing that new material evidence was available, that law or established policy had not been interpreted or applied correctly, or that new or unsettled questions of policy of an exceptional nature were involved. The Commissioners rarely exercised this power.[20]

Criticisms of the former system

According to Richard A. Merrill in a report prepared for the Administrative Conference of the United States,[21] three major criticisms were made of this system: (1) it permitted employees to be removed or otherwise disciplined "on the basis of illegitimate and unsubstantiated charges," (2) it provided "insufficient safeguards against unfairness," and (3) it was too "complicated and duplicative," with excessive delays in the disposition of cases.[22]

---

[20] Comptroller General of the United States, *Report to the Congress, Design and Administration of the Adverse Action and Appeals Systems Need to be Improved* (Washington, D.C.: General Accounting Office, February 5, 1974), pp. 45–51.

[21] See Richard A. Merrill, "Procedures for Adverse Actions against Federal Employees," *Virginia Law Review*, 59, No. 2 (February 1973), 196–278.

[22] Ibid., 205.

The sole statutory criterion for justifying adverse actions is "efficiency of the service." Merrill found that the basis for adverse actions was "routine inefficiency" in about 9 percent of the contested cases; misconduct, both on and off the job, in almost 46 percent of the cases, and unspecified "'other'" reasons in 27 percent of the cases. Agencies were taking disciplinary action for "reasons . . . removed from the central criterion of substandard performance," increasing the "risks of official interference with purely private behavior," yet neither the agencies nor the Commission had developed adequate standards for clarifying what was meant by "efficiency of the service."[23] Also, Commission regulations did not make absolutely clear that the employing agency had the "burden of coming forward with evidence and the burden of persuasion."[24]

In a study released in 1974, the General Accounting Office (GAO) reported that "the issue of the timing of the hearing is the most sensitive and controversial issue in the adverse action and appeal system."[25] In his report for Ralph Nader, Robert G. Vaughn stresses that since in most cases the employee is separated before the hearing, during his appeal he "may be without a job, without an income, and with his savings rapidly vanishing."[26] Merrill comments that "removal from government employment for cause carries a stigma that is probably impossible to outlive."[27] Reviewing recent federal lower court decisions, he concluded that the "constitutionality of the prevailing practice in most agencies is at best uncertain" but noted that the Supreme Court had not ruled on this issue.[28] (The Court has since ruled, in *Arnett* v. *Kennedy* (discussed in detail in Chapter 11), that pretermination evidentiary hearings are not required under the Constitution.)

Agency hearing officers were considered inadequately trained and were viewed by many employees as manage-

---

[23] Ibid., 236.
[24] Ibid., 251.
[25] Comptroller General of the United States, *Report to the Congress*, p. 2.
[26] Robert Vaughn, *The Spoiled System: A Call for Civil Service Reform* (Washington, D.C.: Public Interest Group, 1972), II–134.
[27] Merrill, "Procedures for Adverse Actions," 204.
[28] Ibid., 243.

ment oriented. Except in the larger agencies, they were part-time employees and had so few cases to handle they did not gain much experience. As to the Commission hearing officers, Vaughn believes they were anxious not to jeopardize their opportunities for advancement within the Commission and could not be depended on to be impartial. Vaughn's thesis is that the Commission itself is management oriented and reluctant to offend its "clientele" — the agency managements.

A well-documented charge was that the entire appeals process took far too long. According to the GAO, "an appeal through one agency and the two Commission levels takes, on the average, over 300 days"; during fiscal 1972 the average time for the agency appeal was 170 days.[29]

The Commission's internal organization was viewed with suspicion for not separating the appeals function from its personnel management responsibilities. Regional hearing officers reported to regional directors, who could change their decisions, and the Appeals Examining Office in Washington reported to the Executive Director.

The policy of not opening the agency or Commission hearings to the public or the press constituted another sore point. The rationale was to protect the employee's privacy, permit calm deliberations, and avoid possible disruption, but this was unconvincing to those who believed the public should be able to observe the hearings. After the decision in *Fitzgerald* v. *Hampton* in 1972,[30] the Commission decided the hearings could be open if the employee so requested, but the hearing officer could close all or part of the hearing to the public as he found necessary in the best interest of the appellant, a witness, or the public. Fitzgerald had been removed from his position by the Air Force through reduction in force. The Commission granted him a hearing, and he requested that it be open to the public.[31]

Agency appellate authorities could and often did moderate

---

[29] Comptroller General of the United States, *Report to the Congress*, p. 10.
[30] *Fitzgerald* v. *Hampton*, 467 F. 2d 755, 767 (D.C. Civ. 1972).
[31] Merrill, "Procedures for Adverse Actions," pp. 246–48.

the penalties imposed on employees, yet the Commission's appellate offices could only affirm or reverse the adverse action and could not order a lesser penalty. Merrill reported that Commission appellate officials often upheld agency penalties they privately believed too harsh; if they considered the agency penalty "grossly excessive," they sometimes reversed "cases on procedural grounds that otherwise might be viewed as harmless."[32]

The Vaughn report describes in detail a number of cases in which, according to the facts as presented by Vaughn, employees were disciplined or otherwise treated unfairly and the Commission generally failed to show a real desire to prevent or correct such injustices. The impression is conveyed that "most employees are mistreated." Disagreeing, Merrill says:

> The data we have assembled do not betray any systematic unfairness of the sort that a suspicious critic might expect to find: the system treats young, low-ranking, and female employees not much differently than employees generally, and, surprisingly, the employee who is not represented (by counsel or otherwise) fares no worse than one who is.[33]

Vaughn's basic case against the Commission is conflict of interest. The Commission provides personnel management services to the agencies and, in his opinion, tailors its personnel regulations and enforcement policies to the needs of this "clientele," yet it adjudicates agency adverse actions. Merrill rejects this thesis, stating that many other federal agencies both formulate policy and adjudicate individual cases testing the application of that policy:

> In these instances, experience and expertise are thought to outweigh the risks of systematic bias, a danger which can be inhibited by appropriate separation of functions and, in the final analysis, cured through judicial review. On this theory, one can justify assigning responsibility for deciding adverse action appeals to the agency most knowledgeable about government personnel policy.[34]

---

[32] Ibid., 159.
[33] Ibid., 205.
[34] Ibid., 265–67.

Vaughn's long-range recommendation is that adverse-action appeals should be one of the responsibilities of a proposed independent five-member Employee Rights and Accountability Board. One member would be appointed by the President, with Senate confirmation; two by the Senate president pro tem; and two by the Speaker of the House.[35]

Recent changes

When EO 11787 revoked EO 10987, which had required agencies to establish adverse-action appeal systems, the effect of the new order was to abolish the agency systems. This answers the criticism of duplication and delays caused by the dual appeal systems. Under the Commission's new regulations,[36] an agency's decision on a proposed adverse action must be made by an agency official at a higher level than the one who proposed the action.

Appeals of agency adverse actions now go directly to the Civil Service Commission, specifically to appeals officers located at field offices throughout the country. These appeals officers are a part of a new Federal Employee Appeals Authority (FEAA), which is separate from other Commission functions and reports directly to the Commissioners. The appeals officers make final appellate decisions for the Commission on the cases they decide, and they have delegated authority to mitigate penalties when it is established that the penalty imposed is not in accord with agency policy or practice in similar situations.

There is also an Appeals Review Board; it, too, is directly under the Commissioners and organizationally independent of the Executive Director and the Commission's regional directors. The Board can reconsider decisions by the appeals officers, but only on very limited grounds, such as proof that new and material evidence is available "that was

---

[35] Vaughn, *Spoiled System,* A–36 through A–59.

[36] U.S. Civil Service Commission FPM Letter No. 772-7, "Abolition of the Agency Appeals Systems and Reorganization of the Commission's Appellate Organization," July 5, 1974. See also Paul Mahoney, "Another Step: Implementation," *Civil Service Journal,* 15, No. 1 (July–September 1974), 1–3.

not readily available when the decision . . . was issued."

The Commission has proposed that as an option adverse actions be made subject to negotiated procedures, including binding arbitration. If the employees appealed under the contract, they could not do so to the Commission. The latter would have the authority to review the arbitral awards if they were contrary to law or regulation, and on other reasonable grounds as prescribed in Commission regulations. The Commission has also said it will propose legislation to clarify the meaning of "efficiency of the service."

BIBLIOGRAPHY

Amundson, Norman. "Negotiated Grievance Procedures in California Public Employment: Controversy and Confusion." California Public Employee Relations, CPER Series No. 6. Berkeley, Calif., 1970.

Arbitration in the Schools. American Arbitration Association, New York, monthly summaries of cases.

Crouch, Winston W., and Judith Norvell Jamison. *Hearings and Appeals: A Guide for Civil Service Commissioners.* Chicago: International Personnel Management Association, 1953.

Donahue, Robert J. "Disciplinary Actions in New York State Service—A Radical Change." *Public Personnel Management,* 4, No. 2 (March–April 1975).

Handling Employee Grievances. Public Employee Relations Library, No. 2. Chicago: International Personnel Management Association, 1968.

Krislov, Joseph, and Robert M. Peters. "Grievance Arbitration in State and Local Government: A Survey." *Arbitration Journal,* 25, No. 3 (1970).

Merrill, Richard A. "Procedures for Adverse Actions against Federal Employees." *Virginia Law Review,* 59, No. 2 (February 1973).

National Education Association, *Grievance Administration: Enforcing Teachers' Contract Rights.* Washington, D.C., 1971.

Nigro, Felix A. *Management-Employee Relations in the Public Service.* Chicago: International Personnel Management Association, 1969. Chap. 8.

Ullman, Joseph C., and James P. Begin. *Negotiated Grievance Procedures in Public Employment.* Public Employee Relations Library, No. 25. Chicago: International Personnel Management Association, 1970.

Ullman, Joseph C., and James P. Begin. "The Structure and Scope of Appeals Procedures for Public Employees." *Industrial and Labor Relations Review*, 23, No. 3 (April 1970).

U.S. Federal Labor Relations Council. *Labor-Management Relations in the Federal Service, Amendments to Executive Order 11491 with Accompanying Report and Recommendations.* Washington, D.C., 1975.

Vaughn, Robert. *The Spoiled System: A Call for Civil Service Reform.* Washington, D.C.: Public Interest Group, 1972.

Zack, Arnold. *Understanding Fact Finding and Arbitration in the Public Sector.* Report prepared for Division of Public Employee Labor Relations, U.S. Department of Labor. Washington, D.C.: Government Printing Office, 1974.

Zack, Arnold. *Understanding Grievance Arbitration in the Public Sector.* Report prepared for Division of Public Employee Labor Relations, U.S. Department of Labor. Washington, D.C.: Government Printing Office, 1974.

Zeidler, Frank P. *Grievance Arbitration in the Public Sector.* Public Employee Relations Library, No. 38. Chicago: International Personnel Management Association, 1972.

Constitutional Rights of the Public Employee

A major reason for the emergence of the new public personnel administration is the judiciary's changed conception of the constitutional rights of the public employee. The employment relationship in government in the mid-1950s, as described by Arch Dotson, was lopsided.[1] The public employer imposed many conditions on public employees which they had to accept to keep their jobs, and the only responsibilities of the government were those stated in statutes and thus subject to revocation by the legislature. The employee did not have any rights in the job based on the Constitution; in fixing the terms of employment, the government could and did deny the employee civil and political rights enjoyed by workers in the private sector.

The due process clause was held not to apply to public employees because, as stated in *Bailey* v. *Richardson* (1951), government employment could not be considered property, it could not be "perceived" to be liberty, and it "certainly"

---

[1] Arch Dotson, "The Emerging Doctrine of Privilege in Public Employment," *Public Administration Review*, 15, No. 2 (Spring 1955), 77–88.

was not life. "Due process of law is not applicable unless one is being deprived of something to which he has a right."[2] Accordingly, public employees were not entitled to substantive or procedural due process; they could, for example, be barred from partisan political activity (substantive) and denied the right to a hearing in loyalty cases (procedural). In 1892 Justice Holmes had stated that "The petitioner may have a constitutional right to talk politics, but he has no constitutional right to be a policeman."[3] As Dotson observed, "from the assertion that there exists no constitutional right *to* public employment, it is also inferred that there can be no constitutional right *in* public employment. The progression is that since there are no fundamental claims in employment, employment is maintained by the state as a privilege."[4]

The scope of judicial review of personnel actions in government was very limited. Anthony L. Mondello, General Counsel of the U.S. Civil Service Commission, said that "for the most part . . . the basic factual merits of controversies between employees and managers, and the range of discipline warranted were left to the discretion of managers."[5]

In the past 20 years, the courts have rejected the view of government employment as privilege and substituted the doctrine that "whenever there is a substantial interest, other than employment by the state, involved in the discharge of a public employee, he can be removed neither on arbitrary grounds nor without a procedure calculated to determine whether legitimate grounds exist."[6] They have been examining the facts in discharge and other cases involving the employment relationship and nullifying the public employer's actions if they are not believed to be supported by the facts. In this chapter, we will cover some of the principal areas in which significant new court doctrines have emerged.

---

[2] 341 U.S. 918 (1951).

[3] *McAuliffe* v. *Mayor of New Bedford*, 155 Mass. 216, 29 N.E. 517 (1892).

[4] Dotson, "Emerging Doctrine of Privilege," 87.

[5] Anthony L. Mondello, "Contemporary Issues . . . ," *Civil Service Journal*, 13, No. 3 (January–March 1973), 43.

[6] David H. Rosenbloom, "Some Political Implications of the Drift toward a Liberation of Federal Employees," *Public Administration Review*, 31, No. 4 (July–August 1971), 421.

■THE PROPERTY AND LIBERTY INTEREST IN PUBLIC EMPLOYMENT

In recent decisions, the U.S. Supreme Court has established that there can be liberty and property interests in public employment warranting the protection of the due process clause. As defined by the Court, property interests are not limited to money, real estate, and physical things but include whatever affects the livelihood of an individual (e.g., welfare benefits, eligibility for occupational licenses). In *Board of Regents* v. *Roth* (1972),[7] the Court identified the attributes of property interests protected by procedural due process. The individual must have more than an abstract need or desire for the benefit in question; he must have a "legitimate claim of entitlement to it," not simply a "unilateral expectation of it." "It is a purpose of the ancient institution of property to protect those claims upon which people rely in their daily lives, reliance that must not be arbitrarily undermined."

Roth, a university teacher who had been hired for the fixed term of one academic year, was given no reason when he was told that he would not be rehired. Under Wisconsin law, the decision whether or not to rehire a nontenured teacher was left to the "unfettered discretion of University officials," and, under Board of Regent rules, no reason had to be given, nor was a review or appeal provided. Roth brought court action in which he charged that the university's failure to give any reason for his nonretention and to grant him a hearing deprived him of procedural due process. Hearing the case on appeal, the Supreme Court majority first established that the *"nature* of the interest at stake" had to be determined; specifically, was Roth's interest within the 14th Amendment's protection of liberty and property? The Court decided that, although there might be situations in which the denial of reemployment would affect liberty, this was not

---

[7] 408 U.S. 564, 92 S. Ct. 2701, 33 L. Ed. 548 (1972). See Russell A. Smith, Harry T. Edwards, and R. Theodore Clark, Jr., *Labor Relations Law in the Public Sector, Cases and Materials* (Indianapolis: Bobbs-Merrill Co., Inc., 1974), pp. 1058–68.

true in Roth's case. The state had not made any charges against him which might reflect upon his good name, reputation, honor, or integrity; it had done nothing to prevent his finding other employment. "It stretches the concept too far to suggest that a person is deprived of 'liberty' when he simply is not rehired in one job but remains as free as before to seek another." The Court made clear that had it found Roth to have a liberty interest, he would have been entitled to notice and an opportunity to be heard although he did not have tenure. As to a property interest, Roth did not have one because the terms of his appointment "secured absolutely no interest in reemployment for the next year." He did have an abstract concern in reemployment but not a "*property* interest sufficient to require the University authorities to give him a hearing. . . ."

De facto tenure

In *Perry* v. *Sindermann* (1972),[8] Sindermann had served for two years at the University of Texas and for four years at San Antonio Junior College before being employed from 1965 on for four successive years at Odessa Junior College under a series of one-year contracts. In May, 1969, the Board of Regents voted not to offer him a contract for the following academic year; no reasons were given and no hearing granted. The district court in which Sindermann brought suit ruled that he had "no cause for action"[9] against the petitioners — members of the board of regents and the president of the college — because Odessa Junior College had not adopted a tenure system.

Sindermann argued that the College had a de facto tenure system, under which he had tenure. In the College Faculty Guide, it was stated: "Odessa College has no tenure system. The Administration of the College wishes the faculty member to feel that he has a permanent tenure as long as his

---

[8] 408 U.S. 593, 92 S. Ct. 2694, 33 L. Ed 2d 570 (1972).

[9] See William Van Alstyne, "The Supreme Court Speaks to the Untenured: A Comment on *Board of Regents* v. *Roth* and *Perry* v. *Sindermann*," *AAUP Bulletin*, 58, No. 3 (September 1972), 276.

teaching services are satisfactory and as long as he displays a cooperative attitude toward his co-workers and his superiors, and as long as he is happy in his work."[10] Guidelines of the Coordinating Board of the Texas College and University System provided that a full-time instructor or teacher of higher rank who had been employed in the state college and university system for seven years or more had tenure. In effect, Sindermann was arguing that in his case there was a mutual expectation of continued employment on his part and that of the school system, and this continued employment could not be terminated except for cause.

The Court of Appeals held that, although Sindermann did not have tenure, the failure to allow him a hearing would violate due process if he could show an "expectancy" of reemployment. It ordered the case remanded for a full hearing of the contested issues of fact. Hearing the case under writ of certiorari, the Supreme Court said that there was a "genuine issue" as to Sindermann's right to continued employment at Odessa, since there could be an unwritten "common law" in a university that certain employees have the equivalent of tenure. It considered this "particularly likely" at Odessa and affirmed the judgment of the Court of Appeals remanding the case to the district court.[11] If Sindermann could prove he had a property interest in reemployment, he would be entitled to a hearing, although not necessarily to reinstatement. The important consideration was that he would be able to challenge the sufficiency of the reasons for his nonretention and argue his case for reinstatement on that basis. The Supreme Court's decision, however, did not require an evidentiary hearing *before* dismissal. The Court made no mention of when the hearing need be held.

In both *Board of Regents* v. *Roth* and *Perry* v. *Sindermann*, the Supreme Court emphasized that the government cannot deny any person, tenured or untenured, his liberty rights and freedom of speech. Tenure affects property rights only.

---

[10] Smith, Edwards, and Clark, *Labor Relations Law in Public Sector*, p. 1072.

[11] Ibid., pp. 1072–73.

The property interest in government employment

In *Arnett* v. *Kennedy* (1974),[12] Kennedy, a nonprobationary employee in the competitive civil service, had been dismissed from his position as a field representative in the Chicago Regional Office of the Office of Economic Opportunity (OEO) for allegedly making recklessly false and defamatory statements about other OEO employees. He had publicly stated that the regional director and his administrative assistant had offered a bribe of a $100,000 grant of OEO funds to the representative of a community action organization if the representative would sign a statement against Kennedy and another OEO employee. When he received the notification of proposed adverse action, Kennedy was advised of his right under Civil Service Commission and OEO regulations to reply to the charges both in writing and orally, but he elected not to do so. Instead he argued that the charges were unlawful because "the standards and procedures established by and under the Lloyd-LaFollette Act for the removal of nonprobationary employees from the federal service unwarrantedly interfere with those employees' freedom of expression and deny them procedural due process of law." (We are now concerned with Kennedy's contention about procedural due process; later in this chapter the constitutionality of Lloyd-LaFollette with respect to freedom of expression will be discussed.)

Kennedy maintained that, since he had a property interest in his job, he was entitled to a pretermination evidentiary proceeding before an impartial hearing officer. The Lloyd-LaFollette Act states that "examination of witnesses, trial, or hearing is not required but may be provided in the discretion of the individual directing" the dismissal; Civil Service Commission regulations provide that the employee is entitled to an evidentiary hearing either before or after the decision to take the action. In OEO the only trial-type hearing available typically was held after dismissal.

The district court ruled that Kennedy was entitled to the evidentiary pretermination hearing. When the case was

---

[12] 416 U.S. 134 (1974).

heard by the Supreme Court on appeal, four separate opinions were filed. Six of the justices concurred that a trial-type pretermination hearing was not required; the remaining three thought it was. *Six justices agreed that Kennedy had a property interest in his employment.*

Justices William H. Rehnquist, Warren E. Burger, and Potter Stewart accepted that Kennedy "did have a statutory expectancy that he not be removed other than for 'such cause as will promote the efficiency of the service.'" However, this right was qualified by the statute itself, which does not require hearings. Hence they held Kennedy was not entitled to any hearing and surely not a pretermination hearing. Kennedy's procedural rights depended on the statute, not the Constitution, a view rejected by Justices Lewis F. Powell and Harry A. Blackmun in their opinion. They could not agree that the "constitutional guarantee of procedural due process accords to appellee no procedural protections against arbitrary or erroneous discharge other than those expressly provided in the statute," and that the "statute governing federal employment determines not only the nature of appellee's property interest, but also the extent of the procedural protections to which he may lay claim." If so, no matter what the nature of the person's property interest, he could be deprived of it without notice or hearing at any time.

Although Powell and Blackmun held that Kennedy's due process rights were determined by the Constitution, not the statute, they also maintained that a pretermination evidentiary hearing depended upon a "balancing process in which the Government's interest in expeditious removal of an unsatisfactory employee is weighed against the interest of the affected employee in continued public employment." The government and the public's interest was to maintain "employee efficiency and discipline"; besides there was the additional expense of a prior trial-type hearing. Kennedy's interest was in avoiding loss of income as he waited for a posttermination hearing, a delay which could be considerable. But, reasoned Powell and Blackmun, he might have "independent resources to overcome any temporary hardship," he might be able to find a job in private enterprise, and, failing all else, he would be eligible for welfare benefits.

In a lengthy separate opinion, Justice Byron White agreed with Powell and Blackmun that Kennedy's due process procedural rights originated in the Constitution, not the statute. He also agreed that a trial-type pretermination hearing was not required, but he believed a "mini-pretermination hearing" of notice and opportunity to respond was required. White's interpretation was that Kennedy had been denied his Constitutional rights because the OEO would have had him respond to the notification of dismissal by appearing before the very person who had ordered him fired—the regional director. White's reasoning was the same as Powell's and Blackmun's on Kennedy's economic problems; he could find employment in the private sector or if necessary "draw on the welfare system."

Justices Thurgood Marshall, William J. Brennan, and William O. Douglas considered previous Supreme Court decisions to be conclusive that Kennedy's property and liberty interests were so great that an evidentiary trial-type pretermination hearing was required. The stigma of dismissal from government employment implicated "liberty interests"; since in posttermination hearings as many as a fourth of all agency dismissals were found to be illegal and there was considerable delay between discharge and the holding of the hearing, the employee's loss of income was substantial. The argument that the employee could go on welfare exhibited "gross insensitivity to the plight of these employees," since welfare applicants "must be all but stripped of their worldly goods" to be eligible for benefits.

The majority decision in *Arnett* v. *Kennedy* created much unfavorable reaction among public employees, not only because of the ruling on Kennedy's procedural due process rights but also because, except for Marshall, Brennan, and Douglas, the Court held that the Lloyd-LaFollette Act provision authorizing removal "for such cause as will promote the efficiency of the service" was not unconstitutionally vague and overbroad when applied to speech. The determinations with respect to property and liberty rights do solidify previous Supreme Court rulings and make clear that they cover both nonteachers and teachers.

■ FREEDOM OF EXPRESSION

Prior to *Arnett v. Kennedy*, the leading U.S. Supreme Court decision on free speech rights of public employees was *Pickering v. Board of Education* (1968).[13] Pickering, a high school teacher in Illinois, was dismissed by the board of education for writing a letter to a local newspaper criticizing the board. Several efforts by the board to raise funds by bond issues had been defeated by the voters. In his letter, Pickering alleged that the superintendent of schools had stated that teachers opposing a bond referendum "should be prepared for the consequences" and claimed that the board was allocating a disproportionate amount of school funds to athletic activities. The Illinois courts upheld the dismissal, rejecting claims of 1st and 14th Amendment protections on the ground that as a teacher Pickering should refrain from making public statements about the school's operation "which in the absence of such position he would have an undoubted right to engage in."[14]

Rejecting the proposition that public employment could be subjected to any conditions, no matter how unreasonable, the Court ruled for Pickering, finding that his First Amendment rights had been violated. However, while teachers could not constitutionally be compelled to relinquish a right "they would otherwise enjoy as citizens to comment on matters of public interest with the operation of the public schools in which they work," the state did have interests as an "employer in regulating the speech of its employees that differ significantly from those it possesses in connection with regulation of the speech of the citizenry in general." What should be balanced in each case was the interests of

---

[13] 391 U.S. 563, 88 S. Ct. 1731, 20 L. Ed. 2d 811 (1968).
[14] Smith, Edwards, and Clark, *Labor Relations in Public Sector*, p. 1027.

the teachers as citizens to comment on matters of public concern and those of the public employer in providing efficient services to the public.

Applying this balancing test, the Court noted that Pickering's statements were not directed to persons with whom he would normally have contact in his daily work as a teacher, so there was "no question of maintaining either discipline by immediate superiors or harmony among coworkers." Furthermore, Pickering did not have such close working relationships with the board or the superintendent as to make personal loyalty and confidence necessary. The Court rejected any inference from the board's position that Pickering could be dismissed for substantially correct statements because "sufficiently critical in tone." While Pickering had stated that the board was spending $50,000 annually for transportation of athletes when the true figure was $10,000, the board could easily have rebutted him by publishing the correct figures. Pickering had done nothing to bring into question his fitness as a teacher; in the circumstances of the case, his statements on school policies enjoyed the same protection as those by any citizen. The Court referred to its decision in *New York Times* v. *Sullivan* (1964), in which it ruled that under the 1st or 14th Amendments public officials are prohibited from recovering damages for defamatory falsehoods relating to their official conduct unless they prove that the statements were made with "knowledge of their falsity or with reckless disregard for their truth or falsity."

In *Arnett* v. *Kennedy*, Kennedy had maintained that the statements he made were protected by the First Amendment and that the Lloyd-LaFollette Act denied employees freedom of expression. The standard, dismissal for "such cause as will promote the efficiency of the service," was too vague; employees had no way of knowing what behavior or speech could cost them their jobs.

Justice Rehnquist, writing on this issue in *Arnett* v. *Kennedy* for six justices, disagreed, quoting a previous decision of the Court to the effect that the "root of the vagueness doctrine is a rough idea of fairness." Congress could not be expected to spell out in detail the prohibited conduct because of the practical difficulties in framing a statute "both general enough to take into account a variety of human conduct and sufficiently specific to provide fair warning that certain kinds of conduct are prohibited." These justices believed the act did not authorize discharge for "constitutionally protected speech," proscribing only "public speech which improperly damages and impairs the reputation and efficiency of the employing agency." In this opinion, Rehnquist was joined by Burger, Powell, Stewart, Blackmun, and White.

Justices Marshall, Brennan, and Douglas disagreed. Noting that the majority had cited the statement in *Pickering* v. *Board of Education* that the government had significantly different interests in regulating the speech of its own employees as compared with the general citizenry, they stressed that *Pickering* also established that teachers may not constitutionally be denied their rights as citizens to comment on matters of public concern and to criticize their superiors. They pointed out that Senator Robert LaFollette, in illustrating the abuses to be "cured by the bill," cited the instance of a postal employee's being dismissed for publicizing insanitary conditions in the Chicago Post Office building, conditions condemned by Chicago public health officers. In their opinion, the majority had evaded the issue by stating that Lloyd-LaFollette could not deny constitutionally protected speech. Since no statute can "reach and punish constitutionally protected speech," the majority had "merely repeated the obvious."[15]

When the decision in *Arnett* v. *Kennedy* was announced, some writers and union leaders interpreted it as a new Court doctrine that public employees could make no criticisms of their superiors and were being gagged. As the preceding analysis shows, the Court did not upset *Pickering* v. *Board of Education;* the balancing test still applies. That test, however, has long been unacceptable to those who believe

---

[15] 416 U.S. 134 (1974).

it leaves too much room for the government to arbitrarily suppress employees' free speech rights.[16] A decision that the Lloyd-LaFollette Act was unconstitutionally overbroad would not have been inconsistent with the balancing test; many people feel the Court should have so ruled.

Application of Pickering

Several related lower federal court and state court decisions have also applied *Pickering*. In *Ring* v. *Schlesinger* (1974),[17] Ring, a teacher in a Navy Department school on Midway Island for naval dependents, had written a letter complaining about the principal, and the school board had found her irresponsible for so doing and recommended her termination. Because she was still serving her probationary period, the appeals court dismissed Ring's contention of due process violations based on a property interest in the position. However, it sustained her claim of violation of free speech, since the letter had been sent to only four persons, three of whom were with the Navy Department and the fourth a representative of the National Education Association, which did not disseminate the letter. The court stressed that a teacher has a right to make statements of public concern and that she had not been charged with inadequate performance of duties. The district court decision was reversed and remanded for trial.

Symbolic speech was involved in *Smith* v. *U.S.* (1974).[18] The appellant was employed as a clinical psychologist in a Veterans Administration hospital, attending to emotionally disturbed veteran patients. He was discharged after being repeatedly requested to stop wearing a peace button while on duty. The district court's ruling that Smith's dismissal was not a violation of freedom of speech was affirmed by the appeals court. The latter's judgment was that Smith's wearing the button while on duty created a material and substantial interference with the performance of duty, and could

---

[16] See Thomas I. Emerson, *The System of Freedom of Expression* (New York: Random House, Inc., 1970), p. 581.

[17] 502 F. 2d 479 (1974) U.S. Court of Appeals.

[18] 502 F. 2d 512 (1974) U.S. Court of Appeals.

also introduce new factors of disturbance that might impair the already precarious emotional state of the patients.

In *Donohoe* v. *Staunton* (1972),[19] the chaplain of a state mental hospital was fired for criticizing the hospital program in a union newspaper and in a speech at a labor convention. Citing *Pickering*, the court said that the state's interest in maintaining discipline or harmony among co-workers and the need for confidentiality had to be considered, as well as the fact that a close working relationship requires personal loyalty and confidence. On the other hand, the employee may be presumed to have greater access to the facts in a particular issue. The court decided that "the interest of society in 'uninhibited and robust debate' on matters of public concern, such as mental health care, and plaintiff's individual interest in being free to speak out on matters of concern to him, outweigh those of the State as employer." Accordingly, the court said, the plaintiff's First Amendment rights had been violated by his removal.

Murray v. *Vaughn*[20] concerned a Peace Corps enrollee (Murray) who had received an occupational deferment from selective service because he was in the Corps. In October 1965 he was sent to Chile, where he served on the music faculty of a university, and in June 1967 he was expelled from the Corps, without prior notice or hearing, for publishing a letter in local newspapers criticizing U.S. policy in Vietnam. His draft board changed his classification to II–A and called him up for induction. Murray brought court action alleging that his constitutional rights were being denied and that the draft board was seeking to enforce the employment policies of the Peace Corps. The court decided that Murray's statements had been made as an individual citizen and thus were protected by the Constitution.

In *Lefcourt* v. *Legal Aid Society*,[21] the plaintiff relied upon *Pickering* in claiming that the Society had no grounds for dismissing him for making critical statements about its

---

[19] 471 F. 2d 475 (7th Cir., 1972).
[20] 300 F. Supp. 688 (1969).
[21] 38 U.S.L.W. 2633 (S.D.N.Y., May 11, 1970), U.S.D.C., S.N.Y.

policies. The court upheld the dismissal; whereas in the Pickering case the employee's remarks did not affect anyone with whom he was in daily contact, Lefcourt had been responsible for a series of incidents which caused disharmony in the organization. *Murphy* v. *Facendia* (1969),[22] concerns a group of Vista volunteers who, during a conference held on government time, drafted and signed a petition against the Vietnam war. Superiors had warned them that signing the document would result in dismissal. The volunteers brought suit to enjoin any dismissals as a violation of their constitutional rights, but the court ruled that the Pickering case did not apply because they had made the statements on official time and had engaged in group action causing a "conflict with their superiors" and adversely affecting Vista's efficiency.

■ LOYALTY OATHS

Prior to 1960, the U.S. Supreme Court upheld loyalty oaths, within a "relatively confined area,"[23] as reasonable regulations for government employment, provided there was no adverse effect on those who during their period of affiliation with a proscribed organization were innocent of its purposes. In *Weiman* v. *Updegraff* (1952),[24] the Court voided an Oklahoma loyalty oath requiring all state employees to swear that they were not, and during the preceding five years had not been, members of any organization listed by the U.S. Attorney General as "communist front" or "subversive." The Oklahoma Supreme Court had construed this oath as excluding persons from state employment solely on the basis of membership, regardless of their knowledge of the purposes and activities of the organizations concerned. The U.S. Supreme Court ruled that the due process clause does not permit a state, in attempting to bar disloyal persons from

---

[22] 307 F. Supp. 353, 355 (D. Colo. 1969).
[23] Emerson, *System of Freedom of Expression*, p. 225.
[24] 344 U.S. 183 (1952).

its employment, to classify innocent with knowing association.

In *Shelton* v. *Tucker* (1960),[25] the Court declared invalid an Arkansas statute, aimed primarily at the NAACP, which required public school and college teachers, as a condition of employment, to file yearly affidavits listing every organization to which they had belonged or regularly contributed during the preceding five years. Although the state had a right to inquire into the fitness and competence of its teachers, to require them to disclose all organization memberships was a violation of the constitutional right of free association, "a right closely allied to freedom of speech and a right which, like free speech, lies at the foundation of a free society."[26] As Thomas Emerson points out, although this decision did not deal with loyalty oaths, it "introduced the requirement that a State oath or program would have to be carefully tailored to cover only those areas that appeared to the Court clearly relevant."[27]

In *Cramp* v. *Board of Public Instruction* (1961),[28] the Florida Supreme Court had held constitutional a state statute requiring all employees of the state and its subdivisions to swear in writing that they had never lent "aid, support, advice, counsel or influence to the Communist Party." The U.S. Supreme Court ruled that the meaning of the oath was so vague and uncertain that the state could not, within the due process clause of the 14th Amendment, force an employee to take it at the risk of subsequent prosecution for perjury or immediate dismissal.

The next loyalty case before the U.S. Supreme Court, *Elfbrandt* v. *Russell* (1966),[29] concerned an oath drafted by the Arizona legislature which was intended to eliminate vagueness. Employees were subject to perjury and dis-

---

[25] 364 U.S. 479, 81 S. Ct. 247, 5 L. Ed. 2d 231 (1960).
[26] Smith, Edwards, and Clark, *Labor Relations Law in Public Sector*, p. 1022.
[27] Emerson, *System of Freedom of Expression*, p. 234.
[28] 368 U.S. 278 (1961).
[29] 384 U.S. 11, 86 S. Ct. 1238, 16 L. Ed. 2d 321 (1966).

charge if they knowingly became members of the Communist Party or any other organization advocating the overthrow of the government. The Court declared the oath unconstitutional, arguing that (1) political groups may embrace legal and illegal aims, and one may join such groups without embracing the latter; (2) those who join an organization without sharing its unlawful purposes and without participating in its unlawful activities pose no threat to constitutional government; and (3) to presume conclusively that those who join a "subversive" organization share its unlawful aims is forbidden by the principle that a state may not compel citizens to prove that they were not engaged in criminal advocacy. The Arizona act unnecessarily infringed on the freedom of political association because it was not "narrowly drawn to define and punish specific conduct as constituting a clear and present danger."

In *Keyishian* v. *Board of Regents* (1967),[30] the appellants, faculty and nonfaculty in the state university system, claimed that the state's loyalty laws and regulations were unconstitutional. Their continued employment had been threatened or terminated when they refused to comply with the university trustees' requirement that each certify that he was not a communist. The state's education law provided that "treasonable or seditious" utterances or acts were grounds for dismissal and required the regents to make a list of subversive organizations, membership in which would be *prima facie* evidence of disqualification. The Court found these provisions were unconstitutionally vague and could have a stifling effect on the "free play of spirit which all teachers ought especially to cultivate and practice." It repeated the *Elfbrandt* doctrine, that mere knowing membership without a specific intent to further unlawful aims of an organization was not a constitutionally adequate basis for sanctions.[31]

Emerson concludes that the impact of these decisions is that the "disclaimer oath is beset with constitutional re-

---

[30] 385 U.S. 589, 87 S. Ct. 675, 17 L. Ed. 2d 629 (1967).
[31] See Smith, Edwards, and Clark, *Labor Relations Law in Public Sector*, pp. 996–1004.

quirements almost impossible to meet."[32] To be proscribed, the advocacy must not only be of the action type but also create a probable danger, and the association must be knowing rather than innocent and active rather than passive, with definite intent to further the illegal objectives of the organization. Since these questions can "really be ascertained only on a case-by-case, rather than a blanket, basis," it is "virtually impossible for either the Federal or a State government to impose a meaningful loyalty oath upon its employees."[33]

■ PRIVATE LIFE AND MORALS

With court sanction, public agencies for many years barred from employment and discharged persons for immoral conduct, which was defined to include extramarital relations and homosexualism, but court decisions in this area have changed significantly. The courts began this shift by requiring the public employer to describe clearly the individual's conduct which constitutes "immoral conduct," as in homosexuality. They then began to reverse disciplinary actions where their review of the facts showed no connection between the employee's behavior and the efficiency of the service. This precedent, established in *Norton* v. *Macy* (1969)[34] by the Court of Appeals for the District of Columbia, is the one now applied.

Norton, an employee of the National Aeronautics and Space Administration (NASA), was arrested by District of Columbia police after he had been observed during the early morning picking up another male in his car. Notified that Norton was in custody, the NASA security chief sat in on part of the police interrogation. Norton was given a traffic summons after he denied making homosexual advances to the male he had picked up. The security chief invited Norton to NASA offices, where he questioned him until

---

[32] Emerson, *System of Freedom of Expression*, p. 241
[33] Ibid., p. 240.
[34] 417 F. 2d 1161 (D.C. Cir. 1969).

6:00 A.M., and during this interrogation Norton admitted to homosexual tendencies and mutual masturbation with males in high school and college. Although he denied being a homosexual, NASA concluded he was and fired him for "immoral, indecent, and disgraceful conduct."

The court voided the dismissal, noting that the agency had said Norton was a good worker and that there were no security risks involved, only the danger of public scandal. Since there was no showing that Norton's conduct had "some ascertainable deleterious effect on the efficiency of the service," the dismissal was arbitrary, particularly since the appellant had not flaunted his conduct.[35]

In *Society for Individual Rights, Inc.* v. *Hampton*,[36] the Civil Service Commission had ordered the plaintiff dismissed from his position as a supply clerk with the Department of Agriculture because at the time of discharge from the Army he had admitted he was a homosexual. The court held that the dismissal was improper, citing *Norton* v. *Macy:*

> The Commission can discharge a person for immoral behavior only if that behavior actually impairs the efficiency of the service. The Commission has not met—indeed, it has not even tried to meet—this standard . . . the Commission must show "some reasonably foreseeable, specific connection between an employee's potentially embarrassing conduct and the efficiency of the service; (it) cannot support a dismissal as promoting the efficiency of the service merely by turning its head and crying "shame."

The plaintiff was ordered reinstated with back pay, and the Commission was ordered to

> forthwith cease excluding or discharging from government service any homosexual person who the Commission would deem unfit for government employment solely because the employment of such a person in the government service might bring that service into the type of public contempt which might reduce the government's ability to perform the public business with the essential respect and confidence of the citizens which it services.[37]

[35] See Smith, Edwards, and Clark, *Labor Relations Law in Public Sector*, pp. 1042–48.

[36] U.S.D.C. N.D. Calif., Civil No. C-73-0139 AJZ (Oct. 31, 1973).

[37] United States Civil Service Commission, General Counsel's Notes, 2, No. 3 (February 1974).

In *Joseph* v. *Blount* (1972),[38] a Post Office probationary employee was fired after he had been arrested in the men's room of a downtown department store and charged with perversion under the California Penal Code. The court upheld the dismissal, holding that the Civil Service Commission and the Post Office did not act arbitrarily or capriciously in concluding that the commission of such acts in a public place was relevant to the employee's fitness for his position.

The courts are also requiring a "rational nexus" between private conduct and performance on the job in cases involving heterosexual activity. In *Mindel* v. *Civil Service Commission* (1970),[39] a postal clerk was removed for living with a young woman "without benefit of marriage." Relying on *Norton,* the court deemed the dismissal a violation of due process and the right to privacy. The plaintiff held a nonsensitive position, his conduct was discreet and not illegal under California law, no notoriety or scandal were involved, and there was no connection with his job performance.

Dress and personal appearance

Recent court rulings have put the burden of proof on the employer to "show that any restrictive dress regulation is not arbitrary, but necessary to prevent disruption."[40] In *Lucia* v. *Duggan* (1969),[41] the plaintiff was clean shaven until he grew a short, neat, and well-trimmed beard over the Christmas holidays. He returned to school and taught for two weeks without disruption, but the school superintendent told him there was an unwritten policy against beards. The board sent him a letter requesting him to shave it off; when he did not do so, it voted to suspend him for seven days, the plaintiff receiving no notice that the board was considering such action. The board later suspended him for two more

---

[38] U.S.D.C. N.D. Calif. No. C-71, 534-SC, December 14, 1972.

[39] 312 F. Supp. 485 (N.D. Cal. 1970). For other cases, see Smith, Edwards, and Clark, *Labor Relations Law in Public Sector,* pp. 1048–56.

[40] June Weisberger, *Job Security and Public Employees* (Ithaca, N.Y.: Institute of Public Employment, New York State School of Industrial and Labor Relations, Cornell University, 1973), p. 29.

[41] 303 F. Supp. 112 (D. Mass. 1969).

days for still wearing the beard and voted to meet again to consider dismissing him.

The plaintiff was not notified of the proposed meeting, but it was publicized locally. He asked that the meeting be postponed so he could obtain legal counsel, but this was not done. At the meeting, he met with the board in executive session and again requested postponement, but it was denied, he was fired, and no mention was made in the minutes of the reason for the action. The court ruled that the plaintiff had been denied due process because he had not been told what the charges were. Furthermore, the absence of a predismissal written or announced policy that male school teachers should not wear beards in the classroom amounted to an indiscriminate merging of a legislative-type function (determining whether wearing of a beard should be grounds for dismissal) and a judicial-type function (deciding whether the teacher was wearing the beard without reasonable explanation and whether the dismissal was suitable).

In *Garrett* v. *City of Troy* (1972),[42] a municipal employee was dismissed for failure to trim or remove his moustache and sideburns. The court held that the removal was not a violation of due process, since the city acted upon the basis of substantial evidence that the employee's appearance caused unfavorable comments by the general public and other city employees and interfered with the proper functioning of the city. What constitutes substantial evidence to one court may not, of course, do so to another.

Being a nudist was the issue in *Bruns* v. *Pomerleau* (1970).[43] The plaintiff, a practicing nudist, claimed that refusal to accept his application as a probationary patrolman violated the 1st, 5th, and 14th Amendments. The police chief defended the plaintiff's rejection, arguing the need to maintain discipline and morals and to have a good public image. The court upheld the plaintiff, noting (1) there was nothing unusual about his background except for being a

[42] 341 F. Supp. 633 (E.D. Mich. 1972).
[43] 319 F. Supp. 58 (D. Md. 1970). See Smith, Edwards, and Clark, *Labor Relations Law in Public Sector*, pp. 1053–56.

nudist; (2) no proof had been supplied that his being a nudist would interfere with performance of police duties; and (3) other police officers and federal employees were members of the same nudist organization.

■ POLITICAL ACTIVITIES

It has been a long-standing practice for the political activities of millions of public employees to be greatly restricted. Historically, the purpose of federal and state legislation providing such restriction was to prevent coercion of public employees in elections and other partisan political activities, assure their political neutrality, and protect the merit system and the efficiency of the service. The Hatch Act of 1939 applies to all employees in the federal executive branch except for the President, the Vice President, and the heads and assistant heads of executive departments and those appointed by the President with Senate confirmation. On the basis of a 1940 amendment, it also applies to state or local government employees "whose principal employment is in connection with any activity which is financed in whole or in part by loans or grants made by the United States."[44] An estimated five million federal, state, and local employees are now covered.

Specifically, the Hatch Act prohibits the "use of official authority or influence for the purpose of interfering with an election or affecting the result thereof," and taking "any active part in political management or in political campaigns." Since the first prohibition deals with action, not thought, it poses no problem for First Amendment rights; the need for the government to protect against such interference is generally not disputed. The second is sweeping, affects thought, and has in the opinion of many made the covered employees political eunuchs.[45] The Act is enforced by the U.S. Civil Service Commission, except that for federal employees not in the competitive civil service the enforce-

[44] Ch. 410, 53 Stat. 1147, Ch. 640, 54 Stat. 767.
[45] "Collective Bargaining and Politics in Public Employment," *UCLA Law Review*, 19, No. 6 (August 1972), 968–69.

ment responsibility rests with the employing department. For federal employees the penalty for violations is removal unless the Commissioners unanimously vote against such action, in which case a minimum penalty of 30 days' suspension must be imposed. In the case of state and local employees, if the Commission finds that a violation has occurred, it decides whether removal is warranted. If it recommends removal but the state or local government employer does not comply, the federal funding agency must withhold from the grant or loan an amount equal to two years' pay of the employee.

A recent political activity poster issued by the Commission prohibits the following: campaigning for partisan candidates or political parties; working to register voters for one party only; making campaign speeches or engaging in other activity to elect a partisan candidate; being a candidate or working in a campaign if any candidate represents a national or state political party; collecting contributions or selling tickets to political fund-raising functions; distributing campaign material in a partisan election; organizing or managing political rallies or meetings; holding office in a political club or party; and circulating nominating petitions and campaigning for or against a candidate or slate of candidates in a partisan election. (The Hatch Act exempts from the political activity restrictions state and local employees in educational or research institutions.)

Subject to departmental regulations, the following activities are permitted: registering and voting according to one's choice; assisting in voter registration drives; expressing opinions about candidates and issues; participating in campaigns where none of the candidates represents a political party; contributing money to a political organization or attending a political fund-raising function; wearing or displaying political badges, buttons, or stickers; attending political rallies and meetings; joining a political club or party; signing nominating petitions; and campaigning for and against referendum questions, constitutional amendments, municipal ordinances, and so on.

To varying degrees, most state and local governments

restrict their employees' political activities.[46] Some have laws more restrictive than the Hatch Act, for example, prohibiting voluntary contributions and permitting employees "only to express their opinions privately," but most states have laws which are more lenient. Generally speaking, the Hatch Act has been a pervasive model for most state and local governments.

The issue of constitutionality

In 1947, in *United Public Workers* v. *Mitchell*,[47] the U.S. Supreme Court, by a four to three decision, upheld the Hatch Act prohibition on "taking an active part in political management or in political campaigns," ruling that it did not violate the First, Fifth, Ninth, and Tenth Amendments. Stating that the "fundamental human rights" concerned were not absolute, the majority defined the Court's task as that of balancing the "extent of the guarantees of freedom against a congressional enactment to protect a democratic society against the supposed evil of political partisanship by classified employees of government." The standard it applied was that the conduct regulated be "reasonably deemed by Congress to interfere with the efficiency of the public service." Since Congress and the President were responsible for efficient public service, if in their judgment efficiency was "best obtained by prohibiting active participation by classified employees in politics as party officers or workers," it saw "no constitutional objection."

In a companion case, *Oklahoma* v. *United States Civil Service Commission*,[48] the Court sustained the provision in the Hatch Act prohibiting state and local government employees in federally aided programs from being active in political management or in political campaigns. While under the Tenth Amendment the federal government could not

---

[46] See Commission on Political Activity of Government Personnel, *A Commission Report*, vol. 2, *Research*, (Washington, D.C.: Government Printing Office, 1968), pp. 91–157, and *UCLA Law Review*, 19, No. 6 (August 1972), 970–83.

[47] 330 U.S. 75, 67 S. Ct. 556, 91 L.Ed. 754 (1947).

[48] 330 U.S. 127 (1947).

directly regulate political activities of state officials and local employees, it could do so indirectly by fixing "the terms upon which its money allotments to States shall be disbursed."

In July 1972, after a long period of rising public employee discontent with the Hatch Act, a three-judge federal district court, by a two to one decision, declared unconstitutional the Hatch Act prohibition of political activity by federal employees. The majority did not question the government's interest in so restricting federal employees; its concern was that the prohibitions lacked precision and that the Act was "capable of sweeping and uneven application." It referred to a provision in the Act adopting by reference all rulings and decisions on prohibited political activities made by the Commission prior to 1940; to understand the law, the employee had to be familiar with some 3,000 decisions made by the Commission between 1907 and 1939. While generally praising the Commission for its enforcement of the Act, it concluded that

> any conscientious public servant concerned for the security of his job and conscious of the latent power in his supervisor to discipline him . . . must feel continuously in doubt as to what he can do or say politically. The result is unacceptable when measured by the need to eliminate vagueness and overbreadth in the sensitive area of free expression. [49]

In 1973, in a six to three decision in *United States Civil Service Commission v. National Association of Letter Carriers, AFL–CIO*,[50] the Supreme Court reaffirmed its decision in *United Public Workers v. Mitchell*. It found that there was nothing "fatally overbroad about the statute" and that the Commission's regulations were "set out in terms that the ordinary person exercising ordinary common sense can sufficiently understand and observe, without sacrifice to the public interest," and were not impermissibly vague. The restrictions on endorsements in advertisements, broad-

---

[49] *National Association of Letter Carriers, AFL–CIO, et al. v. United States*, D.D.C. July 31, 1972.

[50] *United States Civil Service Commission v. National Association of Letter Carriers*, 93 S. Ct. 2880, 37 L. Ed. 2d 796 (1973).

casts, and literature, and on speaking at political party meetings in support of partisan candidates for public or party office, the major areas of difficulty, were "clearly stated, they are political acts normally performed only in the context of partisan campaigns by one taking an active role in them, and they are sustainable for the same reasons that the other acts of political campaigning are constitutionally proscribable."

In a case decided on the same day, *Broadrick* v. *Oklahoma*,[51] the Court also upheld the section of Oklahoma's merit system law containing Hatch Act–type political activity restrictions. The Court majority ruled that the statute contained explicit standards, the prohibitions were confined to clearly partisan political activity, and the activities in which the particular plaintiffs were engaged were not constitutionally protected.

These two decisions greatly disappointed public employee leaders and others who had been optimistic that the Court would reverse its 1947 rulings. Their reasoning was that the Hatch Act was outmoded because political patronage had declined and the number of public employees had grown so greatly as to remove from active political participation a substantial proportion of the total citizenry. In 1947, the Court was applying the privilege theory of public employment, which had been discarded. In *Pickering*, it put the burden on the state "to affirmatively demonstrate that its interest in restricting the first amendment rights of public employees was significantly greater than its interest in limiting the same speech of any other citizen."[52] The Hatch Act prohibitions were not limited to cases "where the expression can be shown to relate to job performance, either by way of indicating the employee's competence, interfering with his capacity to carry out orders, or impairing his relations with the rest of the organization."[53] To protect public employees from political coercion, they had been

---

[51] 93 S. Ct. 2908, 37 L. Ed. 2d 830, 41 L.W. 5111 (1973).
[52] *UCLA Law Review*, 19, No. 6 (August 1972), 1000.
[53] Emerson, *System of Freedom of Expression*, p. 590.

stripped of their political rights, "as much as if an unpopular minority were protected from hostile violence by being forbidden to meet in public." Even Justice Stanley F. Reed, who wrote the majority opinion in *United Public Workers* v. *Mitchell*, had said that "political neutrality is not indispensable to a merit system."[54]

In late 1975, the House of Representatives passed a bill repealing the Hatch Acts, but as this is written President Ford has indicated he will veto the bill. Repeal was strongly supported by the AFL-CIO. One of the fears is that repeal would burst open the already expanded political activities of employee unions, and they would coerce their members to be active politically in union causes.

Support for liberalization of the political activity restriction is not limited to the unions. In Fall 1967, the Commission on Political Activity of Government Personnel established by Congress in 1966 recommended changing the law to "specify in readily understandable terms those political activities which are prohibited, and specifically permit all others."[55] The Commission also recommended allowing federal employees to "join a political party or other party organization and actively participate in its affairs, while not on duty, except to serve as an officer"; permitting them to serve as delegates to political or constitutional conventions "so long as such service does not interfere with the time and attention required as Federal employees"; and freeing them to become candidates for and to serve in local offices when conflicts of interest are not involved and there is no interference with the "time and attention such employee is required to devote to the work of the employing agency."[56] They could not become candidates for or hold any office other than local ones or manage campaigns for candidates for federal or state elective offices. These proposals do not go as far as many Hatch Act critics would like. It is certain

---

[54] Ibid., p. 591.

[55] Commission on Political Activity of Government Personnel, *A Commission Report*, vol. 1, p. 4.

[56] Ibid., pp. 46, 48.

that the pressures to open up political freedom for public employees will continue, in legislatures and the courts.

An amendment to the Hatch Act contained in the Federal Campaign Act passed in late 1974 permits state and municipal government employees in federal grant-aided programs to participate in partisan political activities.[57] Specifically, they now may serve as officers of political parties, solicit votes in partisan elections, organize and reorganize political groups, promote and participate in fund-raising activities of partisan candidates and political parties, act as challengers or poll watchers during partisan elections, drive voters to the polls in such elections, initiate or circulate partisan nominating petitions, and serve as delegates, alternates, or proxies to political party conventions. The only remaining prohibitions are being a candidate for elective office, soliciting contributions while on the job, and using official authority to influence nominations or elections. This amendment came as a surprise; the conference committee inserted it in developing compromise legislation. However, where more restrictive state laws governing political activities of public employees exist, the state laws remain in effect.

■ THE RIGHT TO ORGANIZE AND STRIKE

In 1935 Congress passed the Wagner Act, which established the right of private-sector workers to "form, join, or assist labor organizations, to bargain collectively through representatives of their own choosing, and to engage in other concerted activities for the purpose of collective bargaining or other mutual aid or protection."[58] As yet, there is no comparable federal legislation granting the same rights to state and local government employees, although bills to accomplish this are under consideration in Congress.

Historically, employee unions were resisted in the federal service, particularly the Post Office Department,

---

[57] Public Law 93-443, 93d Congress, S. 3044, Title IV, October 15, 1974.
[58] Section 7, Labor Management Relations Act, 1974, as amended by Public Law 86–257, 1959.

until passage in 1912 of the Lloyd-LaFollette Act. This act prohibits the removal or reduction in rank or compensation of any postal employee for joining any organization not affiliated with an outside body which imposes an obligation to engage in, or support, a strike against the United States. Although postal workers alone were specified, in later years this statute was interpreted by extension to apply to all federal employees. For most federal employees, collective bargaining rights were not granted until President John F. Kennedy's Executive Order 10988 in January 1962 (see Chapter 1). Employee unions were also generally resisted in state and local governments, and it was not until 1959 that the first state passed legislation authorizing collective bargaining for employees under its jurisdiction. There has been a long battle to obtain recognition of unions and collective bargaining rights, and in many state and local governments it continues.

The rights to organize and to collective bargaining

The right to organize has been established by the courts as a constitutional right of association under the 1st and 14th Amendments since *McLaughlin* v. *Tilendis* (1968).[59] The plaintiffs, two probationary teachers in the Cook County, Illinois, school system, charged they had been terminated for union activity, and a district court upheld the school authorities, stating that the plaintiffs had no right to join or form a labor union. In reversing the district court, the court of appeals pointed out, "Just this month the Supreme Court held that an Illinois teacher was protected by the First Amendment from discharge even though he wrote a partially false letter to a local newspaper in which he criticized the school board's policy" (*Pickering*). There was no showing that the plaintiffs' activities had interfered with the "proper performance" of their classroom duties. "If teachers can engage in scathing and partially inaccurate public criticism of their school board, surely they can form and take part in

---

[59] 398 F. 2d 287 (1968).

associations to further what they consider to be their well-being."

As to the trial judge's concern that the union might engage in strikes and other action affecting the "very ability of the governmental entity to function," the court of appeals, citing the Supreme Court's ruling in *Elfbrandt* v. *Russell*, said that even if the record had showed that the union had been "connected with unlawful activity," they could not be charged with "their organization's misdeeds" simply because of their membership. In 1969, *McLaughlin* v. *Tilendis* was cited by the court of appeals in a ruling that the city of North Platte, Nebraska, had violated the constitutional right of association of two employees in the street department who had been discharged for joining a union (*American Federation of State, County, and Municipal Employees, AFL–CIO* v. *Woodward*).[60]

In *Atkins* v. *City of Charlotte* (1969),[61] both the right to organize and the right to bargain collectively were at issue. One North Carolina statute prohibited state and local government employees from becoming or remaining members of labor organizations which were, or became, affiliated with any national or international union that had collective bargaining as one of its purposes. A second statute declared illegal any agreement or contract concerning public employees between any state or local agency and a labor organization. The plaintiffs, members of the Charlotte Fire Department, complained that these statutes were overbroad and violated the 1st Amendment and the due process and equal protection clauses of the 14th Amendment. They wanted to become members of a local which would become affiliated with the International Association of Firefighters.

The district court hearing the case found the statute denying organization rights "void on its face as an abridgment of freedom of association protected by the First and Fourteenth Amendments. . . . The flaw in it is an intolerable 'over-

---

[60] 406 F. 2d 137 (1969).
[61] 296 F. Supp. 1068 (1969).

breadth' unnecessary to the protection of valid state interests." Expressing a social policy view, the court said, "It is beyond argument that a single individual cannot negotiate on an equal basis with an employer who hires hundreds of people. Recognition of this fact of life is the basis of labor-management relations in this country." The city of Charlotte itself had admitted in its brief that organization rights of public employees were being increasingly recognized and that collective bargaining might be beneficial in many situations for municipal firefighters, but it feared that national affiliation could lead to strikes and "fires raging out of control." The court did not "question the power of the State to deal with such a contingency," but the statute made association with any labor union illegal, even unions opposed to strikes.

In regard to the right to collective bargaining, the court's view was that this right, "so firmly entrenched in American labor-management relations, rests upon national legislation and not upon the Federal Constitution." There is nothing in that Constitution which "entitles one to have a contract with another who does not want it," so it was "but a step further to hold that the State may lawfully forbid such contracts with its instrumentalities."

The right to strike

The present position of the courts is that public employee strikes are illegal unless allowed by statute (a few state legislatures have passed legislation providing a limited strike right). In recent years, the unions have been making strong efforts to have statutes outlawing public employee strikes eliminated and to obtain permissive strike legislation. In the courts, they have been seeking recognition of a constitutional right to strike.

A U.S. district court ruled that there was no constitutional right to strike in 1971, in *United Federation of Postal Clerks v. Blount.*[62] The United Federation of Postal Clerks sought invalidation of portions of several federal statutes that

---

[62] 325 F. Supp. 879 (D.D.C.) Aff'd 404 U.S. 802 (1971).

denied federal employment to those participating in any strike against the U.S. government or asserting a right to such strikes. The plaintiff contended that the absolute prohibition of strike activity contained in these provisions violated employees' rights of association and free speech and denied them equal protection of the law. It also argued that the language "to strike" and "participate in a strike" was vague and overbroad and violated both the First Amendment and the due process clause of the Fifth Amendment.

The court pointed out that under the common law neither public nor private workers had a constitutional right to strike, and collective action on their part often was considered conspiracy. When the right of private employees to strike was granted, it was by statute (in the National Labor Relations Act); since public workers "stand on no stronger footing in this regard," in the absence of a statute they do not have the strike right. Since there is no constitutional right to strike, it is not "irrational or arbitrary for the government to condition employment on a promise not to withhold labor collectively." As to the plaintiff's argument that the provisions were constitutionally overbroad in applying to all employees "regardless of the type or importance of the work they do," it made no difference whether their jobs were essential or nonessential, or whether similar jobs were performed by private workers who can strike. Where fundamental rights are not involved, a particular classification does not violate the equal protection clause if "any state of facts reasonably may be conceived to justify it." Therefore, "there is latitude for distinctions rooted in reason and practice, especially where the difficulty of drafting a no-strike statute which distinguishes among types and classes of employees is obvious."

Concerning the contention that the word "strike" and the phrase "participate in a strike" were vague, the court did not agree. The definition of strike in the Taft-Hartley Act— "any concerted stoppage of work by employees . . . and any concerted slowdown or other concerted interruption of operations by employees"—was evidence that the meaning of the word was clear. As to "participation," the government during the oral argument had represented that this meant striking, i.e., action in concert with others to withhold services, and the court said:

> We adopt this construction of the phrase, which will exclude the First Amendment problems raised by the plaintiff in that it removes from the strict reach of these statutes and other provisions such conduct as speech, union membership, fund-raising, organization, distribution of literature and informational picketing, even though those activities may take place in concert during a strike by others.[63]

The district court's decision was later affirmed by the U.S. Supreme Court in a one-line judgment.

■ PROTECTION AGAINST ARBITRARY OR DISCRIMINATORY ACTION

The U.S. Supreme Court's concern for constitutional protection of public employees was expressed by Justice White in *Arnett* v. *Kennedy:*

> . . . the concern of the Court that fundamental fairness be observed when the State deals with its employees has not been limited to action which is discriminatory and infringes on constitutionally protected rights. . . . It has been observed that "constitutional protection does extend to the public servant whose exclusion pursuant to a statute is *patently arbitrary* or discriminatory."[64]

In *Donovan* v. *USA* (1969),[65] the plaintiff, who was serving as a probationary employee in the Federal Aviation Administration (FAA) and whose responsibilities included drafting guidelines and procedures for the supervision of concessionaires at the capital airports, was also given the task of rewriting the FAA manual. He had received one hour's instruction in the operations of the concessionaires, none on the style or content of government reports. A recommendation of his superior, who had been absent for

---

[63] Smith, Edwards, and Clark, *Labor Relations in Public Sector,* pp. 669–73.

[64] 416 U.S. 134 (1974).

[65] 298 F. Supp. 674 (D.D.C. 1969).

three months, that Donovan be enrolled in a FAA writing course had been denied. Later, on two occasions, Donovan's superiors had expressed dissatisfaction with his work. They met with him and finally decided on dismissal, following proper procedures in this respect, but the court voided the termination because the agency had not followed its own regulations requiring training of its employees. In *Burroughs* v. *Hampton* (1972),[66] a removal case, Burroughs, a civilian pilot with the Army, had been charged with falsification of official flight time records, not maintaining proper fuel reserves, and failure to report an accident properly. Finding no substantial evidence in the record to support the charges, the court ruled that the agency had acted in an arbitrary and capricious manner.

In *Johnson* v. *Angle* (1971),[67] the Board of Education of Lincoln, Nebraska, had dismissed the plaintiff, a tenured mathematics teacher, on grounds of incompetency and failure to show evidence of professional growth. The board gave no specific findings of fact, basing the dismissal on Johnson's manner of teaching, his handling of students, and his relationships with parents. The court voided the dismissal as a denial of due process, stating that the professional growth standard could not be used since Johnson could have no idea what it meant. Also, a "Contract Termination Procedure" booklet had been promulgated and distributed with the apparent approval of the school board and should have been used in terminating his contract. The school authorities said the booklet was unofficial, but the teachers had not been so informed, and they relied on it.

■ A NEW JUDICIAL POLICY?

A recent decision of the U.S. Supreme Court, *Sampson* v. *Murray* (1974),[68] has led to speculation that the Court may be advising the lower courts "to back off on employee cases

---

[66] District Court, E.D. Virginia.
[67] 341 Supp. 1043 (D.C. Neb. 1971).
[68] 415 U.S. (1974)

—and stop interfering with the administrative functions of federal agencies."[69]

Murray, a probationary employee, had been working in the Public Buildings Service, General Services Administration (GSA), after previous service in the Defense Intelligence Agency. She was given notice of discharge, the reason stated being her "complete unwillingness to follow office procedure and to accept direction from [her] superiors." When her counsel discussed her case with a GSA personnel officer, he was shown a memorandum upon which the dismissal was based which had been prepared by a Public Buildings Service officer. Since this memorandum relied upon information about the respondent's previous employment with the Defense Intelligence Agency as well as about her conduct on the job in the Public Buildings Service, the counsel requested that she be given a detailed statement of the charges and an opportunity to reply. Such procedures are required under Civil Service Commission regulations when the reason for terminating a probationary employee is "for conditions arising before appointment."

The counsel's request was denied and the respondent appealed to the Commission, alleging that her termination had not been effectuated in accordance with the proper procedural requirements. While this appeal was still pending, she filed court action for a temporary restraining order against her dismissal, claiming that her "prospective discharge would deprive her of income and cause her to suffer the embarrassment of being wrongfully discharged." The district court granted the restraining order and scheduled a hearing for a temporary injunction. At this hearing, the court asked to hear the testimony of the discharging official in person before resolving the case; the government declined to produce him, the court ordered the temporary injunction relief continued, and the government appealed to the Court of Appeals for the District of Columbia. The court of appeals upheld the district court, whereupon the

---

[69] "View of Court Ruling, Hands Off in Firings," *Federal Times*, March 3, 1974.

government appealed to the Supreme Court, which by a six to three vote ruled in its favor.

The Supreme Court majority ruled that a district court has no authority to review agency action until such action has become final, because otherwise it cannot be authoritatively said that the applicable regulations were not followed. To justify injunctive relief, there would have to be a showing of irreparable injury, and it had not been made in this case. The court of appeals had been wrong in intimating that either loss of income or damage to reputation provided a basis for temporary relief; besides, "whatever damage might occur would be fully corrected by an administrative determination requiring the agency to conform to the applicable regulations." The majority decision emphasized the "obviously disruptive effect" which the temporary injunctive relief "was likely to have on the administrative process" and referred to the "well established rule that the Government has traditionally been granted the widest latitude in the 'dispatch of its own internal affairs.'"[70] This decision has an ominous ring to those who have been pleased with the role of the judiciary in recent years in examining more closely the personnel side of the public employer's "internal affairs."

BIBLIOGRAPHY

Adler, Joseph, and Robert E. Doherty (eds.). *Employment Security in the Public Sector: A Symposium.* Ithaca, N.Y.: Institute of Public Employment, New York State School of Industrial and Labor Relations, Cornell University, 1974.

Chanin, Robert H. *Protecting Teacher Rights, A Summary of Constitutional Developments.* Washington, D.C.: National Education Association, 1970.

Commission on Political Activity of Government Personnel. *A Commission Report,* vol. 1, *Findings and Recommendations;* vol. 2, *Research.* Washington, D.C.: Government Printing Office, 1968. Vol. 2 contains an extensive bibliography.

Dotson, Arch. "The Emerging Doctrine of Privilege in Public Employment." *Public Administration Review,* 15, No. 2 (Spring 1955).

---

[70] 415 U.S. (1974).

Goodman, Carl F. "Decisions of the 1973-74 Term, Public Employment and the Supreme Court." *Civil Service Journal*, 15, No. 1 (July–September 1974).

Goodman, Carl F. "Judicial Trends In Public Personnel Management." *Public Personnel Management*, 4, No. 5 (September-October 1975).

Grossman, Harry. "Public Employment and Free Speech: Can They Be Reconciled?" *Administrative Law Review*, 24, No. 1 (Winter 1972).

Martin, Philip L. "The Constitutionality of the Hatch Act: Second Class Citizenship for Public Employees." *University of Toledo Law Review*, 6, No. 1 (Fall 1974).

Nelson, Dalmas H. "Political Expression under the Hatch Act and the Problem of Statutory Ambiguity." *Midwest Journal of Political Science*, 2, No. 1 (February 1958).

Nelson, Dalmas H. "Public Employees and the Right to Engage in Political Activity." *Vanderbilt Law Review*, 9, No. 1 (December 1955).

Nigro, Felix A. *Management-Employee Relations in the Public Service*. Chicago: International Personnel Management Association, 1969. Chap. 4.

"Project, Collective Bargaining and Politics in Public Employment." *UCLA Law Review*, 19, No. 6 (August 1972).

Rosenbloom, David H. "Citizenship Rights and Civil Service: Old Issue in New Phase." *Public Personnel Review*, 31, No. 3 (July 1970).

Rosenbloom, David H. *Federal Service and the Constitution: The Development of the Public Employment Relationship*. Ithaca, N.Y.: Cornell University Press, 1971.

Shaw, Lee C. "The Development of State and Federal Laws." In Sam Zagoria (ed.), *Public Workers and Public Unions*. Englewood Cliffs, N.J.: Prentice-Hall, Inc., 1972.

Smith, Russell A., Harry T. Edwards, and R. Theodore Clark, Jr. *Labor Relations Law in the Public Sector, Cases and Materials*. Indianapolis, Ind.: Bobbs-Merrill Co., Inc., 1974.

U.S. Department of Labor, Division of Public Employee Labor Relations. *Summary of State Policy Regulations for Public Sector Labor Relations, Statutes, Attorney General Opinions, and Selected Court Decisions*. Washington, D.C.: Government Printing Office, 1975.

Weisberger, June. *Job Security and Public Employees*. Ithaca, N.Y.: Institute of Public Employment, New York State School of Industrial and Labor Relations, Cornell University, 1973.

Yaffe, Byron. "Free Speech Rights of Public Employees." *Journal of Collective Negotiations in the Public Sector*, 1, No. 4 (Fall 1972).

The Future
of Public Personnel
Administration

12

In any discussion of the future of public personnel administration, there must first be agreement on goals—the direction in which the field should move. It is also essential to
define responsibilities clearly to avoid working at cross
purposes. Once goals and responsibilities are determined,
the necessary characteristics of all those with personnel
management responsibilities can be formulated.

■ PUBLIC ATTITUDES TOWARD GOVERNMENT

Current attitudes toward government and government
personnel also have a bearing on the future of public personnel administration. In late 1973, the Senate Subcommittee
on Intergovernmental Relations made public the results of a
survey of public attitudes it had contracted for with Louis
Harris and Associates, Inc.[1]

---

[1] See *Confidence and Concern: Citizens View American Government,
Hearing before Subcommittee on Intergovernmental Relations of the
Senate Committee on Government Operations*, 93rd Cong., 1st sess.
(Washington, D.C.: Government Printing Office, 1974), and *Confidence*

Among the principal findings was that, for the first time in ten years of opinion polling on the topic by the Harris organization, more than half of all Americans were disenchanted with government.[2] "By any standard," public confidence in the leadership of almost every American institution surveyed had declined since 1966. While most had gained "a little in public esteem" in 1973, except for medicine and local trash collection none had the respect of the majority of the public.[3] The confidence level of the executive branch of the federal government was only 19 percent, eight points lower than in 1972. Only 17 percent felt that "the best people are attracted to serve in public life," although 89 percent thought this goal could be achieved; similarly, whereas no more than 18 percent accepted that "government is the most exciting place to work," 68 percent believed it could develop such attraction.[4]

No more than 36 percent considered that "most public officials are dedicated to helping the country," but 88 percent thought that this goal could be attained.[5] In response to the question, "What do you feel are the two or three biggest problems facing the country you would like to see something done about?" The two top items in the responses were "economy/inflation," 72 percent, and "integrity in government," 43 percent. As to the "qualities which best describe the kind of people who should work in the government," the percentage responses were: 66 for honesty, 56 for dedication to hard work, 51 for desire to help people, 41 for intelligence, 35 for courage, 28 for concern about freedom, 27 for being public spirited, and 24 for efficiency.[6]

In interpreting the findings for the Senate subcommittee hearing on the report, Harris said:

---

and Concern: Citizens View American Government, A Survey of Public Attitudes, Senate Subcommittee on Intergovernmental Relations, 93rd Cong., 1st sess. Parts 1 and 2 (Washington, D.C.: Government Printing Office, 1973).

[2] *Confidence and Concern: Survey of Public Attitudes,* Part 1, p. vi.

[3] *Confidence and Concern: Hearings before Subcommittee on Intergovernmental Relations,* pp. 7, 8.

[4] *Confidence and Concern: Survey of Public Attitudes,* Part 1, p. 33.

[5] *Confidence and Concern: Hearing before Subcommittee on Intergovernmental Relations,* p. 12.

[6] *Confidence and Concern: Survey of Public Attitudes,* Part 1, pp. 48–49.

> While disenchantment among the public runs deep, it is im-
> portant to point out that this disaffection is far more directed
> at the leadership of our institutions than at the institutions
> themselves. In other studies, we have found no more than 5
> percent of the public at all ready to scrap the major institutions
> that make up our voluntary, essentially privately oriented
> society. In this study itself, 9 in every 10 people, a high
> number, expressed the cardinal article of faith that govern-
> ment can be made to work efficiently and effectively, and
> within the parameters of liberty a free people require. But
> there is a mood of skepticism about current leadership of
> nearly all institutions, and just below the surface a growing
> willingness to throw the rascals out. The people want change,
> not to overthrow the system, but to make it work the way they
> think it should.[7]

Harris was reporting the continuation of public disen-
chantment with government which had become pronounced
years before. The Watergate controversy, although a serious
aggravating factor in this discontent, was not the initial
precipitant. As the disclosures continued and it was revealed
that in filling many of the key political policy-making posts
the all-important qualification had been devotion to the
administration rather than competence, it became clear that
there had been a sharp deterioration in the quality of such
personnel. While previous administrations of both political
parties had made many poor appointments to these policy-
making positions, the Nixon administration, preoccupied
with White House control of the agencies, appeared to have
established a new or at least exaggerated political loyalty
test in filling them. The general public may have been more
concerned about the abuses of power, violations of law, and
unethical conduct, but many informed people became convinced that decision making at the top levels in the agencies
in too many cases had been in the hands of unqualified persons. A panel of the National Academy of Public Administration, in its report to the Senate Watergate Committee,
stated that "One does not know how many or how prevalent
these kinds of appointments were, but the parade of wit-

---

[7] *Confidence and Concern: Hearing before Subcommittee on Intergovernmental Relations*, p. 9.

nesses before the Senate Select Committee was not reassuring."[8] As the details of the patronage rings instigated and directed by the Nixon White House (see Chapter 1) are revealed to the public, it is likely that disillusionment with government will grow.

Thus in the mid-1970s, public personnel administrators, along with other government officials, faced deepening attitudes of distrust of government at the same time patronage inroads at the federal level were adversely affecting the morale of federal workers. Nor was the public distrust limited or confined mostly to the federal government; the Harris poll showed that local government had only 28 percent public support, and state government 24 percent.[9] The public tends to see local leaders as promising action they never deliver, and 10 percent of the people view local government as being "'inefficient and inept' in the way it is run."[10] At the state level, the public tends to be critical of "politicians out for themselves" and claims that "we have Watergates of our own right here in this state."[11] Of course, public personnel administrators alone cannot be expected to be able to correct all the conditions that account for these adverse public attitudes (which still continue according to Harris organization findings since the 1973 survey). They do need to understand the numerous factors that affect the personnel function in government and should seek to mark out the most constructive role possible for themselves in this environment.

■ GOALS

A frequent criticism of personnel workers is that their interests are too "narrow," implying that they are versed in just one phase of the personnel operation or are not sufficiently

---

[8] Frederick C. Mosher and others, *Watergate, Implications for Responsible Government* (New York: Basic Books, 1974), p. 67.

[9] *Confidence and Concern: Survey of Public Attitudes*, Part 1, p. 38.

[10] Ibid., p. 43.

[11] Ibid., p. 45.

concerned with employees as people. Leaders in the personnel field have themselves been vocal in making this criticism and in urging their associates to develop a broader, more positive view.

Well-founded as these criticisms have been, it is becoming increasingly evident that the real problem lies in the failure of both practitioners and theorists in public personnel to see the field in its totality. The systems resource model for organizational effectiveness presented in Chapter 2 provides such a total view because it relates the personnel function to the external and internal factors that affect the formation of personnel policy.

Personnel workers may be broadly trained in recruitment, examinations, classification, training, and other specialties within the profession and cognizant of the psychological needs of employees. Nevertheless, they will fail to have maximum impact unless they have a detailed understanding of the relationship between organizational effectiveness and the personnel function. The "map of the organization's terrain" in Figure 3 in Chapter 2 shows how the core technology, goals, and human resource needs of the organization interact with all the various sectors of its task environment. Public personnel workers may regard this figure as so broadly constructed that it has little application to them. Obviously, it is not a series of job descriptions for different kinds of public personnel workers. Nevertheless, if they examine it closely, they will be better able to relate their individual assignments to the strategic elements in personnel administration and manpower management in the public service.

Figure 3 outlines the shape of the arena within which the public personnel function is enacted. This arena is complex and not very "neat." Yet we believe it more accurately reflects the true nature of the public personnel administrator's job than does any series of specialized functions neatly folded into a hierarchy of formal responsibilities. Large bureaucratic systems are of necessity composed of specialized roles, but it is the interrelations between these functions that provide the organization with its dynamics and put it into action. Intelligent action demands comprehension of these interrelations and an understanding of the stresses, strains, and conflicts which inevitably flow from interactions between people, groups, and organizations. The personnel administrator, acting within his or her area of specialization or as a member of a larger management team, must be able to grasp the factors operating in a given situation and translate this understanding into viable courses of action. Complexity and uncertainty are to be expected. As James D. Thompson puts it, "the central function of administration is to keep the organization at the *nexus* of several necessary streams of action; and because the several streams are variable and moving, the *nexus* is not only moving but sometimes quite difficult to fathom."[12]

Public personnel specialists, like everyone else, have the right to their own opinions. However, once goals for the organization have been determined through the public policymaking process — which means with the participation of all those concerned in the community — they should work with other organization members to achieve those goals. If they are to do so willingly, they must have a thorough understanding of the origins of all the tension-creating inputs of the task environment. Agency managements have a responsibility to explain policy decisions and indicate the ways in which new inputs can be absorbed.

Many public personnel workers who are steeped in the civil service tradition will continue to resent special programs for minority groups, women, veterans, the unemployed, and the underemployed. Perhaps these conflicts cannot be resolved without changing long-held concepts of merit systems. We think otherwise, but the important point is that for public agencies to be effective they must make intelligent adaptations to needs of the external environment as they develop.

The goal of public personnel administration is to contribute to organizational effectiveness, to help the organiza-

---

[12] James D. Thompson, *Organizations in Action* (New York: McGraw-Hill, 1967), p. 148.

tion survive, grow, change, and innovate as necessary. If external and internal extractive capabilities are developed well, the possibilities of meeting the needs and expectations of the public, the agency management, and the employees will be improved. The first step is to revitalize the public personnel function by selecting and training personnel administrators who are capable of handling a broadened definition of what public personnel is all about and by carefully evaluating the relationship between the "personnel office" and its environment.

■ PERSONNEL WORKER PREPARATION

Some years ago a work group of the Society for Personnel Administration concluded that "there is no known single appropriate experiential background or educational pattern for personnel workers or administrators."[13] The same view generally is held today in the personnel profession, although increased emphasis is being placed on the need for creativity, propensity for serving as change agents, and dedication to public service. It is now assumed that personnel workers will be college educated and will have broad training in the social sciences, some courses in government and public administration, and some knowledge of subjects traditionally associated with personnel work, such as psychology, economics, and labor relations.[14]

Like all other public employees — indeed, like other adults in today's complicated world — public personnel workers should find the role of perpetual learners congenial. This role requires participation in appropriate in-service training programs, but even more it calls for self-development through reading, taking part in community affairs, being open to exposure to societal problems, and becoming more aware of other people. A known and respected personnel specialist should be regarded as having

---

[13] Society for Personnel Administration, *Professional Standards for Personnel Work*, Pamphlet No. 3 (Washington, D.C., 1956).
[14] See "Personnel Opinions," *Public Personnel Review*, 31, No. 3 (July 1970), 208–11.

well-above-average capacity, insights, and interests in relating to other people and understanding human problems.

■ RESPONSIBILITIES

It has often been charged that personnel administrators are too far down in the organizational hierarchy to influence decisions, and even when they are situated close to the policymakers, their advice is not sought or is disregarded. This may be true, but within many agencies little attention has been given to fashioning clear, coherent personnel policies and developing appropriate internal processes which will implement them. The tendency has been for agency heads to pass down new directives dealing with personnel matters without clarification as to how they fit into or affect existing policies. Neither personnel workers nor line managers are briefed on the reasons for the new policies, nor are they urged to do everything possible to accommodate them with the old ones. When policy is made bit by bit, sometimes under conditions of extreme haste, organizational effectiveness is impaired.

It is realistic to assume that many decisions on personnel policies will continue to be made without sufficient participation by the personnel office. Undesirable as this is, there must also be an understanding that the real personnel managers in any organization are the line administrators and the supervisors. Organization decisions are made by the agency's top management, of which the personnel director may be one part, but these decisions are executed on a daily basis by supervisors at all levels of the organization. Thus both agency management and supervision must understand the implications of the interrelations shown in Figure 3. This may seem to diminish the role of the personnel worker but basically it does not, because by establishing the importance of the *personnel function*, it gives them the opportunity to become more valuable to top management and to supervision. Through their roles in training programs, personnel workers can play a big part in improving the overall capability of the agency in personnel matters.

Collective bargaining has resolved some of the role ambiguity of the personnel technician in relation to management on the one hand and the workers on the other. Although contracts can be negotiated which serve the needs of both management and the unions, collective bargaining is pursued as an adversary relationship in which the roles of the parties are very clear. However, the bargaining table relationship does not characterize all the activities of the personnel office. If public service management and personnel specialists are to develop incentive systems which provide for mutually profitable exchanges between the organization and its members, personnel workers must be employee as well as management oriented. Thus the responsibility of the personnel specialist is not to serve the interests of management alone. In addition, both management and the employees should be public-service oriented, so demonstrably so that they may be able to reduce public distrust in government. Experience shows that it is easy in certain transactions for management and employees to form a closed system, leaving out the public, but in the long run such conduct weakens the organization and, if persisted in, can lead to its demise.

In the years immediately ahead, the ability of the unions to share personnel responsibilities with public management will be tested. Although union leaders (and some management officials) may extol the benefits of collective bargaining as joint decision making between the parties, to date there have been only the beginnings of what could become very extensive cooperation in such areas as training, safety, equal employment opportunity, and the implementation of personnel policies generally. In labor relations programs such as that in the federal government, the legal requirement for management to confer with the unions before making changes in personnel policies has served to make the unions important participants in the personnel function. Even where items may not be negotiated because they are reserved as management rights, the strength of the unions can dissuade management from making certain kinds of personnel decisions, as in subcontracting and layoffs. If the unions exercise this role responsibly, as many now do, personnel policies may become better conceived and executed.

The relationships of central personnel agencies with line departments constitute a special problem which has become more pressing in recent years as criticisms of the "establishment" have increased. If the Nader report on civil service reform[15] mentioned in Chapters 3 and 10 is correct, these agencies minister to the needs of what they consider their clientele, the agency managements. Far from regulating them, the central agencies seek to minimize their mistakes. One can disagree with much of Nader's indictment of the performance of the U.S. Civil Service Commission in its relations with the agencies but still concur that the Commission combines inconsistent functions which should be separated. The report of the National Academy of Public Administration panel states that:

> Its [the Commission's] duties are a strange mixture of quasi-judicial, quasi-legislative, and administrative functions. On the one hand it is a Presidential staff agency, guided and constrained by the policies of the incumbent President. It is also a principal instrument in establishing or proposing legislation and regulations applying to the civil service. And it is the major enforcement and appellate agency for assuring compliance with those laws and regulations.[16]

While the panel was not prepared to make specific recommendations for reorganizing the Commission, it urged that serious consideration be given to establishing a separate agency for the "monitoring, investigative, and adjudicatory functions" involved in:

1. Maintaining merit standards.
2. Preventing political influences in competitive service personnel actions.
3. Serving as an appeals court for disciplinary actions

---

[15] Robert Vaughn, *The Spoiled System: A Call for Civil Service Reform* (Washington, D.C.: Public Interest Research Group, 1972).

[16] Mosher and others, *Watergate*, p. 75.

and complaints of discrimination and other unfair treatment.

4. Serving as an ombudsman for federal employees in personnel matters generally.[17]

It was reported that on several occasions Commission Chairman Robert E. Hampton had tried unsuccessfully to obtain White House action against political referral units in certain agencies,[18] and it was obvious that so long as the Commission maintained its role of personnel arm of the Presidency—a legitimate one for determining personnel policies—its regulatory functions would be inhibited.

The modern approach to personnel administration calls for relating the public personnel function very closely to the chief executive of the governmental jurisdiction. Watergate made it clear that in the federal government the investigative, regulatory, and adjudicatory activities could no longer be retained as part of the "personnel arm" of the Chief Executive without considerable loss of public confidence in the entire personnel function.

There are obvious limits on what a central personnel agency, or even the separate agency suggested above, can do to curb the bureaucratic "lawlessness" referred to in the Nader report. That report is concerned not only with agency violations of personnel laws and regulations but also with their use of administrative discretion to prevent the proper execution of government programs, as in the regulation of various economic interests. It postulates that in order to be able to deter unfettered discretion and punish officials who fail to respect legislative intent, Congress would have to pass new legislation. The proposed Employee Rights and Accountability Board would be far more than a personnel agency in the traditional sense; rather, it would be designed as "an independent agency congressionally mandated to control executive behavior."[19]

---

[17] Ibid., pp. 75–76.
[18] Arthur Levine, "'I Got My Job Through Creep.'" *The Washington Monthly*, 6, No. 9 (November 1974), 45–46.
[19] Vaughn, *Spoiled System*, pp. vi–15.

No matter what kind of new administrative machinery is created, all abuses of administrative discretion, all dishonesty, all unethical conduct, and all incompetence in government will never be eliminated. This is not to take a pessimistic view but rather to call attention to the key consideration: attracting and retaining in government persons of high integrity and competence. Administrative machinery and sanctions are important, but the controlling factor is the kind of human material the employee represents.

■THE NEED FOR MORE EXPERIMENTATION

In reviewing the public personnel literature of recent years, we have been struck by the paucity of new breakthroughs, new ventures. In no way do we want to minimize the hard work and the hard thinking that have gone into the improvement of traditional personnel methods and techniques, nor do we value new ventures per se. Yet, with so many problems to be solved and so many intensified criticisms to be answered, the only promising new technical development (apart from the test validity research mandated by the courts and administrative agencies) appears to be the assessment center.

The idea of the assessment center is being used in several federal, state, and municipal agencies, primarily to assess potential for promotion to supervisory and management positions and as a vehicle for management training. The distinguishing characteristics of the assessment center are that participants are observed over a longer period than under traditional procedures, and they are rated primarily on their performance in various situational exercises which simulate critical aspects of management activity. The assessment process usually lasts one to three days, the assessors being specially trained, higher level managers; a common arrangement is six assessors and 12 participants. Some research studies have shown the assessment method to be more valid than panel interviews and psychological tests because it provides a more sustained opportunity to study the candidates, and the simulated exercises elicit a variety of responses.[20]

While the assessment center approach may seem only commonsense, it is innovative compared with traditional civil service procedures, which have been partial, step-by-step, and frequently superficial. If similar experiments were conducted with other phases of the personnel program, it is possible that many more of the traditional methods, which were developed to meet the problems and needs deemed important many years ago, would be replaced with more effective techniques. Admittedly, many of the problems are stubborn and unyielding, and solutions may not be easily forthcoming. Still, the "new personnel administrator" should characteristically be open to experiment and constructively critical of the old methods.

■ ADMINISTRATIVE ETHICS

Watergate and related developments focused attention on administrative ethics, an appropriate topic with which to end this book. There are many constraining factors on what government can achieve in this area, because it is a subsystem of the society in which individuals are reared, educated, and molded in many ways. It is said that ethics in government can be no better than they are in the society, but it is also true that public officials can set the tone for the rest of the community. Certainly government can exercise care to employ persons of integrity and can encourage its employees to maintain high ethical and other standards of performance. Watergate indicated that the major problem was in the personal deficiencies of many appointees to political policy-making posts, but there have been enough examples of dishonesty, unethical conduct, arbitrariness, and public-be-damned attitudes by career officials at all levels of government to make it evident that public personnel administra-

---

[20] See William Byham and Carl Wettengell, "Assessment Centers for Supervisors and Managers," *Public Personnel Management*, 3, No. 5 (September–October 1974), 352–73. Contains an extensive bibliography.

tion needs to concentrate on improving the personal qualities of career personnel. An awareness that organizations—be they public or private—are *moral* as well as *technical* orders, and that the ethical quality of the ways administrative ends are pursued is just as important as the goals themselves, is central to this effort.[21]

Certain proposals of the National Academy of Public Administration panel are instructive in the matter of administrative ethics. In general it recommended careful selection of political appointees, both as to competence and ethical qualities. Specifically, it recommended that:

1. The major party organizations maintain lists of best qualified persons for such appointments.
2. There be an assistant to the President who would keep a roster of the "best qualified possible appointees to executive and judicial offices."
3. The Senate make a more thorough review of the qualifications of nominees to positions as heads and sub-heads of agencies.
4. Prior to appointment, nominees for the "more specialized political posts" be screened by nonpartisan panels of experts.
5. "New political appointees be encouraged or even required to attend educational briefing sessions concerning their responsibilities and particularly their relations with career personnel." These sessions would include "ethical conduct," the "importance of responsibilities to the public," and relationships with career personnel.[22]

For both noncareer and career personnel, the panel recommended:

1. An improved code of ethics (a ten-point code was adopted by Congress in 1958).

---

[21] Abraham Kaplan, *American Ethics and Public Policy* (New York: Oxford University Press, 1963).
[22] Mosher and others, *Watergate*, pp. 68–69.

2. The new code be incorporated into the oath of office sworn to by all new officers and employees.

3. A Federal Service Ethics Board, similar to those already functioning in some state and local governments, be created to set general guidelines and "investigate particularly important and difficult ethical questions that are brought before it."

4. An ombudsman for the entire government or one in each agency be appointed to "consider complaints of ethical violations."[23]

The panel emphasizes that much depends upon the values people have internalized before they enter government service. As one way of dealing with this, it urges that educational institutions which prepare students for public jobs should give more attention to public service ethics in their programs of study.[24] Reacting to adverse publicity over the sizable number of lawyers involved in Watergate, leaders in the legal profession have made the same suggestion to law schools.

The ethical problem in government has many ramifications and must to be attacked in many places, and the public service personnel office is only one of numerous participants in these efforts. In its recruiting, placement, training, promotion, disciplinary, and other activities, as well as in its advisory role to management, it can play an effective and even decisive role. Even one bad key appointment avoided can save an agency serious ethical problems, and this is only one point at which the personnel office can exert its influence to protect the integrity of the agency. This role of the personnel office is limited by the outlooks and preferences of the agency head and the political leadership, which is why the quality of this political personnel is so critical.

The challenge to public personnel administration is massive, with implications reaching far beyond the offices of public bureaucracies. Throughout this book, we have at-

---

[23] Ibid., p. 125.
[24] Ibid., pp. 125–26.

tempted to communicate a sense of urgency to the reader. If personnel administrators are willing to accept the difficult intellectual and practical task of meeting the challenge, we believe they will find public personnel a rewarding, dynamic field of endeavor. The future of public administration as an occupational area depends, of course, on the insight and imagination of those who choose to enter it as professionals.

BIBLIOGRAPHY

Cleveland, Harlan. *The Future Executive.* New York: Harper & Row, Publishers, 1972. Part III.

Frederickson, H. George. "Education for the Personnel Function." In *Public Personnel Administration—Threshold or Crossroad?* Chicago: International Personnel Management Association.

Howard, Ann. "An Assessment of Assessment Centers." *Academy of Management Journal,* 17, No. 1 (March 1974).

Macy, John W., Jr. *Public Service, The Human Side of Government.* New York: Harper & Row, Publishers, 1971. Chap. 22.

Mosher, Frederick, and others. *Watergate, Implications for Responsible Government.* New York: Basic Books, 1974.

Nigro, Felix A. "The Implications for Public Administration." In Felix A. Nigro (ed.), "A Symposium, Collective Bargaining in the Public Service: A Reappraisal." *Public Administration Review,* 32, No. 2 (March–April 1972).

Parker, John D. "Public Personnel Administration in the Year 2000 A.D." In Gilbert Siegel (ed.), *Human Resource Management in Public Organizations, A Systems Approach.* Los Angeles: University Publishers, 1972.

Rosen, Bernard. "A Plus for Effective Government." *Civil Service Journal,* 15, No. 2 (October–December 1974).

Waldo, Dwight. "Reflections on Public Morality." *Administration and Society,* 6, No. 3 (November 1974).

Name Index

Subject Index

BOOK MANUFACTURE

The New Public Personnel Administration was typeset, printed and bound at Kingsport Press. Internal and cover design was by Don Walkoe. The type is Caledonia with Helvetica display.